HUMAN RESOURCE
FORECASTING
AND
STRATEGY DEVELOPMENT

GUIDELINES
FOR
ANALYZING AND FULFILLING
ORGANIZATIONAL NEEDS

EDITED BY

Manuel London, Emily S. Bassman,

AND

John P. Fernandez

Q

QUORUM BOOKS

New York • Westport, Connecticut • London

Library of Congress Cataloging-in-Publication Data

Human resource forecasting and strategy development : guidelines for
  analyzing and fulfilling organizational needs / edited by Manuel
  London, Emily S. Bassman, John P. Fernandez.
      p. cm.
    Includes bibliographical references.
    ISBN 0–89930–436–2 (lib. bdg. : alk. paper)
      1. Manpower planning—United States.   2. Labor demand—United
  States.   3. Strategic Planning—United States.   4. Employment
  forecasting—United States.   I. London, Manuel.   II. Bassman, Emily
  S.   III. Fernandez, John P.
  HF5549.5.M3H825   1990
  658.3′01—dc20   89–24365

British Library Cataloguing in Publication Data is available.

Library of Congress Catalog Card Number: 89–24365
ISBN: 0–89930–436–2

First published in 1990

Quorum Books, 88 Post Road West, Westport, Connecticut 06881
An imprint of Greenwood Publishing Group, Inc.

Printed in the United States of America

The paper used in this book complies with the
Permanent Paper Standard issued by the National
Information Standards Organization (Z39.48-1984).

10 9 8 7 6 5 4 3 2 1

CONTENTS

Contents   vii

ILLUSTRATIONS

FIGURES

TABLES

EXHIBITS

PREFACE

As we move into the twenty-first century, corporations are recognizing the need to plan in advance to meet their human resource (HR) requirements. Changing characteristics of the workforce and new skill demands require consideration of the availability of people to meet changing corporate needs. In the past, HR forecasting was a matter of understanding economics and labor force demographics. Today and in the future, organizations must use multiple disciplines to understand global population changes, social values, family patterns, educational goals, career expectations, labor relations, and business developments in an international economy.

HR forecasting and planning is especially crucial because employees are and will continue to be the determining factor of a firm's competitive advantage. In a world in which new technology is quickly adopted by major competitors across the globe, having employees with the right abilities, skills, and motivation is critical to corporate success. Consequently, organizations must forecast their needs for different types of employees, consider the extent to which current employees have the skills needed today and for the future, and examine labor force availability. Planning is necessary to establish ways to meet HR needs through employee selection, employee development, educational support, and other initiatives. Therefore, HR planning must become an integral part of corporate strategy development and implementation.

The book is for HR managers, personnel directors, business planners, and executives who are in charge of corporate strategy and business direction. It is for public agency officials and legislators who influence government funding for education and training and who manage organizations with changing HR requirements. The purpose of the book is to inform these planners, managers, and policy-setters about current trends and actions that can be taken now to ensure organizational vitality and success.

The book contains original articles by leading experts. Examples come from major corporations such as Baxter Travenol and AT&T. Multiple disciplines are represented, including sociology, psychology, economics, demographics, and management. The authors take an international perspective and recognize the changing business environment and new directions for employee development. The book is meant to be practical. Each chapter outlines issues, presents examples, and offers guidelines or recommendations for action.

The genesis for the book was the re-establishment of the HR forecasting and planning function in AT&T after the Bell System divestiture. Before divestiture, HR planning entailed developing an annual five-year plan to project the number of people needed at different levels of the corporations in each of the major entities of the Bell System. Each entity was asked for a forecast, and the data were aggregated at the corporate level. Projections were based on anticipated corporate changes when they were known. In many cases, projections were based on assumptions of a continuing steady state or steady growth. This forecasting was generally limited to internal analysis. Computer programs were developed to analyze the demographic characteristics of the employee body and examine likely race, sex, and age mixes in different geographical regions at different levels of attrition owing to retirement eligibility and changes in organizational need. In general, the HR function in the corporation was guided more by responding to immediate needs for more or less employees than by long-term plans.

Shortly after divestiture, AT&T's HR function continued to be highly reaction oriented. The emphasis was on meeting immediate business needs. The firm had to cut costs dramatically, and it did this partly through financial incentives to encourage, and in some cases require, employees to retire early. In contrast, some parts of the business needed more employees with specialized skills and experience (e.g., programming, customer interface, sales, product development, and credit management). This led to rapidly implemented recruitment and hiring programs. Some thought, although probably not enough, was given to coordinating employee needs throughout the company by encouraging retraining and transfers where there were force imbalances. In addition, some consideration was given to long-term needs, suggesting that hiring contract employees in some disciplines might be better than hiring permanent employees because job security could not be guaranteed. In general, there was a change in the culture that employment in AT&T no longer meant job security for life, and that employment security meant having skill and knowledge that contributed to the needs of the enterprise.

About two years after the divestiture, AT&T had the time to begin considering better ways to organize and perform the HR function. As the company began formulating a clear business strategy, top officers recognized that having employees with the right mix of skills would be key to accomplishing business objectives. HR managers were included in business planning sessions, and they began to understand the need to redefine the role of the personnel department in formulating and implementing business strategy. A HR strategy group was established, and one division of this group, headed by John Fernandez, was responsible for HR forecasting and planning. He recruited Manuel London and Emily Bassman, and others who were then in other parts of the personnel department to form the new HR Forecasting and Planning Group.

One of our first tasks was to examine competitive analogues. That is, we wanted to see what other major firms did in the area of HR forecasting and planning. We visited firms in a variety of industries. We also attended a number of conferences and several workshops sponsored by the Human Resource Planning Society. In addition, our education was fostered by several consultants who offered advice and information.

One of our early findings was that there is no uniform method or process for doing HR forecasting and planning. Some companies prided themselves on sophisticated methods for analyzing current employee skills and matching employees to job vacancies. Other firms used complex mathematical models to predict the number of employees they would need during a planning period of five or more years. Other companies did little internal analysis but conducted detailed environmental scans to track trends in the labor force and predict the number of people who will be available for employment and the skills they will have.

Our field research led us to design a comprehensive HR forecasting function that included internal force tracking and analysis and environmental scanning. Also, we established a consulting function to work with our business units to help them project their needs for people in relation to their specific business objectives. In addition, as a means of educating professionals in the HR community throughout the corporation, we held several conferences on environmental trends and HR planning methods. These conferences invited outside speakers to describe what they were doing in their own firms or in their consulting practices. Many of these outside speakers are represented in this volume. Our goal in these conferences, and in this book, was to communicate leading edge thinking, current data, and practical examples to business and HR managers.

As mentioned above, the HR forecasting and planning function was part of a strategic HR department. As such, we participated in a team effort to formulate the organization's HR strategy during a time of major corporate change owing to deregulation, technological advancements, and pressing competition. This strategy team was composed of headquarters HR department staff. As the work progressed, input was sought from a wider group of HR and line managers, and eventually plans were shared with the company's top offices. Our goal was to envision the firm's business activities during the next five years and to form a HR strategy that would achieve the organization's goals. We needed to think about the type of corporation we wanted to become, given industry trends and corporate resources. We also needed to consider the HR management activities that were necessary in the short term. Moreover, we needed to draw on an analysis of environmental trends that addressed the availability of talent outside the firm and the competition for that talent.

This strategy formulation effort focused our attention on the strategic value of human resources as an extension of the company's business plans and as a key resource for accomplishing those plans. However, this was not an easy process. We had to create our own methods and continuously share our ideas with one another and our colleagues in other departments. There were seemingly endless meetings during which we debated broad strategic direction and fine-tuned words and phrases in our strategy document.

This book builds on this experience by describing ways to collect environmental data and formulate HR strategies recognizing current and anticipated changes in the environment and the organization. There are five parts to the book. Part I covers environmental scanning techniques. It examines ways to search the environment for trends that may influence the availability of employees with need skills and the motivation of employees to do the required work. The three chapters in this section explain how to identify environmental trends, including demographics of the labor force now and in the future, and how to apply this information to developing HR strategies.

Part II considers ways to analyze the organization's HR needs. The two chapters here indicate how to analyze employee demographics (e.g., age; eligibility for retirement in five and ten years from now; number of women, minorities, and older workers at different organizational levels; number of people who are unlikely to advance to higher levels) and how to use information about employees' job attitudes to plan for the future and design HR programs that will retain and motivate needed employees.

The three chapters in Part III describe ways that organizations formulate HR strategies in response to environmental trends and organizational goals. This section emphasizes that HR professionals are strategists and change agents who must understand and influence the organization's overall mission and strategy.

The fourth part of the book provides examples of HR implications of organizational change—the effects of these changes on employees and the need for new HR policies and programs. One chapter considers ways to avoid layoffs and, when this isn't possible, provide support for laid-off employees and the survivors. Another chapter describes a merger of two large organizations. The chapter highlights ways to involve employees at all organizational levels in the process, thereby fostering their commitment and loyalty to the new, combined organization and treating all people, including those who need to find other employment, with dignity. Another chapter shows how a corporation's government and community affairs department explored the need to re-orient their goals and, as a result, the change in the nature of employees' responsibilities and what was expected from them.

The last part of the book describes organizational reactions to changing environments. The chapters in the section cover ways to take advantage of an aging workforce and how organizations design new working relationships in response to family needs, specifically work-at-home jobs that take advantage of the latest computer and telecommunications technologies. The final chapter of the book is an in-depth examination of employee and organizational responses to perhaps the most critical problem facing U.S. organizations in the 1990s—the increasing cultural diversity of the workforce.

We believe that this book provides a practical view of the input needed for meaningful HR plans and what to do to generate these plans. The chapters describe ways to gather information and resources that are readily available, often from published reference material from such sources as the U.S. Census Bureau and the Daily Labor Report published by the Bureau of National Affairs. Suggestions are made for collecting data pertinent to specific needs—that is, doing "homemade" environmental scans of periodicals, newspapers, and other reference material. Creative ideas are presented for using the information, such as developing scenarios of alternative futures and considering the implications for human resources. Other chapters examine current social, economic, and technological trends from a worldwide perspective. Again, the focus is on the implications of these trends for HR practice.

The chapters on analyzing employee characteristics describe how corporations take an inventory of the skills in the organization. The examples show how that information can be used to help people plan their careers and to help departments ensure that people with the right skills are available when they are needed. Chapters demonstrate the importance of analyzing employee skills and organizational needs under changing conditions; for instance, when two corporations are merging and fewer employees are needed.

The essence of meaningful HR planning is linking business plans to HR plans. This is the theme of the chapters on HR planning, with the emphasis on understanding business directions and ways to include HR professionals in the planning process. Examples show how this can be accomplished, and how business planners can be sensitized to the value of environmental scanning and accounting for existing employee skills in developing and executing business plans.

In the future, organizations will achieve competitive advantage by attracting and retaining the most competent and motivated employees. This will require understanding employees' desires and needs for such programs and benefits as child care, flexible work schedules, cafeteria benefits, and corporate-supported education. Organizations will have to track the attitudes, ambitions, and needs of employees and prospective employees (people the organization wants to attract). Moreover, organizations will have to react quickly to institute programs that match employees' current expectations.

This book shows that HR professionals play key roles in organizations as strategists, educators, program designers, implementers, and evaluaters. HR professionals play the dual roles of representing the needs of the organization and representing the needs of employees. HR professionals pay attention to immediate corporate requirements as well as to the long-term viability of the enterprise.

We are grateful to have the support and encouragement of a number of forward-thinking business managers and HR professionals. They encouraged us to learn from sources outside our company and from employees in our company through force analyses, attitude surveys, and focus groups. They were receptive to trying new ideas and including us as they initiated new business directions. This was an exciting time of thinking, designing, creating, and implementing, and our efforts were enriched by a spirit that expected everyone to contribute their best efforts.

We thank our directors, John Petrillo, James Pagos, and Michael Goodman, for their encouragement and the opportunities they provided. Also, many colleagues were a source of stimulation and support, principally, Tapas Sen, Mirian Graddick, Jeannette Galvanick, Joseph L. Moses, Simon Krieger, and William Luithle. The members of our HR Forecasting and Planning group were valuable contributors to our enthusiasm and success, especially Linda Shanosky, Maria Verna, Carlos Cantu, John Schaut, James Shillaber, Julie DeAngelo, and Barbara O'Neal. Finally, we thank the chapter authors, who inspired us with their vision and who have provided exciting, practical ideas for HR planning as we move into the twenty-first century.

Part I

Environmental Scanning

This first section describes the importance of searching for trends in the environment that may influence the availability and motivation of people with the skills needed by the organization.

Joseph F. Coates and Jennifer Jarratt begin the section with a chapter based on their experience studying trends that suggest future developments. They describe two environmental scanning studies sponsored by companies that pool their resources in a consortium to fund the research. Coates and Jarratt outline how these scans were organized, including the time line, how materials were gathered, and how members of the consortium were involved in analyzing and interpreting the data to derive implications for human resource (HR) programs. Their methods for judging a trend's likely impact on the company and the importance of the trend over time should be valuable to HR managers who are asked by line managers or executives about the implications of an event, such as a Supreme Court ruling on equal employment opportunity, or a trend, such as the increasing age of the workforce. Moreover, the environmental scanning process is a way to change people's thinking about HR within an organization. Indeed, it can be the first step toward introducing changes and establishing new directions in recruiting, management development, and other areas of personnel management.

In the next chapter Troy Duster and David Nasatir, both sociologists, apply demographic analysis to a specific geographical region: California and the Pacific Basin. They argue that labor force trends in that region foretell what is likely to happen in the rest of the country because of the diversity of the California population and the importance of the Pacific Basin area for economic development. In fact, more than 10 percent of America's labor force of the year 2000 is alive and living in California or about to move there. This labor force reveals a greater diversity than can be found in the labor force of today, suggesting that the culture as well as the composition of corporate America may be starting a rapid and profound change. The authors describe trends in the number and educational levels of Chicanos and Latinos, Asians, women, and older workers. They recommend that, given an increasingly diverse population, corporations should broaden and intensify their recruitment activities to identify talent for entry-level positions. In general, diversity in the labor force should be viewed as an opportunity rather than as a problem. Creating a culturally diverse organization to match the cultural diversity of suppliers and customers will be a HR strategy that enhances employee motivation and productivity and generates a competitive advantage for the firm.

Emily Bassman, who has managed HR forecasting and planning activities for AT&T and Pacific Bell, considers how to tie environmental trends, information about the demographic characteristics of the organization's employees, and HR strategy. She discusses how organizations can generate age distributions of their current employee body to develop predictions of retirement, mortality, and hiring during the next five to ten years. Information about the age of the work force combined with information about future shortages of entry-level workers and decreases in the skill levels of new work force entrants suggest the need for HR programs that retain older workers longer, provide flexibility of labor availability by rehiring retirees temporarily as needed, and provide learning and growth opportunities for mid- and late-career employees. (In a later chapter Manuel London describes how Grumman Corporation initiated programs for the continued development and productivity of older workers for these reasons.) Bassman concludes the chapter with steps for finding and using environmental scanning and employee demographic data.

CHAPTER 1 _____

SEARCHING FOR TRENDS IN THE HUMAN RESOURCES ENVIRONMENT
_____ JOSEPH F. COATES AND JENNIFER JARRATT

In the past five years, J. F. Coates, Inc., has looked at the future of human resources in large North American corporations through two scans of the external environment. These scans, based on current literature, yielded reports on trends that affect the workforce and on the implications of those trends for corporate human resource (HR) planners. This chapter reviews the origin of those scans, the methods and techniques that were developed to do them, and the relationships with clients that contributed to the final products. Several of the lessons learned from the process are noted.

J. F. Coates, Inc., is one of a half dozen organizations in the United States that studies and explores the future as its primary activity. Sometimes studies of the future, although becoming better known and more familiar, seem esoteric and mysterious to those who have not been involved in one. Therefore, in all of its approaches to the future, J. F. Coates, Inc., urges its clients to participate as much as possible in the process.

Consequently, the participation of clients in the two environmental scans described here was designed into the projects from the beginning. Client interests and responses, as well as likes and dislikes, shaped the boundaries and dimensions of the scan, influenced the development of clear and precise trend statements, and helped to tailor the final reports. In exploring any aspect of the future, the two crucial problems are establishing legitimacy and credibility. "Who is presenting this material?" and "Why should I believe it?" Less exacting are the collection, organization, processing, and handling of relevant data and information. Therefore, a primary focus in each of these scans was on creating a participatory process that would enable clients to answer these two questions first for themselves and later for their organizations when they came to use the material in their work.

Table 1.1
Two Environmental Scans of the Future of the North American Workforce

	Scan 1	Scan 2
Year	1985	1988
Length of Project	10 months	9 months
Title of Report	The Future of Work & Workers in the American Corporation	Human Resources Scan '88
Scanning Period	Jan. 1983-July 1985	Jan. 1987-Sept. 1988
Clients	Environmental Scanning Association (18 corporate HR planners)	Eight large No. American corporations
How Sponsored	Competed	Solicited (by JFC, Inc.)
Final Products	500-page report on 47 trends, separate summary Briefing charts	500-page report on 37 trends organized in 7 themes, summary
Typical Client Use for the Product	As database for company-wide task forces on HR future.	Briefing charts 40-minute videotape As information base for HR staff and senior managers

The two scan projects illustrate the use of systematic futures thinking in the service of organizational decisionmaking. Table 1.1 summarizes key facts about each project.

The Environmental Scanning Association (ESA), a consortium of eighteen *Fortune* 500 companies, is a well-established group of corporate HR planners in a broad range of businesses from retailing to manufacturing to raw materials and energy production. The ESA had already contracted for one environmental scan completed in the previous year. They contracted with J. F. Coates, Inc., to produce a new scan. They intended to use the participatory process proposed by J. F. Coates, Inc., to improve their interchanges and cohesion as a working group.

The second project two years later was sponsored by eight corporations recruited by J. F. Coates, Inc. Based on experience with the ESA, it was clear that a multiclient study offers the benefits of a large project at a relatively low individual company cost. It also provides opportunities for exchanges of information, realizations, and learning for the participants and the scanners. The first benefit is increasingly important in belt-tightening times. On the second benefit, it is our observation that people in large organizations understand how to communicate within their own culture, but find that communication across company boundaries is by no means easy or relaxed. Consequently, one of the values reported by our clients was in establishing links outside their own companies. Evidence of this was plain in the second project, whose sponsors had no history together, as had the ESA. During the first meeting, after participants had met one another and exchanged experiences, they were quick to offer their corporate sites and hospitality for subsequent meetings.

ORGANIZING THE SCAN

Unlike other futures studies, or other research, an environmental scan is usually limited to looking at current published literature and other immediately available sources, such as Census Bureau reports. It does not attempt historical analysis, original field or experimental research, or the searching out of all possible information on a subject. The scan identifies and examines current trends in order to explore their implications for the future.

The scans were similarly organized. Each one began with a preliminary meeting for the sponsors to meet the scanners and one another and to establish how the scan would be done and what it would cover. At this meeting, five more meetings were scheduled. In four of those meetings the participants would review and discuss the trends developing from the scan. At the final meeting, J. F. Coates, Inc., would give a briefing on the scan and deliver a draft report. A further briefing, at the individual client's own organization, was arranged on request for the participants of HR Scan '88. It is worth nothing that there was no expectation on the ESA's part that J. F. Coates, Inc., would give briefings on the scan to member companies. As an established organization, the ESA had its own structure, capable of contracting for studies that members then used as they pleased. It elected a task force to do most of the work of reviewing the trend materials. This task force reviewed the draft report, thus enabling a final report to be delivered at the last meeting and the project to be concluded then with a final briefing.

The first meeting in each project covered important details and evoked the clients' expectations for the scan, as well as their ideas on how they would use the final product in their own organizations. The ideas that came out of this discussion, and the discussion itself, demonstrated what became increasingly useful to the participants throughout both projects—an exchange of information and ideas on communicating HR initiatives and plans within the corporation.

The principal output of the first meeting was an agreement on subjects of interest (and those of little or no interest). The range of publications—journals, newspapers, periodicals—to be scanned was established, as well as the recognition that *ad hoc* commission reports, government documents, association literature, and so on would be acquired as the scan progressed.

The last meeting with the clients included a briefing. In the HR Scan '88 project, there was an opportunity for last-minute questions, and suggestions for the final report. Also handled were such matters as aesthetics, and the relative use of charts and graphs. The intermediate meetings in both projects were work sessions. In preparation, the trends, as they had so far evolved from the scan, were mailed to each client. Participants were given a three-ring binder to collect and store their materials. Ten days to two weeks in advance, a packet of trend materials was mailed with a letter urging clients to read the materials and prepare for discussion of these trends at the next session. At all times, participants took these instructions seriously, although sometimes the number and variety of trends sent to them overwhelmed their ability to be equally attentive to each item. Frequently, a client would circulate trend pieces to a colleague in the company with expertise in a specific area, such as labor relations, and bring that additional opinion to the next meeting.

Because some trends were more interesting and their content possibly more controversial than others, a vote to determine the rank order of discussion was taken at each session. The highest voted item was discussed first. Described below are some of the techniques used in those discussion sessions.

The principal aim of the working sessions was to present material that would open up discussion, evoke agreement, disagreement, endorsement, questions, and uncertainties. What seems critical in those discussions is obvious in retrospect: the use of "trigger" words that set off furor and excited response; the desire of some clients to have more quantitative or less quantitative material; and the desire of some clients to have almost no hortatory words, such as "should," "must," "ought," but rather to have options presented in the indicative case.

The interactions of the group were useful in sharpening their judgment and opinions about the development and importance of trends, and in highlighting diverging opinions. This divergence was a basis for discussion. The meetings were mutually educational. Originally in the *HR Scan '88* project, one representative from each company was to participate in the meetings and have a designated backup, in view of the likelihood that everyone would not always be able to attend every meeting. As it turned out, most of the participants chose to have both of their representatives attend all sessions. This had the added value of exposing both to the group's interaction and so being able to carry on the discussion with a colleague outside the sessions.

SOME PRINCIPLES

Running through the process were some principles, including the following:

- *Allow no surprises.* Experience says that a negative and precipitous closure of the mind may follow unexpected, surprising, or shocking information. Consequently, in each of the working sessions, material difficult to accept was presented repeatedly, from different points of view. The object was not so much to build acceptance of the trends or their implications, but to open minds to alternatives.

- *Offer a positive alternative.* Negative material, that is, material that carries a heavy burden of undesirable implications, is readily and easily rejected, forgotten, ignored, or denied, unless at the same time there is presented some possible and plausible way to deal with the impending problem.

- *Account for divergence.* A multiclient project has to fit the collective overlap of interest and at the same time be tailored to include some of the divergences. For example, in *HR Scan '88* one client was Canada-based and four others had operations in Canada. An unplanned supplement of Canadian data had to be pulled together, paralleling the main report. The effort to keep in mind the North American, rather than just the U.S., workforce when thinking about future trends was salutary for the whole group.

CONDUCTING THE STUDY

On both scans, the work team consisted of the two authors assisted by three junior professionals. For a richer and fuller background, we set a starting date for scanning nine months earlier, going back to scan material almost a year in advance of the beginning of the project. This was not particularly difficult or demanding and did greatly enrich the pool of information and add some depth to the trend material.

Each person was assigned responsibility for doing some part of the catch-up scan, covering the previous nine months. They made notes on or reproduced anything of interest. Their choice of what to keep was open-ended and judgmental. All of the material collected was sorted into folders with broad, evolving topical headings, about 160 topics. As the scan proceeded, materials were clipped or copied from newspapers and periodicals, read by at least one person other than the scanner who clipped the items, and sorted into the folders. As the folders filled, the scanners were acquiring a sense of some specific trends that could be identified from the articles and clips that were rapidly piling up.

In preparing for meetings, a general rule was to identify trends across a range of topics. For example, one trend would be pulled from office technologies, one from a folder on developments in human resources, perhaps one on demography, another on changes in international markets, and so on. The topic folders would be assigned to one or more people to read and think about. Those staff would bring back to the team a working trend statement. One person was assigned to prepare a one-page outline based on the stated trend. This outline was reviewed and discussed by the team. The author expanded and revised a draft based on the discussion. This cycle was repeated at least twice and, in some cases, as many as four times. With the process completed for a package of trends, the drafts would be mailed to clients.

What is true about futures research in general and was validated in the scans is that trends do not speak for themselves. They do not jump out of a pile of data. Identifying and defining a trend, testing it and evaluating it is a partially creative and partially empirical process. The statement of a trend and its direction evolves out of accumulated information. The way in which that statement is framed can be modified to fit the circumstances, to fit client needs (note: needs, not wishes), and to be salient, uniform, and in a style compatible with other trends.

Trend identification is an art form. As with any art form, it cannot be totally validated by the competence and skill of the creator, but must stand some test of the intellectual marketplace, in this case the test, review, and evaluation by clients with a knowledge of the field, here that of HR planning.

Format became particularly important in the preparation of trend analyses (see Exhibit 1.1). The aim was to use figures and charts, to be punchy, brief, and accurate. In interpreting the data and describing the implications for human resources, it became necessary to be scrupulous in separating data supporting what had been identified as a trend from potential implications. Clients wanted to know when they were reading facts and data and when they were reading speculation, opinion, or wild conjecture. To solve this problem, implications were presented on three levels. In the first set were those implications strongly supported by data. For example, demographic data clearly implied that to do business in the Southwest, a corporation must accommodate the Spanish language and the Hispanic workforce in a variety of ways. The second level of interpretation was less supported by the data, but was drawn from other factors, theories, or information in the scan itself. The third level involved matters that were more speculative, with few objective indicators of likelihood, but in many cases representing possibilities that were potentially of much greater importance. This sorting of the implications into three categories satisfied most participants, except those clients who wanted to see the implications rank-ordered. To meet this need, the authors scored each implication on two low-to-high ranges, assigning scores of 1 to 5 each for likelihood of occurrence and for importance to the corporation. Thus some implications with a high likelihood were not of especial importance, and more speculative possibilities might have a low possibility of occurrence, but be of extremely high importance if they did occur. This scoring was used only in the first scan. It was probably requested because among the eighteen members of the ESA, several who were not on the task force or able to attend all the meetings had less information on or trust in the subjective judgment of the scanning team; therefore, they wanted to see some more objective measure of value. As well, in a scan with hundreds of implications, scoring enabled easier identification of key points.

The number of trends that evolve out of a scan can be large. Client interests and time limited the number presented in the final reports, but there were still forty-seven in the scan for the ESA, thirty-seven in *HR Scan '88*. In the

Exhibit 1.1
How Trends Are Treated in This Report

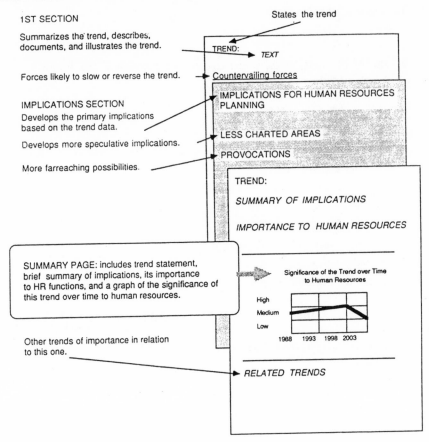

1ST SECTION

Summarizes the trend, describes, documents, and illustrates the trend.

Forces likely to slow or reverse the trend.

IMPLICATIONS SECTION
Develops the primary implications based on the trend data.

Develops more speculative implications.

More farreaching possibilities.

SUMMARY PAGE: includes trend statement, brief summary of implications, its importance to HR functions, and a graph of the significance of this trend over time to human resources.

Other trends of importance in relation to this one.

States the trend

TREND:
TEXT
Countervailing forces

IMPLICATIONS FOR HUMAN RESOURCES PLANNING

LESS CHARTED AREAS

PROVOCATIONS

TREND:

SUMMARY OF IMPLICATIONS

IMPORTANCE TO HUMAN RESOURCES

Significance of the Trend over Time to Human Resources

High
Medium
Low
    1988   1993   1998 2003

RELATED TRENDS

earlier scan, it was possible to re-use and adapt a topical structure already developed for the ESA by the author of its previous environmental scan. In *HR Scan '88*, it became attractive to organize the trends in seven theme sections. It is difficult to remember thirty-seven trends; it is a lot easier to remember seven themes, especially if some, or all, carry a clear, powerful message.

A look at the substance resulting from the scanning process may be helpful at this point. In the scan for the ESA, the trends were reported in seven categories:

1. Workforce demographics
2. Economic conditions
3. Legal and regulatory

4. Technological innovation
5. Workforce social trends
6. International developments
7. Human resources management

In one of the categories, international developments, for example, ten trends were noted:

1. Continuing decline of U.S. dominance
2. Faster global communication
3. Interdependence of resources, economies, skills, finances, and production
4. Global unemployment
5. New sources of economic, industrial, and technological strength
6. United States tries to hold the line
7. Creeping protectionism
8. Increasing vulnerability to disruption
9. Increased political use of trade and industrial policies
10. Continuing integration of politics and business

In *HR Scan '88*, the seven themes were the following:

1. Diversity in the workforce: Flexibility in management
2. The integration of home and work life
3. Globalization: Integration of the economy into the world economy
4. Integration of HR planning with business unit planning
5. The changing nature of work implies re-educating and training the workforce
6. Striking a balance between cost and demands for benefits
7. The corporation interacts with the social agenda in new ways

These themes do not represent trends, but the categories under which the trends were organized. However, the themes themselves do contain substantial information. If one absorbs these themes, they become effective bases for thinking, planning, and organizing material.

Theme three, for example, included four trends:

3–1. Mergers and acquisitions continue, with more foreign actors involved

3–2. Workforce and market demographics in Europe and Asia present new opportunities

3–3. Sweeping changes are altering market basics

3–4. Worldwide technical and scientific competence will sharpen competition

Exhibit 1.2
The Nine Box: Relating Likelihood to Importance

HIGH ----------- Impact on the Company ---------- LOW

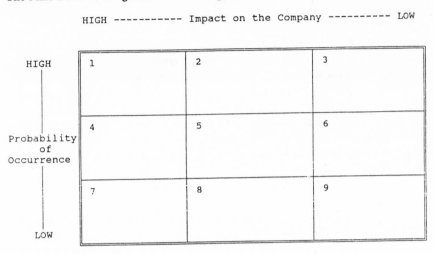

Exhibit 1.3
Importance over Time

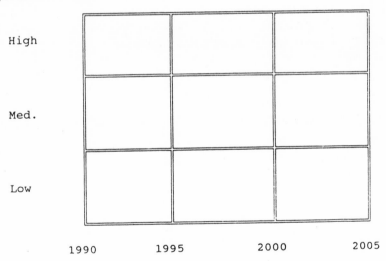

SOME TOOLS

At the work sessions with clients, the discussions were wide-ranging and thoughtful. There was no need to stimulate response. However, it seemed wise, given everyone's concern about credibility and legitimacy, to build in some structures that would evoke responses from everyone along particular dimensions—the trend's overall importance to HR planning, for example, or its likelihood of occurring. *Voting to rank order* the trends for discussion has already been mentioned. Another tool that was quite valuable was the *nine box* (Exhibit 1.2). This box treats two dimensions, importance to the corporation and imminence or likelihood of the trend continuing to develop or mature. Each trend discussed was assigned by each participant to a nine box. With a show of hands, a pattern of the whole group's judgment could be drawn. Based on their choices, a further discussion of the trend would begin, not with the tightest clustering of votes, but with the outliers. For example, in a particular vote, most of the votes were in boxes four and five, with one or two in one and nine. Rather than start where there was agreement, and thus perhaps suppress the views of the outliers, or cause them to modify their opinions, the discussion would be enriched if those who cast votes in one and nine were asked first for their comments.

A third tool valuable in wrapping up and concluding discussion as well as in shaping views of a trend was the *time line* (Exhibit 1.3). Putting this diagram up on a flip chart and giving each participant a marker, each one was asked to set up and draw a line of the future history of the trend over the years indicated on the chart. That future history was based on the individual's assessment of the trend's importance to his or her own corporation. Homogeneity or uniformity is rare with the time line or the nine box. Their principal values are to shape discussion and show participants that reasonable people in their own field, human resources, can hold widely different views about the same subject. A minor value of the time line was to get people out of their chairs after hours of intense discussion and, second, to express their views graphically, rather than in talk. Interestingly, with the time line and the nine box, participants report deciding on the shape of the line or where they'll put their X only an instant before acting. The exercise crystallized judgment.

SOME OBSERVATIONS ON SOURCES

The sources scanned were from a similar list in both scans, although several publications investigated for the ESA scan were dropped because of low yield. In reviewing the value of the various materials, formal, technical, and professional journals were of relatively lower interest than had been anticipated. By their nature, these journals tend to publish historical analysis, and draw on older and already well-known material. Books played no special part in either scan, although any particularly new and timely book was glanced through. Newspapers were a valuable source. Routine reading of *The New York Times, The Washington Post, The Wall Street Journal,* and *USA Today* produced hundreds of items. Magazines were useful. One of the factors to cope with in a scan is redundancy, particularly across the more news-oriented publications. In some cases when there were several magazines covering the same topic, such as business, we chose one and took a cursory look at the others. When practical and possible, we went back to original sources to document or expand on trends.

A lot of useful and relevant one-time publications, government documents, and commission reports, from both public and private sources, were published either immediately before or during the two scan periods and were, therefore, available to mine for material. The Carnegie Foundation for the Advancement of Teaching's report, *Corporate Classrooms*, published in 1985, is an example. Periodicals of the federal government provide important baseline data. Typical of these is the *Statistical Abstract of the United States*, published annually by the Commerce Department. We came upon these largely through previous knowledge of them, announcements, or visits to the Government Printing Office, except in the case of congressional documents, where we met with or talked with committee staff.

THE FINAL DELIVERY OF RESULTS

The final deliverables on the projects were, as one would expect, a document of about 500 pages and a summary, in one case 40 pages and in the other 32 pages. Each summary was more or less exemplary, rather than a digest, of the report. In addition, charts from the final briefing were made available so that the client could use them in its own internal briefings. In *HR Scan '88*, an internal briefing at the time and place of the client's choosing was offered as well as a video summary. The company briefings varied from relatively small—20 persons—to large—approaching 100 persons. In each case, the group was specifically assembled to hear about the 1988 HR scan. These briefings ran for two to three hours and involved extensive questions and discussion. Their primary purpose was to stimulate the audience to, as a minimum, read the summary and dip into, if not read, the full report.

Each client followed different strategies in using the material from the scan internally. Some made it available through their own internal newsletters; others disseminated the material through announcement or through copies to selected people. Others tore the report apart and fed varying groups of trends into their activities, planning, training, task forces, workshops, and briefings to senior managers.

Probably the most prevalent use was to change people's thinking about human resources within an organization. This was seen as a first step toward introducing changes and new directions, such as in recruiting or management development. The extent to which a scan can become an authoritative source to guide planning varies. An executive from one of the ESA companies who had not been involved in the scan reported two years later to one of the authors that the report had become his organization's "bible" on the future workforce.

The ESA retained ownership of their final product. This probably guaranteed exclusive use to members, although after about a year, copies of the scan began appearing at non-member corporations, probably through the network of professional friendships and contacts. *HR Scan '88* participants own their scan results for a year, after which ownership returns to the authors. It is the authors' belief that much of the scan's effectiveness as a corporate tool lies in its being communicated as widely as possible internally, and therefore its content will eventually become public. This expectation should be anticipated and included in planning.

SUMMARY OBSERVATION

The process above describes as reliably and fully as possible in this brief chapter what was done, how it was done, and why it was done. The reader should keep in mind that if he or she duplicates this process, by no means will an identical product necessarily result, for two reasons. First, the authors and the authors' team bring to such projects years of experience in futures research and practice in organizing, presenting, and analyzing material from a futures point of view. Second, the process of conducting a multi-client study itself is one of constant learning in both directions and constant response to augment what works well and to correct what works poorly. It cannot be too firmly emphasized that social, psychological, and small-group process were a major factor in the success of each of these projects. That the sponsoring participants got to know one another quite well and to enjoy an intellectual and professional intimacy not available to them through the mere exchange of printed material was an outstanding value of each project. For most of us, in understanding the future, process dominates content.

This is not to say that the results of a scan are random, erratic, and completely open-ended. On the contrary, attempting to define from a large pool of material what is potentially important creates wide latitude for what is selected and why. The skill of framing useful and reliable trends must vary. The interpretation of the implications of those trends will be different. They may, for example, concentrate more intensely on some areas. Again, some analysts may focus on the same subject, but identify or emphasize either a complementary or different set of trends, or give a somewhat different emphasis to the trend study. Identifying the trend and interpreting it is an artful, skillful, creative process, which is validated by standing the test of close scrutiny, evaluation, and utility.

culture and heritage. So, too, will the skilled labor force working
ields, unless there are major, unforeseen changes in immigration
and birth rates. The Immigration and Naturalization Service re-
at 56 percent of the 11,241 immigrant scientists and engineers
to the United States in 1986 were born in Asia, and 33 percent
tal intended to reside in California.

all the more remarkable in that, while Asians constitute only 2
f the U.S. population, and only about 7 percent of the California
n, in the fall of 1986, Asians constituted 26.5 percent of the fresh-
s at the University of California at Berkeley, 33 percent of the
class at the University of California at Irvine, and between 8 and
t of the freshman classes at Harvard, Stanford, Yale, Massachu-
tute of Technology, and Brown (Nakao 1987; Wang 1988).

6, 14 percent of all adults in the United States (and 20 percent of
ren under seventeen) came from either African American, Latino
, Native American, or Asian American groups. By the year 2000,
ne-third of all school-age children will come from these groups.
eau of the Census, 1986). Already, in the twenty-five largest met-
areas of the nation, more than half of the public school students
m the racial and ethnic groups mentioned above. By the year 2000,
ately 42 percent of all public school students will come either from
ups or from white families who fall below the poverty line (U.S.
f the Census, 1987).

are the implications for human resource (HR) planning, whether
ademic or corporate setting? Two major strategies merit consid-
Traditionally, many universities and corporations have intensified
rts to recruit elements of the labor pool that differ as little as
culturally, from those currently employed. This requires broad-
d intensifying search activities as acceptable candidates constitute
maller percentage of the otherwise qualified labor pool, a strategy
creasingly costly.

ternative strategy has been to recruit from the pool of those qual-
the extent necessary (or possible), some attempt (formal or infor-
ld then be made to urge new hires to adapt to the existing corporate
as much as possible, often at some cost to the individual. In an
gly tight labor market, however, it may be that the institutional
vill be forced to adapt. People may choose to migrate to more
l employment contexts rather than bear the continuous aggravation
derstanding, misinterpretation, and, in some cases, mischief.

than 10 percent of America's labor force of the year 2000 is alive
g in California, or about to move there (see Figure 2.2). A look at
r force reveals much greater diversity than can be found in the
ce of today and suggests that the culture as well as the composition

CHAPTER 2

CALIFORNIA AS THE FUTURE OF THE LABOR MARKET: WORKPLACE DIVERSITY—BARRIER OR OPPORTUNITY?

TROY DUSTER AND DAVID NASATIR

By far the most populous state in the union, with more than twenty-eight million residents, California already has ten million more residents than New York. In addition to its absolute size, California is also growing more rapidly than the second largest state. The population of California has grown by over half a million residents per year, on the average, during the current decade. Immigration, both from foreign nations and from other parts of the United States, has accounted for most of this increase. People are attracted to California.

For more than a generation, between 1960 and 1987, 55 percent of the increase in the state's population has been due to migration; only 45 percent of the growth during this period may be attributed to the excess of births over deaths. Indeed, the greatest foreign migration to California since the restrictive immigration legislation of 1924 took place in the 1970s.

Because migration and immigration have been such important factors in California's growth, the ethnic mix of the state has changed dramatically in recent years. In the first half of the 1980s the white population of the state decreased from 67 to 62 percent and the black population, from 7.4 to 6.7 percent. During the same period, the Chicano and Latino population of the state increased from 19 to 23 percent and the total percentage of Asians and others in the population grew to 8.6 percent.

Differential fertility rates have also contributed to the changing makeup of the state's generally aging population. The effects of these differential rates will be most clearly observable in the next twenty years as the children of the Chicano and Latino population themselves reach childbearing age (see Figure 2.1).

The vitality of the state's economy may be attributed, in substantial mea-

Figure 2.1
Ethnic Composition of Major Age Groups, California, 1985

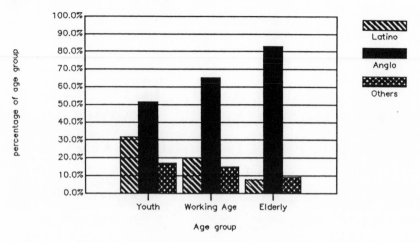

Source: Adapted from Hayes-Bautista et al. (1989).

sure, to the concentration of new immigrants in urban ethnic enclaves, in much the same way as New York's economy was fueled a century ago. Southern California has the largest concentration of Koreans outside of Korea, the largest concentration of Nicaraguans and Salvadorians in the country, and the second largest concentration of Armenians outside of Armenia. San Francisco has the greatest concentration of Chinese outside of Asia, with rapid growth occasioned by recent upheavals on the mainland and the impending takeover of Hong Kong. Singapore and Taiwan also add to the continuous flow from this region. The immigrants come to the cities to join most of the residents of California, who live in metropolitan areas; only New Jersey has a higher percentage of its population living in urban areas.

California's migration-driven population growth has intersected clearly with the character of its economic growth and development. Thurow, Heilbroner, and others have all pointed to the fact that new economic growth in California is in light and medium industries. What was earlier designated as a blighted area in Los Angeles, for example, is now a center of commercial and financial revitalization in employment, investment, and retail trade based, in some measure, on the concentration of an ethnic community (Light and Bonacich 1988).[1]

Throughout California substantial new financial investment has accompanied extensive suburbanization. Fresno and Bakersfield, which until the 1970s were treated as backwater agriculture and oil energy support for rural and industrial growth, have recently experienced substantial growth in micro

---

electronics, office services, and wholesale t: these areas of growth was fueled in part by new investment in housing.

In 1987, the growth rate of the California national economy. Civilian employment, one economic health of the state, advanced at 5. than the 3 percent growth rate of the nati California's construction sector increased at in 1987, also remarkable when compared w the rest of the nation.[2] While the service sect imately one-third of this growth, there are industries may play a larger role in the future

The influence of the University of Californi Davis campus, in particular, has played a la aqua-culture (growing fish and lobster), disea grated pest management programs to use a m and natural ecosystems control. The University Congress for a million-dollar-per-year funding to facilitate the sale of California agricultural countries (Japan, Taiwan, South Korea, Hong laysia).

The Bay Area, with the San Francisco and University of California, complementing nearb frastructure for the largest center of commercia in the country. There is a similar development Stanford and Berkeley combine to develop ne science, electrical engineering, and computer sci frastructure in these areas for nearby Silicon Va

AGING, EDUCATION, AND RECRUITMEN CORPORATE WORLD

Many of the issues that will be faced in the co be seen in the world of education. In many wa changing nature of the California student body a California institutions of education provides lead to view the changes that will occur in the corpor

Like its academic counterpart, the corps of Am More than half the nation's university professors tirement age within the next decade. The contents replacement, however, look very different indeed place. In California, the composition of students m nical, and engineering subjects, for example, sugg of the next generation of professors in these fields

---

of Asia
in these
pattern
ported
admitte
of this

This
percen
popula
man c
freshn
19 pe
setts I

In
the cl
Amer
almo
(U.S.
ropo
come
appr
these
Bure

W
in t
erat
the
pos
eni
an
tha

ifie
ma
cu
in
cu
cc
of

a
t
l

Figure 2.2
California Population, 1985 (1) vs. 2000 (2)

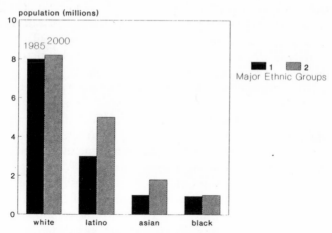

Source: Adapted from Employment Development Department, *Annual Planning Information*, State of California, 1988–89 (July 1988), p. 1.

of corporate America may be at the beginning of a rapid and profound change.

One example of the kind of change that may occur can be seen by looking at the feminization of the workplace that has occurred during the past decade. This process will continue, as women are likely to account for more than 60 percent of the growth in the labor force during the next ten years (Bianchi and Spain 1986). The changes that have accompanied the increasing number of women in the corporate world have been well chronicled (Kanter 1977). A recurring observation is how women in the corporate setting are subject to pressures to behave like men, who previously provided the only model of corporate life.

The complement has been somewhat less remarked upon; how has the corporate culture itself been altered as the proportion of its members who are women has grown from a relatively low figure to one that may soon approach parity?

Executives may initially become aware of the process in an individualized manner. Specific changes occur in the choreography of everyday life in parts of a corporation as managers, peers, and subordinates accommodate to the personal habits and characteristics of individual women replacing individual men in the ordinary process of corporate staffing and mobility. The generality of this accommodation is less visible.

It is impossible, however, to ignore cultural changes as the overall proportion of the corporate staff that is female increases. Accommodations must be made, and accommodations are made. These accommodations range from realignment of the physical infrastructure (from toilet facilities and office furniture) to realignment of corporate policy (from maternity leave to child care and paternity leave). Effects are seen in matters as diverse as language, dress, and managerial style. Changes, adaptations, and accommodations are an inevitable consequence of the increasing presence of a distinctive feminine culture in the workplace.

None of the above can come as a surprise to anyone with experience in the corporate setting that extends beyond the past decade. What may come as a surprise is that the degree of diversification in the next decade is more likely to increase than stay as it is or diminish.

More than 20 percent of the growth in the total U.S. labor force through the year 2000 will be made up of immigrants. As noted earlier, this figure is likely to be higher in California. The process of cultural accommodation outlined above will operate in a manner similar to the feminization of the workplace, and it will operate similarly in response to the expected 20 percent growth in the native nonwhite component of the labor force.

The proportion of Chicanos and Latinos in the California population is increasing for two reasons: first, Chicano and Latino fertility is higher than Anglo fertility and, second, Mexican and Latin American immigration continues at a relatively high rate. Regarding fertility, for the past century, the exception to nearly eighty years of declining Anglo fertility was the baby boom, which lasted from approximately 1946 to 1964. Given some modest assumptions about fertility and immigration, a reasonably conservative estimate of Chicano and Latino population growth would be from 5.6 million in 1985 to 12.3 million by 2030, or from 21 to 38 percent of the total population. This growth will be concentrated in the younger age groups (see Figure 2.3).

Chicano and Latino population growth will occur at that very time when the baby boom generation will be aging. It has been pointed out (Hayes-Bautista et al. 1989) that by the year 2010, California, in all likelihood, will become highly stratified by age and ethnicity.

LATINOS IN THE CALIFORNIA ECONOMY

The changing composition of California's labor force represents a key concern for both public policy and the private sector. With the importance of well-trained and educated population for the state's economic health and future firmly established, Latinos in the aggregate face consignment into low-wage or low-growth sectors of the California economy at the same time that they constitute the fastest-growing segment of California's labor force.[3]

This development warrants serious consideration and could easily shape planning and investment strategies. Without some direct intervention, California's labor force will increasingly lack the skills and educational attain-

Figure 2.3
Projected Ethnic Composition, California, 2030

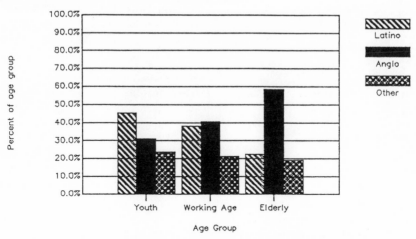

Source: Adapted from Hayes-Bautista et al. (1989).

ment necessary to meet the challenge of technological advancement, balanced growth, and international competition.

The growing importance of Latinos occurs at a time when California's link to the international economy is rapidly expanding. In 1986 alone, Mexico and California were involved in 3.8 billion dollars of international trade, and the state recently opened a trade office in Mexico. International competition and the worldwide reorganization of manufacturing place considerable pressure on the California economy to maintain an innovative edge in the areas of high technology, information services, and the new manufacturing industries (see Table 2.1).

CALIFORNIA LABOR FORCE TRENDS

The great majority of Latinos have traditionally been employed in either the primary sector (extraction or agriculture) or the secondary sector (manufacturing) of the economy. However, economic growth is occurring most rapidly in the tertiary, or service, sector. As is true for the nation as a whole, California has witnessed a decline in employment in large-scale manufacturing. Employment opportunities are greatest in communications, computers, banking, finance, and high technology, but, as will be clear from the discussion that follows, without a considerable shift in the trajectory that we have witnessed for the past decade, these jobs will only rarely go to Latinos.

More than any other group, the Mexican and other Latin American origin

Table 2.1
Employment by Major Industry, California, 1985–1995

Industry Title	Employment	Percent
Total All Industries	10,964,900	100.0%
Mining	50,510	0.5%
Construction	482,260	4.4%
Manufacturing	2,089,380	19.1%
Transportation, Commun., & Utilities	565,010	5.2%
Trade	2,615,310	23.9%
Finance, Insurance, & Real Estate	730,140	6.7%
Services	2,637,760	24.1%
Government	1,794,530	16.4%
1995	Employment	Percent
Total All Industries	14,172,150	100.0%
Mining	44,710	0.3%
Construction	575,020	4.1%
Manufacturing	2,493,5201	7.6%
Transportation, Commun., & Utilities	681,120	4.8%
Trade	3,451,090	24.4%
Finance, Insurance, & Real Estate	958,210	6.8%
Services	3,876,850	27.4%
Government	2,091,630	14.8%
CHANGE, 1985-1995	Employment	Percent
Total All Industries	3,207,250	29.3%
Mining	(5,800)	-11.5%
Construction	92,760	19.2%
Manufacturing	404,140	19.3%
Transportation, Commun., & Utilities	116,110	20.6%
Trade	835,780	32.0%
Finance, Insurance, & Real Estate	228,070	31.2%
Services	1,239,090	47.0%
Government	297,100	16.6%

Source: Adapted from Hayes-Bautista et al. (1989).

workforce is concentrated in such blue-collar occupations as operators, laborers, and craft and low-wage service workers. Over 60 percent of the second- and third-generation Mexican American labor force has been employed in such blue-collar occupations from 1940 to the present, a level higher than that of any single group in California's population (Hayes-Bautista, Schink, and Chapa 1989, p. 11). Occupations for a large proportion of Mexican Americans are concentrated in declining blue-collar manufacturing employment. A full 50 percent of California's Latinos are foreign-born. Although the large proportion of unskilled or low-skilled immigrants may explain some of this stratification, third- or later-generation Latinos

Table 2.2

California's Major International Trading Partners by Value of Trade, 1982–1986

Imports to California (in billions of dollars)			
Nation	1982	1985	1986
Japan	12.9	27.8	31.6
Taiwan	3.1	6.7	7.9
South Korea		4.2	5.1
Hong Kong	1.6	2.8	3.0
West Germany		2.7	3.3
Mexico		1.7	2.0
Singapore	0.8	1.5	2.1
Malaysia		1.3	1.4
Indonesia		1.1	0.6
United Kingdom		1.1	1.2
Canada		1.1	1.1
Australia	0.3	0.6	0.6

Exports from California (in billions of dollars)			
Nation	1982	1985	1986
Japan	6.9	7.5	7.7
Australia	2.2	3.0	2.6
South korea		2.7	2.4
Singapore	2.0	3.0	2.0
Mexico		1.9	1.8
Taiwan	1.4	1.5	1.7
West Germany		1.3	1.7
United Kingdom		1.6	1.6
Hong Kong	1.2	1.2	1.3
Malaysia		1.0	1.1
Canada		0.7	0.7
Indonesia		0.3	0.3

Source: Adapted from Hayes-Bautista et al. (1989).

continue to possess significantly lower rates of educational and professional attainment and lower levels of household income.

According to projections by the State of California Department of Finance, U.S.-born and immigrant populations of Latin American and Asian origins are likely to represent more than 70 percent of overall labor force growth in the 1987–95 period, with Latinos accounting for nearly 40 percent of this growth.

TRADE WITH THE PACIFIC BASIN: CALIFORNIA DIVERSITY AS OPPORTUNITY

It will be noted from Table 2.2 that from 1982 through 1986, California's major trading partners were in the Pacific Rim and, increasingly, Mexico.

Most dramatic is the relationship with Japan, in which 12.9 billion dollars in imports constituted 58 percent of California's foreign imports in 1982. In the four short years to 1986, that figure had skyrocketed to nearly thirty-two billion dollars in imports. This actually represents a decline to 53 percent of the total, but this is obviously a function of increased trade around the globe, not a slowing of trade with Japan. The Pacific Rim countries constitute over 85 percent of all foreign imports to California.

Thus one of the most noteworthy insights to be gained from viewing California as a leading indicator of changes in tomorrow's labor market (and associated corporate response) is the growth and persistence of heterogeneity as a fundamental and enduring characteristic.

The median age of the California population has risen from a low of 28.1 in 1970 to 29.9 in 1980, and is projected to be 36.7 in the year 2020. This figure is due in large measure to the aging of the white population of the state while entry level positions are more and more likely to be filled by young people from a minority (particularly Chicano or Latino) background.

In every major school district, non-whites are either the majority or approaching the majority of the students enrolled in the primary and secondary schools. Many have a low level of educational attainment and a high rate of abandonment from the formal education process. As a consequence, the part of the labor pool that is growing the fastest will enter the labor market with skill levels and mathematical abilities that are unsynchronized with projected needs for increased skills.

DIVERSITY AS PROBLEM VS. DIVERSITY AS OPPORTUNITY

There is considerable public rhetoric about the virtues of living and working in an environment that is socially diverse (by gender, ethnicity, culture, age, race, etc.). However, managers of organizations and institutions are more likely to confront the issue of diversity as a problem to be solved, circumnavigated, or avoided. Despite the rhetoric, cultural diversity is less likely to be seen as a prized possession, a rich potential reservoir of human talent to be drawn upon. There is seemingly more comfort, and certainly less work and "management," in a homogeneous workforce or student body.

Thus a common managerial approach is for each of various branches or divisions to deal with a different type of input and attempt to transform that variant into a common type that can be dealt with in a common manner by all other elements of the organization. The U.S. school system, for example, has frequently been challenged to adjust to a population of students who spoke no common language, shared few common values, and differed enormously in the command of the symbolic systems of the larger society. Special classes, tracking, and the development of special schools for specific subgroups was the conventional response to heterogeneity—until the position of a single dominant culture began to become less clear. English-speaking European immigrants and their children no longer constitute the majority of the clients for public schools in Los Angeles, and that will soon be the case for California as a whole.

It has proved impossible to create a multiplicity of specialized schools to work only and exclusively with distinct subgroups, transforming the "raw material" of education into a sufficiently common core to permit higher levels of the educational enterprise to continue by offering materials as if to a uniform population. The new recruits to the labor force in the next decade will be predominantly women and people of color. Nationally, about half of the labor force growth between 1990 and 2000 will be made up of Chicanos, Latinos, and blacks. Schools are learning to deal with heterogeneity, but it is still true that about half of each group's seventeen-year-olds are functionally illiterate or close to it. Thus the labor market is likely to develop in ways that rely on a highly educated, rapid-learning elite and a mass of low-level employees who require constant retraining or replacement.

The challenge that confronts the nation, but especially California, is to find ways of intercepting a developing stratification that, in the aggregate, coincides with ethnicity, culture, and race. The concentration of Asian and Pacific Islanders in the United States is dramatic, with more than 35 percent living in California alone and another 35 percent concentrated in just four other states (Hawaii, New York, Illinois, and Texas).[4] The educational achievements of Asian and Pacific Islanders have been well chronicled, but one feature is especially noteworthy in the context of their demographic concentration. A full 33 percent of Asian and Pacific Islanders are college graduates, more than double the rate (16 per cent) for the nation.

With the Pacific Rim an increasingly important trade region for the United States, the utilization of the many linguistic and cultural skills of this ethnically diverse, highly educated population would seem obvious. A homogeneous organization or state population could hardly be expected to handle the languages of trade with the Pacific Rim (Mandarin, Cantonese, Japanese, and Korean) without years of special study. However, rather than tapping the resource of employee diversity, traditional managers may be inclined to erect a "glass ceiling" to thwart the mobility of those who have these skills, in the interest of maintaining and preserving the cultural homogeneity of the upper management enclave.

"MULTI-SKILLING" AND EMPLOYMENT SECURITY

The direction of the most progressive corporate leaders has been to try to create internal labor markets and training mechanisms within their corporate settings. This takes two forms. One is to develop an approach based on "multi-skilling," in which workers are moved horizontally from sector to sector of the company, rather than on hiring and firing in response to shifts in labor cycles. This has been occasioned by a shifting emphasis among employees from job security, narrowly defined in terms of protection of a specific job, to employment security. The latter concept is more fluid, and permits the company to move to a second strategy: the development and utilization of education and training opportunities, stipends, incentives, and support. Education and retraining can be internal to the company, or it may be more feasible to subsidize the education of current employees by providing released time and tuition support at nearby institutions. It is likely that a new profile of the model work history will be a willingness to learn new skills and adapt to new kinds of work settings. For example, following an early assessment by researchers at Hewlett-Packard, there is an emerging consensus that three years is the typical limit before knowledge of contemporary (moderately advanced) software becomes obsolete.

FINANCIAL AND INDUSTRIAL CENTERS

The locus of American financial and industrial activities can no longer be considered to reside exclusively in the United States. It is clearly located at various points on the Pacific Rim. The Japanese have the greatest share of retail banking in the United States in California. By 1988, Japanese companies owned, wholly or partly, 435 manufacturing firms in the United States, double the number owned in 1980. General Motors and Toyota now collaborate on the production of automobiles at the new American Motors plant in Fremont, California. In this setting American workers labor under the direction of Japanese managers who use a management style more common in Japan than in Detroit.

To get a sense of the expanding market potential, we need only note that West Germany's Volkswagen, in a joint venture with Shanghai Volkswagen, has issued bonds worth 29.5 yuan, or about eight million dollars. Funds will be used to expand a plant that made 10,000 cars in 1987 and that planned on producing 60,000 in 1990. The events of the spring of 1989 have obviously altered any projections that are based on a stable political and social circumstance, but the American desire to reach out to the Chinese marketplace remains strong.

SUMMARY AND CONCLUSION

California (and the United States) must address an apparent contradiction or a potential collision of social and economic realities. The economy is growing and relatively healthy. Current growth, however, is based primarily in the service sector, and the predominantly white workforce of the higher-paying jobs in this sector is aging. Meanwhile, the Chicano and Latino population is relatively youthful, and growing at a much faster rate. It is members of the youthful Chicano and Latino population who will be available to fill most of the jobs that will become available in this economy.

As noted earlier, the educational preparation of young Chicanos and Latinos is not well suited to the labor force needed to sustain the nature and direction of current economic growth. Meanwhile, the educational preparation of the Asian population appears to be well suited for technical and managerial jobs. As a result, we find ourselves well on our way to a workforce that is stratified by ethnicity and race. This workforce resembles an hourglass in which there are many relatively unskilled jobs on the bottom filled by Chicano and Latino youth, few middle-level jobs, and a relatively large number of highly skilled jobs on the top, filled by whites and Asians. In such a world, overwhelmed by the immediate demands of political realities, we run the serious risk of overlooking the rich potential for long-term development that workplace diversity can provide.

NOTES

1. We refer in particular to "Koreatown," where the rate of growth exceeds that for Los Angeles County.

2. Employment Development Department, *Annual planning information, state of California, 1988–89* (July 1988).

3. This segment is indebted to a discussion in *The challenge: Latinos in a changing California*, The Report of the University of California, SCR 43 Task Force (Berkeley, CA: 1989).

4. U.S. Bureau of the Census, *We, the Asian and Pacific Islanders* (Washington, D.C.: Government Printing Office, 1986).

REFERENCES

Bigham, Joe. 1989, June 10. UC aims at farm trade in Pac Rim. *Oakland Tribune*, p. C1.

Bianchi, Suzanne M., and Daphne Spain. 1986. *American women in transition*. New York: Russell Sage.

Employment Development Department. 1988, July. *Annual planning information, state of California, 1988–89*.

Hayes-Bautista, David E., Werner O. Schink, and Jorge Chapa. 1988. *The burden of support: Young Latinos in an aging society*. Palo Alto, CA: Stanford University Press.

Hayes-Bautista, David E., Arturo Gomez-Pompa, Juan Vicente Palerm, Jaime E. Rodriguez, Vicki Ruiz, David J. Sanchez, Jr., Alex M. Saragoza, and Faustina Solis. 1989. *The challenge: Latinos in a changing California* (Report of the University of California SCR 43 Task Force). Berkeley: University of California Press.

Johnston, William B., and Arnold H. Packer. 1987. *Workforce 2000: Work and workers for the 21st century*. Indianapolis, IN: Hudson Institute, 1987, p. 89.

28   Environmental Scanning

Kanter, Rosabeth M. 1977. *Men and women of the corporation*. New York: Basic Books.

Kasarda, John D. 1989, January. Urban industrial transition and the underclass. *The Annals of the American Academy of Political and Social Science* 501, 26–47.

Light, Ivan, and Edna Bonacich. 1988. *Immigrant entrepreneurs: Koreans in Los Angeles, 1965–1982*. Berkeley: University of California Press.

Maxfield, Betty D. 1981. *Employment of minority Ph.D.s: Changes over time*. Washington, D.C.: National Academy of Sciences.

Nakao, Annie. 1987, May 3. Thorny debate over UC: Too many Asians? *San Francisco Examiner*, pp. A1–2.

U.S. Bureau of the Census. 1986. *We, the Asian and Pacific Islanders*. Washington, D.C.: Government Printing Office.

U.S. Bureau of the Census. 1986, November. *Projections of the Hispanic population: 1983–2080* (Current Population Reports, Ser. P–25, No. 995). Washington, D.C.: Government Printing Office, T 14, p. 64.

U.S. Bureau of the Census. 1987, August. *Money, income and poverty status of families and persons in the U.S.: 1986* (Current Population Reports, Ser. P–60, No. 157). Washington, D.C.: U.S. Government Printing Office, T 18, p. 30.

Wang, L. Ling-Chi. 1988. Meritocracy and diversity in higher education: Discrimination against Asian Americans in the post-Bakke era. *The Urban Review* 20, no. 3, 1–21.

CHAPTER 3 _____

STRATEGIC USE OF
ENVIRONMENTAL SCANNING DATA
_____ EMILY S. BASSMAN

In recent years, environmental factors have changed the demographic mix
of the workforce in terms of age, race, ethnicity, and skill level owing to
educational preparation. Environmental scanning has grown in importance
as the rapid pace of technological change has altered the business environment, social institutions, and demographic realities. A major driver in this
awakening interest has been the transition from plentiful entry-level labor
because of the large baby boom generation (born between 1946 and 1964)
to a situation of scarce entry-level labor because of the much smaller number
of "baby busters," born after 1964.

Many corporations have expanded their environmental scanning efforts
in recent years beyond the disciplines where such scanning normally occurs
(e.g., marketing and product development) into new areas, such as human
resources and strategic planning (see also Burack and Mathys 1987, 1989;
Walker 1980). The most forward-looking and strategically well-integrated
companies have done this all along. Jain (1984) found that companies that
were relatively advanced in their scanning and forecasting approaches were
also the companies that utilized the longest time horizons in their scanning
work. This chapter provides guidance in utilizing environmental scanning
information in human resources and in tailoring such information to the
strategic needs of the organization. A model has been developed to enable
the linkage between environmental data and the strategic direction of the
organization.

GETTING STARTED

The wide array of data available on population and workforce issues
must first be organized to focus the information search. In one company

that recently revitalized environmental scanning, a major strategic thrust was globalization. This strategy drew their human resource (HR) planners to look at global HR issues, including demographics of targeted countries. Another strategic goal was to develop organizational capability in data networking, which led them to explore productivity issues, including office automation. Whatever the specific strategies are, environmental scanning efforts must link environmental information closely to the strategic direction of the company. If the company expects to be doing little domestic hiring, for example, information concerning the effect of the baby bust on availability of entry-level workers may not be seen as relevant. Reducing the massive amount of available information into a few main topic areas will enhance the effectiveness of not only the data search, but also the presentation of the material. The above-mentioned company's HR scan was organized into five topical areas: demographics, globalization, productivity, health care, and legislation. Other companies, with different strategic directions, will need to organize environmental scanning information differently.

FINDING AND USING EXTERNAL DATA

Where does one find the information? There are many resources available, including U.S. government and foreign government agencies, HR associations, private research organizations, consultants, futurists, think tanks, and various publications. In a recent study by Graddick, Bassman, and Giordano (1989), corporate HR planners named a variety of sources in their environmental scanning activities. The HR planners interviewed representatives of nineteen manufacturing or service sector companies in the United States. Table 3.1 ranks the sources used and the percentage of companies in the sample that reported using each source.

Finding the appropriate information is an important first step in the strategic process. However, what happens next may be even more important. Graddick et al. (1989) also asked their respondents to rate their companies on how well environmental scanning and HR planning were integrated into business planning, and compared companies with high scores with those with low scores. Although high-scoring companies did not differ from low-scoring companies in the number or type of sources used to gather data, there were large differences in how they then used the information. High-scoring companies tended to share information directly with top management as a strategy for gaining their commitment, and they tended to customize the information to raise issues and stimulate action. Companies that scored low in integration with business planning tended not to meet directly with top management or focus on specific implications and next steps.

Table 3.1
Sources Used to Gather Information

Source	Percent of Companies	

Human Resources Associations
  E.G. Environmental Scanning Assn
  Human Resources Institute
  Human Resources Planning Society
	74%	(N=14)

Business Press	68%	(N=13)

Government Sources
  E.G. Bureau of Labor Statistics
  Bureau of the Census
  State Agencies
	47%	(N=9)

Internal Sources
  E.G. Library Sources
  Internal Demographics
  In-House Business Research
  Employee Surveys
	37%	(N=7)

External Consultants	32%	(N=6)

General Professional Associations
  E.G., The Conference Board
  Business Roundtable
  American Management Association
	32%	(N=6)

Academic Information/Studies	21%	(N=4)
Exchange of Information w/Competitors	11%	(N=2)
Professional Connections	5%	(N=1)

Methods used to communicate the information also differed between high-scoring and low-scoring companies, as demonstrated in Table 3.2.

One other difference between high-scoring companies and low-scoring companies deserves mention here. The high-scoring companies tended to score high as well on their level of senior management commitment to researching and solving problems relating to the changing demographics. Whether this is a cause or an effect of the previously mentioned strategies or whether both are caused by some other factor cannot be determined from this study alone. However, at least one company's innovative use of demographic information has been aimed specifically to raise awareness

Table 3.2
Scoring of Companies on Communication Methods

High-Scoring Companies	Low-Scoring Companies
o Presentations/Executive summaries to top management	o Monthly newsletter to all managers
o Senior level discussions	o Checklist for HR planners
o Strategic reports to Chairman	o Just talking to managers
o Presentations to managers as part or core curriculum	

among top management, and thereby gain their commitment to support a new HR planning process. This example is discussed in the next section.

USE OF INTERNAL DEMOGRAPHICS

One strategy that has been used successfully to engage top management's interest in the changing demographic outlook is the use of demographic information and projections concerning the company's own employee body. Data concerning the age structure and ethnic or gender composition of the employee body are fairly easy to obtain from mechanized information systems. Other data such as household composition and employee values may be more difficult to find, and may need to be collected.

Age

The most straightforward age measure that can demonstrate changes over time is a simple age distribution. The current age distribution can be compared with one from a past year or with a projection of the age distribution for a future year. Large companies generally have people (usually in the benefits or actuary group) who generate these age-related projections. Using a model that builds in assumptions about retirement, mortality, and hiring, it is possible to generate estimates about the demographic composition of the employee body at some future date. Unless a company has a particularly youthful workforce, these projections are likely to show significant aging as the population and workforce of the United States age. Because of this, other age-related measures, such as retirement eligibility, can show some dramatic changes for the future. Retirement eligibility is a measure that considers both age and years of service with the company in determining when a person could retire with full pension benefits. Information on years of service can be fed into the above-mentioned model to generate projections of the proportion of the employee body that will be eligible for retirement at a future date. One can compare this with the proportion of the employee body that is currently eligible for retirement. In an aging workforce, the proportion of retirement-eligible employees will probably increase in the future.

HR planners in one company used retirement-eligibility projections to stimulate top management's commitment to supporting more active HR planning. In this company, the aging of its workforce was projected to result in a large increase in retirement eligibility between 1988 and 1998. This figure alone was startling enough to engage top management's interest. When combined with information about future shortages of entry-level workers because of the baby bust, and decreases in the skill levels of new workforce entrants, these figures brought home the implications of an aging workforce more dramatically than national workforce data alone ever could have. Top management's commitment to working these issues within the business was gained and their receptivity to HR planning issues increased. What followed was a process of developing an HR strategy for the business that was socialized at the highest levels in the corporation.

Which particular internal demographics will have the most impact in stimulating change depends on the strategic direction of the company and the unique corporate culture. If top management has identified particular aspects of the company's culture that, if not altered, could interfere with achievement of the strategic direction, this information should be used to help guide the choice of internal demographics to study.

An example of internal demographics being used to support this strategic process is the case of a company that was trying to reduce the number of management layers in order to be closer to the customer and more competitive. The culture of this company, however, traditionally had valued upward movement over any other kind of development, and this was identified as a problem in the context of the strategic need to de-layer. Because of the career-plateauing problem that was gaining attention outside the company because of the aging of the baby boom generation, this company's HR planners decided to look at the situation within the company.

Analyzing the age distribution in the company, they discovered that just under 70 percent of the company's employees were baby boomers (nationally, a little more than half of the workforce are baby boomers). This meant that the company's strategic direction could cause a career-plateauing problem of more than average severity for its employees. When brought to the attention of senior management, this implication reinforced the importance of initiating a cultural change in the company. Senior management, aware of how the age distribution could influence what they wanted to achieve, began to seriously examine what they needed to do to support the cultural change necessary to value forms of development that don't include upward movement.

The cultural change that is needed for this company and for many other companies faced with the same problem will be enormous, even transformational. Much has been written about the phenomenon of career plateauing (Bardwick 1986) and about career development, career growth, and career patterns (Brousseau 1984; Driver 1979; Driver and Brousseau 1988; Driver, Brousseau, Von Glinow, and Prince 1981; London 1983, 1985, 1987; London and Bray 1984; London and Mone 1987). Because of the aging of the baby boom generation, there is currently a high degree of interest in possible career-plateauing problems and the growing criticality of supporting alternative career patterns (Bardwick 1988; Brousseau 1989; Driver 1985). Many companies, because of their hierarchical organizational structures, are growing increasingly concerned about the plateauing problem, especially for baby boomers (Graddick et al. 1989), and are beginning to socialize the idea that "up is not the only way." Many of these companies, however, must struggle with cultural values that narrowly define career success as upward movement within the organizational hierarchy. Because this value is so deeply embedded within the company's culture and tied to both formal and informal reward systems, it is difficult to establish a new value around alternative career patterns (e.g., lateral development within a field of expertise). It will be particularly difficult for officers in a large, strongly hierarchical company to change their values around upward movement, since they themselves have achieved career success by progressing to the top of the hierarchy. Because of this, the needed cultural change is likely to occur first in smaller, more entrepreneurial firms that have grown from relatively recent start-ups.

Diversity

Another example of a company's use of internal and external demographic information to support a strategic direction is one high-tech firm's response to growing diversity in the workforce (Jerich 1989). In addition to analyzing its own demographic composition, this company looked at the results of its employee attitude survey by demographic group (e.g., women and minorities). What they discovered was that although the attitude survey results did vary by group, there weren't any groups within the company, including the "majority," who truly felt empowered. Senior management decided that they wanted every employee to feel empowered. Furthermore, one of their strategic directions was to expand globally. Their response to these findings in the context of their strategy was to develop a vision for the company that articulates how valuing diversity and empowering every employee to fully develop his or her talents will give the company a competitive advantage in the global marketplace.

Workforce Planning

Recent environmental and demographic changes have stimulated a more comprehensive planning approach in many companies. One company has integrated diversity into a fifteen-year workforce balance program (Graddick et al. 1989). Projections are made relative to the type of diverse balance the company would like to reflect in its workforce over the next fifteen years. Top management annually reviews staffing decisions made by managers to see how they track with those projections. Particular attention is paid to jobs that traditionally have been overwhelmingly staffed by men or by women, as well as jobs that have been devoid of minorities. The underlying assumption and strategy are that diversity provides strength, both in creating innovative ideas and in responding to a diverse marketplace.

The skill level of the workforce is a growing concern in U.S. business. Because of declining skill levels observed in recent hires, as well as rapidly changing technology and an increasingly competitive business environment, many companies have undertaken comprehensive workforce planning efforts. Two of the companies in the study by Graddick et al. (1989) have projects under way designed to identify critical jobs over the next three to five years and the skills that will be required for those jobs. They are also tracking movement within each business unit: who is coming into the organization, where they are from, and who is leaving and why. In one of these companies, the project was initiated at the request of the president of the company; of major concern to senior management was the availability of people with basic skills.

Internal demographics can also be used to support specific initiatives designed to respond to changing external demographics. One company undertook a comprehensive survey of its employee body, their demographic and lifestyle characteristics (e.g., single, married, single parent, dual-income couples, number and ages of children, and use of child care providers), and needs related to those characteristics. They then used this information to design flexible policies that were aimed at supporting the work and family needs of an increasingly diverse employee body. Because of its full employment practice, this company consciously creates an environment that will attract, motivate, and retain the best talent. Supporting the work and family needs of its employee body was seen as a necessary response in order to continue to be competitive in attracting and retaining talented people.

SUMMARY

This chapter has discussed how to find and use environmental scanning and demographic data for the strategic benefit of the organization. The model developed can be described by the following seven steps:

1. *Identify the major strategic thrusts of the company.* Refer to the company's business plans, and generate HR implications of those plans.

2. *Organize environmental information around the strategic direction of the company.* Reduce and categorize the massive amount of data available in order to tailor it to be relevant to the company.

3. *Identify aspects of the corporate culture* that could get in the way of the realization of the strategic direction. If the officers have identified any of these potential roadblocks, use those.

4. *Analyze the internal demographics of the company.* Pay special attention to any measures that are relevant to points 2 and 3 above (e.g., aging, career plateauing, and skill levels).

5. *Identify the external or internal data that have the most potential impact* on the company's successful achievement of its strategic goals. Customize the information to the company's needs. Generate specific implications and recommendations.

6. *Share the information directly with top management.* Use mechanisms appropriate to your own corporate culture (e.g., share directly with the vice-president of human resources and develop a strategic plan for getting the information to other officers).

7. *Follow up.* Develop action plans in the areas where change is indicated.

Implementation of these steps will vary according to the unique corporate culture of the company, the credibility of the HR organization, the value system of top management, and so on. Frequently, use of this model will generate implications that point to the need for significant cultural change. HR planners should, therefore, consider ahead of time what resources (external or internal) will be needed to facilitate managing change in the company. By using an approach such as the one outlined here, HR planners can succeed in bringing human resources to the planning table early in the business-planning cycle. In this way, HR issues can be used to influence the strategic direction of the company.

REFERENCES

Bardwick, J. M. 1986. *The plateauing trap.* New York: Amacom, American Management Association.

Bardwick, J. M. 1988, December. *Plateauing 1988: What it is and what corporations are doing about it.* Discussion paper prepared for the Work in America Institute.

Brousseau, K. R. 1984. *Guidelines for a corporate rewards policy.* Los Angeles: Decision Dynamics Corporation.

Brousseau, K. R. 1989, April 30. *Career dynamics in the baby boom and baby bust era.* Presented at the Fourth Annual Meeting of the Society for Industrial and Organizational Psychology, Boston.

Burack, E. H., and N. J. Mathys. 1987. *Human resource planning: A pragmatic manpower planning approach* (2nd ed.). Lake Forest, IL: Brace-Park.

Burack, E. H., and N. J. Mathys. 1989. Environmental scanning improves strategic planning. *Personnel Administrator, 34* (4), 82–87.

Driver, M. J. 1979. Career concepts and career management in organizations. In Cary Cooper (ed.), *Behavioral problems in organizations* (pp. 79–139). Englewood Cliffs, NJ: Prentice-Hall.

Driver, M. J. 1985. Demographic and societal factors affecting the linear career crisis. *Canadian Journal of Administrative Sciences, 2,* 245–63.

Driver, M. J., and K. R. Brousseau. 1988. *Four career concepts.* Santa Monica, CA: Decision Dynamics Corporation.

Driver, M. J., K. R. Brousseau, M. A. Von Glinow, and J. B. Prince. 1981. *The career concept questionnaire.* Los Angeles: University of Southern California, Graduate School of Business Administration.

Graddick, M. M., E. S. Bassman, and J. Giordano. 1989, April 30. *Demographics and their impact on industry.* Presented at the Fourth Annual Meeting of the Society for Industrial and Organizational Psychology, Boston.

Jain, S. C. 1984. Environmental scanning in U.S. corporations. *Long Range Planning, 17* (2), 117–28.

Jerich, B. A. 1989, May 10. Address at The Conference Board's Second Annual West Coast Conference on Key Issues in Human Resources Management, Los Angeles.

London, M. 1983. Toward a theory of career motivation. *Academy of Management Review,* 8(4), 620–30.

London, M. 1985. *Developing managers.* San Francisco: Jossey-Bass.

London, M. 1987. Employee development in a downsizing environment. *Journal of Business and Psychology,* 2(1), 60–73.

London, M., and D. W. Bray. 1984. Measuring and developing young managers' career motivation. *Journal of Management Development, 3,* 3–25.

London, M., and E. M. Mone. 1987. *Career management and survival in the workplace.* San Francisco: Jossey-Bass.

Walker, J. W. (1980). *Human resource planning.* New York: McGraw-Hill.

Part II

Analyzing Human Resource Needs

This second part of the book builds on the first part by more in-depth exploration of how to use internal and external labor force analyses to establish human resource (HR) strategies.

In the first chapter, Christie Teigland, an economist, and Lori Hewig, a statistician, describe HR forecasting and planning for New York State government. People are a strategic resource in New York, given that the state government employs more than 200,000 persons and that an estimated 80 percent of the state operations budget is devoted to personnel. The forecasting effort began with an examination of New York's changing population profile, including age demographics, minority representation, immigration, and labor force participation rates for women. Economic and technological trends were also considered. In addition to the environmental analysis, New York State developed an employee data base to do the types of internal analyses suggested by Bassman in Chapter 3. For instance, in order to plan for the future, the state needed to know who its workers are: their ages, their tenure with state government, their geographical distribution, and the number of women compared with men as well as the number of whites compared with minorities. Teigland and Hewig emphasize the need to develop an information system with accurate historical information on the organization's workforce. This chapter is valuable because, similar to the state of California, highlighted in Chapter 2 by Duster and Nasatir, the occupational trends in New York State government mirror trends in the economy as a whole in such areas as the growth rate for managerial occupations and the high demand for health care professionals. The chapter also demonstrates how major policy changes of government affect the deployment of the workforce. As an example, the decision to open new correctional facilities influences the increasing need for employees to staff these new facilities. Finally, Teigland and Hewig outline a HR planning model for succession planning, policy formation, workforce reductions, budgeting, training, and recruitment in light of the forecasted need for and supply of labor.

William Schiemann, an industrial and organizational psychologist with expertise in employee attitude surveys, describes how to use employee attitude data to understand employee needs and develop HR strategies in response. Although a different approach to the use of internal and external demographic analysis described in the previous chapters, this chapter shows the importance of tracking employee attitudes to understanding the needs of employees for revised or new HR programs. Understanding employees' attitudes, expectations, and norms can help in understanding and *predicting* individual behaviors, especially behaviors associated with productivity, such as work performance, absenteeism, and likelihood of staying with the organization. Indeed, attitudinal analyses can be expanded to include other key groups, such as customers, shareholders, financial analysts, the media, and community leaders. Each of these groups can have a significant effect on organizations. For instance, buying decisions affect production needs, which in turn influence the type of employees required. Schiemann describes several ways to measure attitudes, including questionnaires, interviews, focus groups, and exploration of archives such as various documents and memos. He stresses the importance of the confidentiality of individual responses to attitude surveys to ensure that people provide accurate information. Projections for the future need to factor in external changes that may affect the workforce, including the influence of likely demographic changes on employee attitudes. This suggests that the environmental trend analyses described in earlier chapters have implications for predicting the future culture, needs, and concerns of tomorrow's workforce. As an example, an increasingly heterogeneous workforce (based on race, sex, and age distributions) may suggest the desirability of awareness workshops to help employees value and take advantage of differences rather than trying to socialize everyone in the organization to the same way of thinking and behaving. Schiemann views attitude surveys as a powerful organizational intervention that allows employees to express their feelings and provides planners with feedback on the organization's policies and programs. A process to periodically track employee attitudes results in "action planning"—continued refinements to programs to ensure their success. The organization's HR department plays a critical role in both designing and administering the attitude surveys (or contracting for this work) and in helping line managers interpret and respond to the results.

CHAPTER 4

PROJECTING WORKFORCE NEEDS IN GOVERNMENT: THE CASE OF NEW YORK STATE

CHRISTIE TEIGLAND AND LORI HEWIG

In his 1988 State of the State message, Governor Mario M. Cuomo said, "As an employer, the state must ensure that its agencies have an adequate supply of workers and managers with the proper skills to provide high quality services. A long-term comprehensive workforce planning strategy is necessary for the effective recruitment, retention and deployment of our employees."

With the recognition that *human* resources are as critical to the survival of an organization as fiscal or material resources, strategic planning for human capital becomes a bottom-line necessity. For New York State government, this challenge is heightened by a fiscal crisis. Given that personnel costs dominate the government's cost of doing business—an estimated 80 percent of the state operations budget is devoted to personnel—it becomes critical to deploy a capable and motivated workforce in a way that is both productive and cost effective.

With an average length of service of 10.3 years, current state employees represent a major investment. Moreover, the substantial and rising costs of examining, recruiting, and training new workers stress the need for more comprehensive management of the state's existing human resources. Consider, as a case in point, the cost savings possible from knowing what current and projected attrition rates are relative to those of other titles, occupations, and regions in the state, as well as relative to industry standards (e.g., those published by the Bureau of Labor Statistics). Research on the causes and composition of attrition can lead to the development of policies designed to reduce costly, undesirable turnover.

This chapter begins with a discussion of the major demographic, economic, and technological forces that underscore the need for strategic human resource (HR) planning in New York State government. First-year steps toward this end are outlined, along with some preliminary results. Many of the results are drawn from the most significant accomplishment in the first year of the state's workforce planning initiative, the publication of New York State's first *Work Force Plan*. The chapter concludes with some discussion regarding the future direction of workforce planning in the state government.

NEW YORK'S CHANGING POPULATION PROFILE

New York, like the rest of the nation, has experienced several important population shifts during this century. Age demographics, minority representation, immigration, and labor force participation rates for women have all changed significantly. These trends will strongly influence the demand for New York State government workers as well as the available supply of labor.

Foremost among these changes has been the shift in the age profile of the population. Although New York State birthrates have steadily declined, there has been an unprecedented growth in the number and proportion of older New Yorkers. The average age of state government employees is 40.8 years, 5 years older than the national labor force average of 36 years. At the same time, between now and the year 2000, there will be a 23 percent decline in the number of working-age youth (ages fifteen to twenty-four) in New York State and a 13 percent decline in the number of workers aged twenty-five to thirty-four.

The aging of the population has a major impact on both the supply and the demand sides of the workforce equation. On the supply side, as the number of young workers entering the workforce decreases relative to the number of vacancies created by those retiring, New York State will experience labor shortages. To the extent that these new workers do not have the skills required for the available jobs, the shortages will be more critical. On the demand side of the equation, we can expect to see an increase in the need for geriatric care and gerontological support systems. This need translates into an increased demand for government services in health care and human services, areas in which employee shortages are already being felt.

Minority[1] populations represent an increasing percentage of the state's total population (from 25 percent in 1980 to a projected 31 percent by the year 2000). With a 23 percent minority representation, the state government workforce is currently more diverse than the national labor force, which has a 13.3 percent representation, and the New York State labor force, which has a 15.8 percent representation.

Another key group that has impact on both supply and demand issues for the state's workforce is the immigrant population. Although this growing population will increase the demand for educational and social services from the state, they also will become an important segment in the labor pool. New York is home to 17 percent of the total immigrant population, trailing only California, which attracts a 25 percent share. According to the 1980 Census, immigrants constituted 13.6 percent of the state population, nearly twice the national average of 7 percent.

The increase in labor force participation rates for women is yet another factor that will greatly alter the current composition of the labor force. The participation rate now is about 50 percent. If, as expected, this rate follows national trends and increases to nearly 60 percent by the year 2000, a significant number of women will be entering the labor force. Furthermore, most of these entrants will be women who have children at home. It is estimated that by the year 2000, 80 percent of all working women will be of childbearing age. There are significant policy implications for New York State government resulting from this shift. The economic imperatives of working women with children are different from those of the traditional labor force. As an employer, the state must identify and satisfy the requirements of this growing and changing sector of the labor force.

Immigrants, minorities, and women are the labor force of the future. Working to integrate these populations into our workforce will no longer be, simply, the socially correct thing to do. Rather, it will become an economic necessity that employers cannot ignore. If we begin to recognize this reality now, New York State will be an employer "out in front" in the scramble to attract and keep qualified workers.

ECONOMIC TRENDS

Although New York State has a higher rate of employment than that of the nation, the state's labor force participation rate lags behind the national rate (61.6 percent for New York State as compared with 65 percent nationwide). Unemployment rates mask the large pool of potential labor force participants by not counting those who have either dropped out of the labor force or never entered it. Thirty-eight percent of working-age New Yorkers are not on payrolls and are not looking for jobs. The situation is even worse in New York City, where the rate is 11 points below the national average.

The labor supply situation is even more severe because a large number of students drop out of high school every year. With an average dropout rate of 33 percent, New York State ranks forty-fifth in the nation. The dropout rate in New York City is even higher. At the same time, new technologies in the workplace require basic reading and math skills as a minimum. Many graduates and dropouts lack even these basic skills. Consequently, as the labor supply shrinks, these less-skilled workers will make up a larger portion of the pool of workers, forcing the overall quality of the labor force to decline. This situation is complicated by the fact that new jobs will require even higher-level skills, including mathematical reasoning, problem-solving skills, and the ability to learn. The Bureau of Labor Statistics predicts that about 38 percent of jobs created between now and the year 2000 will require one or more years of college. The Hudson Institute predicts that 60 percent of these new jobs will require reading and writing skills possessed by only 22 percent of the available labor pool.

The economic scenario for the state indicates slower growth, higher inflation, lower unemployment rates, and higher wages for 1989. For New York State government, this means that it will be more difficult to recruit and retain workers, and careful attention needs to be paid to the allocation of increasingly scarce human and financial resources. One goal of workforce planning is to help ensure that the hard choices facing the state will be made with the benefit of information.

OCCUPATIONAL TRENDS

A snapshot of national occupational statistics for 1989 shows that clerical jobs will require the largest number of workers, followed by professional and technical workers, with service occupations the third fastest growing occupation. Managers and officials will account for more than 10 percent of demand, and blue-collar jobs will constitute 20 percent, or one in every five occupational opportunities.

Looking forward to 1995, the Bureau of Labor Statistics projects the rates of growth for some occupations to slow considerably. Emerging technology will require a rethinking of how work is done and who does it. As a consequence, many jobs have been restructured over the past decade, and many more will undergo substantial change over the next ten years. For example, the rapid spread of computerized office equipment and the automation of clerical tasks will result in a slower growth rate in the large number of clerical workers through 1995. Hence, the administrative support group's share of total national employment will decrease from 17.5 percent in 1984 to 16.7 in 1995. The impact will be even greater for New York State government, where office and clerical workers make up 22 percent of the workforce. This is an excellent example of the need to identify the generic skills held by this group of workers and to match them to areas in which there is forecasted need. In this way, the state can provide the necessary retraining to avoid losing valuable workers through displacement.

Some of the specific titles with the largest expected job growth through 1995 include titles for which New York State government will be in direct competition with the private sector (e.g., registered nurses, janitors and cleaners, accountants and auditors, secretaries, and computer programmers). All of these are among the twenty largest job titles in New York State, and together compose 45 percent of the workforce. This fact clearly demonstrates the necessity for New York State to be able to estimate the demand for and supply of workers in these occupations. The ability to foresee critical shortage areas at all levels of government gives the state the lead time to react in ways that satisfy its responsibilities to agencies, to employees, and to its taxpayers.

In light of the trends described above, New York State government can no longer function competitively and efficiently without a strategic plan to guide HR management and policies. It faces both a supply and skills gap that could lead to labor shortages and structural unemployment. Clearly, employers who believe that we continue to face a "buyer's market," where qualified employees can be purchased as needed, will jeopardize the future of their organizations.

EXPANDING OUR WORKFORCE INFORMATION SYSTEM: THE VALUE OF STRATEGIC INFORMATION

New York State must develop the capacity to forecast workforce trends and to conduct rigorous, ongoing analyses of government's labor supply and demand. It must be able to anticipate workforce issues and initiate proactive policy and program interventions. To accomplish this, the state must have accurate and complete information about the major forces that affect its workforce.

Data gathering is a critical part of the workforce planning process. This effort has focused on four main areas: (1) New York State government workforce data; (2) demographic data on New York's labor force; (3) general economic data; and (4) agency-supplied data on workforce needs arising from changing programs, functions, and policies.

In order to plan for the future of the New York State government workforce, it is necessary to first know who its workers are: How old are they? How long have they worked for state government? What is the number of women compared with men, whites compared with minorities? How is the workforce distributed geographically?

A major focus in year one of workforce planning has been on the development of a data base containing accurate historical information on the New York State government workforce. This data base will ensure the availability of consistent and comparable historical trend data that will in turn allow tracking of the movement and turnover of employees and estimation of the need for employees in various titles, occupations, and geographical areas. When this information is completely assembled, it will provide a much-needed capacity to analyze the state government workforce. How has the current workforce changed over the past five years and what significant trends, patterns, and potential problems are surfacing?

Some preliminary analyses indicate that occupational trends in state government have mirrored trends in the economy as a whole. For example, the largest rates of growth have been in managerial, professional, and office and clerical occupations. There is a particularly high demand for nurses, as demonstrated by a 25 percent growth in three large nursing titles over the past five years. The state will be in intense competition with the private sector for nurses and other high-demand health care professionals in coming years.

In addition, the major policy changes of government are evident in their impact on the deployment of the state workforce. With the opening of eight new correctional facilities, the Department of Corrections accounted for 32 percent of the growth in the New York State government workforce from 1984 to 1988. Also, the state's deinstitutionalization policies, whereby select mentally ill or mentally retarded clients are transferred from institutions to community residences for treatment, have reduced the representation of paraprofessional jobs from 19 to 17 percent of the workforce.

The variety of geographical work locations of state employees and changing demand for workers in these locations also have important implications for strategic workforce planning in New York State government. Dramatically different labor supply situations and the resulting disparity in wage rates and living costs will strongly affect agencies with operations concentrated in high-cost areas and tight labor markets. Without major interventions, these problems will only worsen in the near future. Whereas there will continue to be functions and services that are critical in the New York City area, New York State does not have the option to "move out"; competitive solutions must be found to address the problems.

Through the application of information addressing the size, composition, and dynamics of the workforce over time, a broad, quantitative view of the workforce can be developed that will aid in the establishment of goals and missions and in the refinement of HR policies, programs, and systems to support them. Such systems will provide state management with information concerning what human resources will be needed and when. Subsequent evaluations of these forecasts and trends will help management decide how best to meet those needs, within the constraints presented.

It is important to remember that planning is directed toward current decisions; to make necessary adjustments now. A workforce information system is being developed that can predict and act on workforce requirements based on demography, changing missions, and prevailing economic conditions. Stabilization of the workforce and the avoidance of staffing crises are the ultimate goals of workforce planning.

FORECASTING HR NEEDS

Moving beyond the basic trend information outlined above, the state must also address other questions, such as: How many people are likely to retire from state service? How many people are likely to resign? What job titles will experience a shortage of employees? A surplus of employees? How

do turnover rates compare among job categories? Among geographical locations? Will a high inflation rate affect the number of employees expected
to retire? The ability to answer such questions will be invaluable to the
workforce planning process. With this foreknowledge, agencies can take
action now in such areas as succession planning, training, recruitment, and
budgeting to ensure that they meet their primary objective: to have the
inventory of personnel they require when they are needed.

One of the ways in which workforce planning will increase the state's
ability to meet immediate and long-term staffing needs is by using analytical
tools and data resources to develop prediction models of the workforce. On
the demand side, these models will project the types of skills and number
of people with those skills needed, as well as identify occupations in which
shortages and surpluses will develop. On the supply side, the dynamics of
the workforce can be forecast with a high degree of reliability through the
use of practical statistical and econometric modeling techniques.

New York State has developed a Work Force Planning Personnel Flow
Model that will describe the existing configuration or profile of an agency
and where the configuration is trending, given current environmental and
policy influences. In order to make informed policy decisions, HR managers
must make some sense out of a complex system of internal employee mobility. In the first projection efforts, a Markov process has been used, which
has proved to be a useful model for the study of complex systems.[2] The
model is an arithmetic simulation of organizational changes over time that
takes into account the following:

- The profile of the agency by title, salary, ethnic and gender distribution, occupational group and geographical location
- Turnover rates based on historical data on separations from state service, transfers,
and promotions
- The age and length of service distribution of employees

Through such modeling efforts, the workforce planning initiative will
achieve one of its major goals: to make workforce information available
and useful to New York State government.

The ability to project labor supply is a crucial component of the entire
workforce planning process for several reasons:

1. *Succession Planning.* Use of a model permits analysis of personnel flows in connection with succession planning as well as with changing projected work loads.
For example, if the forecasted labor supply for a particular title is not enough
to satisfy the agency's anticipated increase in work load, the agency must act to
fill these vacancies. Its options include hiring new employees, training existing
employees in other titles to perform the necessary job, and promoting those at
lower levels in the title series. If a shortage is predicted, the answer may not be

to merely employ more people at the title in question. It may be more advantageous, or even necessary, to bring new personnel into lower-level titles in earlier periods. This action would enable the agency to follow a policy of promotion from within to fill vacancies, hence saving valuable recruitment dollars and time. Moreover, such a policy would benefit the employees by increasing their opportunities for upward mobility in their careers. One invaluable use of the Markov-type model is its ability to show the period-by-period effects that hiring trainees would have on the composition of the workforce in the future.

2. *Strategic Planning.* An important application of the model is to aid in the development of HR policies. By projecting what an agency will be like in future periods under current policies, practices, and attrition experience, the model will provide a rational basis for forecasting recruitment needs throughout an agency and, in aggregate, the state. The utilization of this relatively simple approach points to the fact that one of the major sources of future labor requirements is the current workforce itself. The final composition of the workforce depends on the employees' transition probabilities, that is, the likelihood, based on past experience and behavior, that a person will change his or her status (i.e., will leave state service, transfer to a new title, get promoted, or retire). Moreover, each probability is subject, to some degree, to control by the agency. Indeed, the extrapolation of the labor supply into the future may point out that current hiring and promotional policies will lead to an imbalance in the workforce. A policy that allows more flexible deployment of the current workforce between titles would help agencies to correct the imbalance without having to resort to hiring or reductions. For example, suppose an agency is projected to experience a shortage of computer programmers over the next year while a different agency is projected to have a surplus of research scientists. A policy of flexible deployment would allow the research scientists with satisfactory programming skills to transfer into the computer programmer title, hence helping to alleviate the labor supply problems for both agencies.

3. *Reductions in Force.* The power of the forecast model in the event of a reduction in force cannot be overstated. In order to plan for a required layoff, an agency must be able to predict the number of employees who can be expected to leave state service voluntarily (e.g., separations owing to retirement and resignation). Also, by studying the historical patterns of employee transfers and promotions and by using these patterns to predict the labor supply available in the future, an agency can identify which titles, if any, will have a surplus of employees. If this identification is done early enough, the agency can target those titles for layoff and provide training or expanded transfer opportunities for employees currently in those titles. Although it would probably not prevent all employees from being separated from state service, this look-ahead capability offered by the use of a personnel flow model will keep losses caused by a reduction in force to a minimum.

4. *Budgeting.* New York State government and individual agencies can use turnover forecasts in their budgeting and benefits planning as well. The model will help to identify long-term trends in payroll and recruitment costs, which will then feed into budget plans. Also, projected characteristics of the workforce in terms

of its age, gender, and length of service distributions will be valuable inputs to determine what needs the workforce will have in terms of benefits.

5. *Training and Recruitment Strategies.* Given the availability of information on the expected demand for labor over the next one to five years, the state, by targeting specific areas of projected need, can focus training and recruitment dollars to ensure that they are spent productively and efficiently. In addition, retraining efforts can focus on training for people with low-demand or obsolete skills to equip them with the skills they need to fill high-demand or newly created jobs. In this way, the state can improve the retention of valuable workers in whom it has already invested a great deal, and hence increase the stability and flexibility of its human resources.

RETIREMENT FORECASTING

With its large share of middle-age workers, the state workforce is especially affected by the "aging of the baby boom" phenomenon. This fact, coupled with the influence of retirement on the movement of employees through an organization, highlights the important role that accurate retirement forecasts play in the state's HR planning effort.

First, retirement forecasts can enhance the state's ability to anticipate and plan for future HR needs at both the state and agency level. By analyzing retirement as a specific type of turnover, it is possible to project expected retirements and retirement rates by title, occupational group, geographical location, and other demographic characteristics.

The benefits of retirement forecasting are several. For one, the model can provide a preview of the potential impact proposed employment and retirement policies will have on the number of retirements and, consequently, the labor supply. If, for example, the state were to adopt a retirement incentive program or were to make changes in provisions for reemployment of retirees, the forecasting model can project how these policies might affect the expected number of retirements and the consequent workforce configuration. Thus, the forecast results can assist policymakers in decisionmaking before adoption and implementation of new or changed employment or retirement policies.

Second, retirement forecasts give managers the lead time to use experienced workers to train their prospective replacements, and hence ensure the continuity of quality service. In general, unanticipated retirements result in a loss of institutional memory and a less experienced workforce. Retirement information enables an agency to make a smooth transition and to maximize the use of valuable training dollars and time.

ENHANCEMENTS

Both demographic attributes of the workforce and economic forces will influence the transition probabilities used to project the labor supply. A future enhancement to the existing model will include adjusting the transition probabilities to incorporate the effects of these factors on employee movements within and out of state government.

For example, research has shown that two of the major demographic characteristics of employees that are strongly related to their propensity to leave are length of service and age. Excluding retirements, employees with short lengths of service will tend to leave more rapidly than those with long lengths of service. This observation holds true for age as well, since age and length of service exhibit a high correlation. Hence, using a single separation rate to describe the departure of a group of employees sharing the same title yet having a wide range of tenures can lead to inaccurate predictions. In order for the transition probabilities to accurately reflect the separation of employees from state service, it may be necessary, especially for large titles or occupational groups, to break down titles by age, length of service, or other demographic traits (e.g., gender and ethnicity) and to establish separate leave rates for each subgroup. This refinement of the model will improve the accuracy of workforce predictions.

Economic conditions will also influence career moves made by employees and changes in staff made by employers. These shifts in employment will reflect the employees' and employers' perceived economic well-being and their typical reactions to changes in key indicators such as interest rates, inflation, and unemployment rates.

To obtain quantitative measures of the impacts that various economic forces will have on employee movement, we will use regression analysis. Basically, regression analysis is a statistical tool that utilizes the relation between two or more quantitative variables so that one variable can be predicted from the other(s). For this application, regression analysis will be used to predict transition rates based on changes in economic variables. For example, economic research points out that during periods of low unemployment, resignation rates within an organization rise, owing to a wider range of outside job opportunities. Using past levels of New York State unemployment with historical data on "quit" rates, a regression analysis will predict, on an agency level, the expected number of resignations for a given level of unemployment.

IMPLICATIONS OF A COMPREHENSIVE STRATEGIC APPROACH: THE BOTTOM LINE

Developing the capacity to make informed decisions regarding HR policies, current and future needs, and the optimal allocation of scarce resources must begin with the development of basic information. Using statistical and econometric modeling techniques, it is possible to emulate the dynamics of the workforce with a high degree of reliability. Models that accurately simulate the effects of policy alternatives are a valuable decision support resource. In addition to facilitating more effective planning, their application can have clear bottom-line implications. With the publication of the first *Work Force Plan*, New York State government is in a better position to ensure that decisions are made with the benefit of information about possibilities and potential outcomes.

NOTES

1. Minority groups include non-Hispanic blacks, Hispanics, Asian and Pacific Islanders, Native Americans, and other races.

2. An excellent discussion of the use of the Markov process to study personnel movements is G. S. Bres III, R. J. Niehaus, F. M. Skarkey, and C. L. Weber, Use of personnel flow models for analysis of large scale work force changes, in *Strategic human resource planning applications*, ed. Richard Niehaus (New York: Plenum Press, 1987).

CHAPTER 5

EMPLOYEE ATTITUDES AND HUMAN RESOURCE STRATEGIES

WILLIAM A. SCHIEMANN

BACKGROUND

The measurement of attitudes in organizations has occurred in firms for more than fifty years, but only recently has the knowledge of employee and customer attitudes been utilized extensively to enhance strategic focus and productivity. For many years, research on the impact of employee attitudes has been controversial and lively. For more than three decades, debates focused on whether attitudes influenced behaviors or vice versa. Although the complete network of attitude-behavior relations is far from understood, what we do know about employee and other stakeholder attitudes and their importance in creating highly effective organizations is impressive.

Although the measurement of attitudes and expectations is not new, the applications of this information are innovative and changing. Today, there are many creative ways to obtain information about employee thinking. Furthermore, as a result of many external forces, employee attitudes and values are currently sporting a higher number of different characteristics than they were a decade or two ago. Most important, however, is the extent to which attitudes are being used not only to assess strategic awareness and progress, but also to effect positive changes in a corporate culture in support of major organizational goals.

This chapter is organized into two parts. In part one, the importance of attitudes in corporate assessment is discussed, including a brief discussion of the impact of attitudes on key outcomes. Alternative ways to measure attitudes are described, followed by a review of several trends that have had an impact on employee and employer needs. A model for understanding the relation between strategic goals, required behaviors, attitudes, and cul-

Figure 5.1
Operational and Strategic Linkages

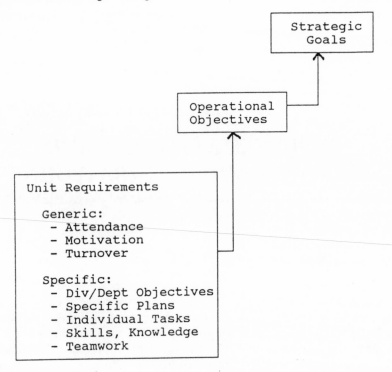

ture is described, including a discussion of the importance of culture in strategic initiatives. The second part of the chapter is devoted to attitude surveys as an intervention to effect positive change. Several examples are presented along with key elements that ensure a successful process. A number of the issues that emerge from these assessments have a direct impact on human resource (HR) planning and systems.

WHY MEASURE ATTITUDES?

Figure 5.1 describes the relation between attitudes, beliefs, and expectations on one hand and organizational goals on the other. Throughout this chapter, discussion will pertain not only to attitudes (whether someone likes or dislikes something), but also to beliefs (e.g., "this organization supports quality" or "we reward innovation"), norms (e.g., "we don't do it this way around here"), and expectations (e.g., "my pay should be related to my performance"). It is this collection of feelings that describe how a person is thinking and how he or she is likely to behave. In Figure 5.1, the chain of attitudes to behaviors to unit objectives to corporate strategic goals is displayed. If the organization is to reach strategic goals, clear operational objectives must be articulated. These objectives, in turn, imply a set of division and department objectives that require focused activities and behaviors to accomplish these ends. A number of these behaviors are generic (e.g., low absence, retention of highly skilled workers, and increased motivation and effort) and others are dependent on specific jobs and objectives (e.g., high safety attitudes and behavior, specific task assignments, objective planning that is congruent with key departmental goals, and cooperation and teamwork with other departments).

An understanding of attitudes, expectations, and norms can help in understanding and predicting individual and organizational behaviors. For example, with the generic behaviors above, attitudes (e.g., job satisfaction and organizational commitment) have been shown to be good predictors of employee turnover, absenteeism, accidents, and unionization success. With respect to specific behaviors, attitudes, and expectations (e.g., regarding rewards and performance demands), awareness of goals and the perceived importance of corporate mission are helpful in understanding past and future performance, cooperative or conflicting behavior, and productive or unproductive cultures.

The understanding of employee attitudes, expectations, beliefs, and norms can, therefore, be quite powerful in understanding many cultural and productivity issues. In many ways, by knowing how the workforce thinks, one can understand the past and predict probable future outcomes. For example, strategic objectives today imply specific focus for tomorrow. It becomes clear that certain cultures and behaviors will foster these objectives and others will not. Employee assessments can provide continual information regarding the current and probable future direction the firm is pursuing.

Although employees are a key stakeholder group, they are not the only one. Assessment of attitudes of customers, shareholders, financial analysts, the media, and community thought leaders can also be critical to organizational mission. Each of these groups can have a profound impact on organizations, and only through a thorough understanding of their thinking can an organization position itself effectively. Employees, however, represent a stakeholder group that is under greater management control, and one that is critical to reaching key outputs.

Customer attitudes are of great importance in buying decisions. The entire field of market research has flourished because of the realization that future buying decisions can be predicted by better understanding the thinking of buyers in key market segments. By combining the assessments of employees and customers, organizations have a powerful operational and strategic tool.

MEASURING ATTITUDES

Attitude or Opinion Surveys

There are many ways to assess attitudes. Surveys are one of the most effective tools for collecting broad information regarding employees, customers, or other publics in a cost-effective manner. A carefully constructed questionnaire that is administered effectively can yield a wealth of precise information about attitudes, intentions, beliefs, expectations, understanding, observed behaviors, and norms. More specifically, such surveys can be targeted to specific populations (e.g., employees and customers) or be designed to assess differences across subpopulations (e.g., executives, managers, professionals, clericals, and hourly employees). These instruments can be broad in coverage or narrowly focused on a particular subject. They can be more strategic or more operational in nature.

For many firms, employee surveys represent one of the few formal upward communication vehicles available. Most senior managers seldom have information that is as representative in scope (of the workforce at large) or as unfiltered as that which is obtained in a survey. In large organizations, research has shown that negative information is continuously filtered on its way up the organization. Unfortunately, this often leaves corporate leaders who are involved in strategic planning without an accurate view of the real beliefs and attitudes across the workforce. That is why successful union organizing efforts are sometimes a surprise to senior management, but seldom a surprise to first-line supervisors.

Quantitative surveys do have their limitations. For example, because of the interest in more precise data on both absolute and comparative attitudes, questionnaires usually contain many closed-ended item (e.g., five-point scales of agree to disagree or satisfied to dissatisfied) that provide numerical benchmarking. Such questionnaires, however, rarely provide the depth of understanding on any given issue because they are not interactive nor do they allow for more complete descriptions of causes, decision processes, contingencies, or trade-offs that individuals consider. An open-ended questionnaire can capture some of this thinking but is difficult to score and can be extremely time consuming and costly. A reasonable number of open-ended items when coupled with closed-ended items can be an effective compromise. These open-ended items must be summarized in some form, usually along the lines of themes or key issues.

Interviews

Another approach to this type of information is interviews. One-on-one interviews can provide greater depth of understanding. For example, an employee can describe why he or she feels positive about a particular issue. Employees can describe how decisions are made or how a given practice came to be.

This information can be useful in preparing a questionnaire that is more focused. Items can be more precisely written when alternative hypotheses are clear. Interviews can also be useful in explaining survey data that have already been collected. Key questions may be raised by the data that can be explored in the interviews.

Focus Groups

One-on-one interviews, however, can be quite costly and time consuming. An alternative is focus groups or simply group interviews. These typically consist of six to twelve employees drawn from homogeneous job groups so that issues common to one population can be explored in depth. Because of the sensitivity to some of the issues discussed in a broad assessment of corporate culture or organizational effectiveness (e.g., quality of management and supervision, pay, and advancement), these sessions are best conducted by an objective source, without higher levels of management present. These sessions are often semi-structured with key issues and questions identified before the sessions, but with enough flexibility to pursue issues to their fullest and allow for unexpected, but related, issues to be covered.

Archival Analysis

Attitudes, beliefs, and expectations can also be assessed through the analysis of documents, procedures, and memos. This is a more process-oriented approach that analyzes the living organization as it documents itself in its formal communication. Unfortunately, this is not where the grapevine lives, and much of the important informal organization cannot be captured. However, such an analysis can shed a great deal of light on values, levels of bureaucracy, speed of decisionmaking, risk orientation, tolerance of ambiguity, awareness and understanding of policies and procedures, and cooperation. What is difficult to ascertain is the extent to which people's underlying attitudes support the visible communications they generate. Also, many groups (e.g., hourly employees and customers) have little written information to analyze.

Confidentiality of Assessment

In all cases, the collection of this information should be voluntary and confidential. Forced participation leads to unpredictable responses, often unrealistically favorable because of fear of retaliation. Confidentiality is also a major concern of most employees and many other stakeholders. People in one-on-one interviews with outside interviewers often describe key events in which a respondent was punished for openly criticizing someone or something. In most organizations in which we have conducted interviews, it is difficult work to convince employees to open up and tell the "real story." Without promises and demonstrations of confidentiality, many employees will not be candid—a useless outcome for assessment and planning.

UNDERSTANDING THE WORKFORCE

What is crucial to the understanding of probable future workforce behaviors is both an understanding of general trends that are taking place in workforce attitudes and values today and the specific profile of a particular firm. For example, it is clear that a number of demographic, educational, and value trends have taken place over the past several decades. These changes have made a dramatic impact on the nature of work in organizations today and will continue to influence the organizations of tomorrow. Senior management in any firm today should be aware of these profound trends, but must also recognize that each workforce has unique characteristics (e.g., experience levels, skills mix, values orientation, demographic mix, and educational level) that require the specific assessment and regular monitoring of their unique profile. It is with this awareness of both societal trends and the specific profile of a given workforce that senior management will be best prepared to understand today's workforce while preparing for the needs of tomorrow.

Many trends impact the workforce as a whole. Demographically, the workforce is aging as baby boomers move through the force. This means that more employees will be clustered in certain career stages with particular expectations. It also implies an older workforce in the next decade that will have a different values profile. Needs structures are also changing, with fewer traditional families. There are more two-earner families, more singles, and more families with dependent parents. This profile will influence the importance and expectations regarding certain benefits and rewards, work location, time flexibility, and work-family trade-offs.

Employees today are more independent and more articulate than their counterparts of twenty years ago. Increasing education levels have created better consumers of information who expect greater participation in decisionmaking and more frequent and open communication. Today's workforce is less likely to sit back and wait to be asked. Of course, this provides excellent opportunities to assess where they stand on given issues and how they are likely to behave in the future. More important, this also affords an opportunity to involve employees to a greater extent in solutions to organizational problems and focus their energy toward corporate goals.

The assessment of attitudes and behaviors of employees or other stakeholders is one important way to gauge strategic and operational congruence. It is like looking into a mirror. These attitudes and behaviors reflect the real culture of the organization—the embodied set of beliefs, attitudes, and values that determine how employees will behave. Will they cooperate as needed? Is key information shared across interdependent units? Are employees willing to go the extra distance to reach key objectives? Do employees understand where the firm is going and why? Are employees motivated by the compensation and reward systems in place? Are corporate

Figure 5.2
Relation of Strategic Goals to Employee Attitudes and Behaviors

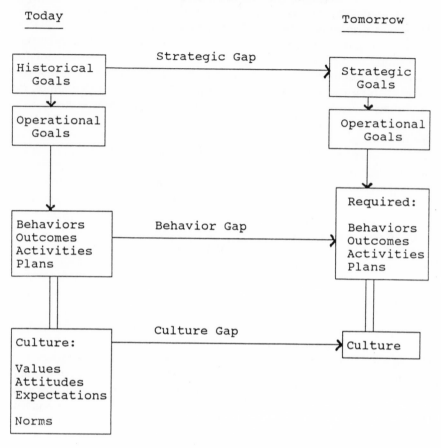

messages credible? Is there adequate risk-taking to foster innovation? Are creative ideas supported? Do employees have clear goals, understand their importance, have adequate information and skills to complete their tasks, and receive clear feedback on ways to improve? Are specific activities that are important to the firm being accomplished?

Figure 5.2 offers a model for thinking about organizational change and growth and the role that employee measurement can play in this process. Organizations are continually revising their goals in a constant interplay with external and internal forces that limit, shape, and support certain directions. As the best scenarios of tomorrow are formulated and strategic goals are established, immediately there are assumptions made about the amount and types of resources that are required to accomplish these objectives. Although some actions depend on capital, energy availability, materials, and market conditions, few plans can be accomplished without successfully harnessing critical labor resources. In fact, as a result of reduced or equalized competition on some of these factors, labor has become a more important element in reaching a competitive advantage. As service industries continue to grow, and service dimensions of non-service industries become more important in differentiating winners and losers, firms that best mobilize their labor resources in support of strategic objectives are most likely to succeed and grow. Only recently have firms focused more attention on the enormous investment in and underutilization of their labor resources.

Therefore, HR objectives and employee behaviors become crucial ingredients in successful plan implementation. However, organizations today do a limited job of assessing their human resources and the ingredients necessary for success.

The advantage is shifting to those organizations in which employee potential is mobilized best. For example, once the strategic plan is agreed on, immediately certain HR needs are implied. This occurs in two ways. A specific set of behaviors, activities, and unit outcomes needs to occur *and* a corporate culture that will support this direction must be crafted. The two must go hand in hand. For example, you cannot ask people to attempt risky activities in an environment of conservativism and risk avoidance. A recent client wanted to create a risk-oriented, innovative, low-bureaucratic, teamwork-oriented environment to foster the growth of critical research and development, marketing, and production activities surrounding a research area that promised to have an enormous market for the firm with the first technical breakthrough. However, they at first tried to establish this orientation within a culture that was fraught with risk avoidance, negativism regarding growth, low teamwork, and enormous bureaucracy. The effort failed miserably. A second attempt to foster this effort in a separate unit with strong management support for this culture succeeded, and led to major growth for the firm and for *all* the employees.

The senior management of a utility realized that the future deregulated nature of the industry would increase competition, open new markets, and require a strong customer orientation. This management team became frustrated because they thought that employees were not listening to the message and were not changing their behaviors. Clearly, one does not turn around ingrained values and attitudes in a few months any more than a captain could turn around a huge ocean-going vessel in several yards. However, further in-depth investigation indicated that although employees had indeed heard and understood the message regarding the need to change, they did not see any visible symbols supporting this message, nor did they see any change in related systems. For example, immediate managers were unsure of the implications and impact on specific operations, the reward system continued to support historical behaviors, decisions were more congruent with the "old" organization, and by and large they saw no real change in senior management behavior—just words! Clearly, the culture did not support the needed changes.

Culture and Focused Behaviors: Requirements for Success

Once the required behaviors and matching culture are ascertained, the firm must assess the gap from today's culture and activities. This requires a systematic assessment of behaviors and the existing culture. Such an assessment might be needed across the entire firm or only in particular business units. This type of gap analysis identifies the changes that will be required to reach key objectives. In some cases, this means minor adjustments; in other cases, it may mean a major overhaul. Ultimately, however, these changes are essential to success, in that they are key elements to reach the agreed on strategic plan. If management believes that the changes are impossible, then the plan needs to be revisited. If management moves recklessly ahead and assumes that the changes will be made when needed, disaster looms.

A firm in the transportation field went through a major transformation resulting from deregulation, with a greater need to increase customer awareness, service, and cost effectiveness. Strategic planning indicated that the successful market of tomorrow required a more flexible set of product offerings, a more congenial and knowledgeable workforce, and higher productivity. Management continuously tried to change key customer service behaviors, improve output, and upgrade staff knowledge. Little was accomplished, and business continued to decline for this firm because there was no commitment to the cultural changes that are essential to success. Rewards did not match the new behaviors or skills, punishment rather than encouragement was the norm, and service failures, rather than successes, received all the attention. Employees naturally shunned customer contact to avoid such situations—a sad story that didn't have to happen. It would have been better for management to revisit the strategic plan and make some hard decisions earlier in the process.

A gap analysis provides a precise blueprint of the type of changes that are required in both culture and behaviors. Such an analysis assesses attitudes, beliefs, norms, expectations, and values on the cultural side and specific behaviors, practices, plans, information, and direction on the behavioral side. The organization is then prepared to develop a realistic action plan for the changes needed. Such a plan identifies the time required to accomplish these changes. Most important, this assessment provides the firm with a clear picture of the baseline today so that changes can be readily identified.

Key elements that might be assessed in a gap analysis include the following:

Cultural Assessment

- Attitudes toward management and supervision, compensation systems, safety, communication, and working conditions
- Values regarding security, pay and benefits, autonomy, advancement, work and family, growth, ethical behavior, and control
- Expectations regarding pay for performance, fair pay, quality performance, training and education, equitable treatment, work load, and level of responsibility
- Beliefs about the performance appraisal process, relations with other departments, management style, communication credibility, competencies, and training quality
- Norms regarding work level, seniority, quality, and cooperation

Behavioral Assessment

- Planned objectives of individuals and business units including short-term and intermediate goals
- Performance levels, including quantity, quality, level of teamwork, and accomplishment of specific outcomes
- Types of behaviors, such as task, interpersonal, and customer
- Turnover and absence
- Safety activities and accidents
- Communication
- Employee relations or unionization and grievance activities

Monitoring the Plan

The next step in the process involves the management of the plan. If the plan is to be reached in the time interval specified, certain milestones must be identified and measured along the way. Again, attitudes and behaviors need to be periodically checked to determine if progress is being made behaviorally and culturally. Have some of the intended changes occurred? In what areas of the firm? Have employees heard and understood certain messages? Are they believed? Are employees more or less positive regarding certain issues than before? What role is management playing in the process? Are resources and rewards moving in tandem with behaviors? Is there adequate feedback?

Periodic surveys of the workforce or specific units can be quite helpful. Targeted focus group interviews can provide in-depth information among different job groups. Interviews with senior managers can identify key concerns and congruence with the "official" position. Barriers can be identified that must be removed in order to reach key goals.

It is important to define the targeted changes *at the beginning* in order to know how close the firm is to achieving its objectives. This is analogous to knowing where one is going on a trip. Baseline data, an understanding of the roads, and knowing how close one is to the goal are all important. Knowing that one has gone 300 miles is almost useless without knowing in which direction the miles have been traveled. The focus should always be in closing the gap between the current state and the desired goal. Few of us would drive to a new city without a good map and sound measurements (e.g., odometer, road markers, fuel gauge, and speedometer), and yet many organizations are driving to their destinations with limited measures and an ill-defined map.

Projecting for Tomorrow

At this stage, it is also crucial for the HR experts to factor in external changes that will have an impact on this workforce. If the plan encompasses five years, for example, the workforce then will not be identical to the one of today. Therefore, while continuing to shape the current workforce, management must be aware of external trends affecting values, attitudes, and expectations that will have an impact on both current employees *and* new hires over the next five years.

It is important to realize that these broad trends may influence your workforce to a *greater or lesser* extent. There is no substitute for continual monitoring of changing attitudes, values, and expectations within a particular workforce. By recognizing now the changes that are coming down the road, managers will be better able to integrate today's plans with tomorrow's workforce.

A California firm recently adopted a new style led by its president that called for less democratic decisionmaking and a more rigid communication style because of increasing customer demands, more structured tasks, and a need for tighter quality standards. Besides, the president's style was far more authoritarian than that of his predecessor. In this firm this approach backfired because it violated the implicit style expectations among the current workforce, many of whom left. It also flew in the face of the cultural values of most potential hires in the geographical area, leaving the firm with limited talent; high recruitment, selection, and training costs; and unacceptable turnover rates. Again, this could have been averted by understanding the culture-behavior-goal gaps.

ATTITUDE SURVEYS AS AN INTERVENTION

Attitude measures (surveys and other assessment instruments) can influence organizations in a number of ways:

- As a cathartic experience
- As a feedback tool regarding corporate culture, organizational health, and planned progress toward goals

- As a catalyst for action planning
- As a tracking system over time

Cathartic Experience

Each of these interventions varies in sophistication and value. For example, completing a questionnaire or participating in a focus group on work issues frequently has a cathartic value beyond the information generated. Many respondents feel relieved that they have finally expressed their views— views that have often been building up inside without a forum for release. Participants leaving focus groups often thank the moderator for "just listening."

This suggests several possibilities. First, many employees (and frequently customers also) do not have others with whom they can share their concerns, with the possible exception of close friends and family when available. Thus, this feedback vehicle allows them to purge feelings that, in many cases, have been heretofore hidden. Certain issues have, in all probability, been festering, and this represents an opportunity to officially let management know their thinking.

Second, it suggests that these upward communication vehicles represent some limited opportunities that employees have to regularly communicate about these issues. Because of status differences, fear of retribution, and poor supervisory communication skills, these issues often are not discussed with immediate supervisors or they have been discussed with no resolution. In either case, such pent-up feelings are unhealthy, likely to create stress, and potentially distracting from primary work focus.

Feedback Tool

As a feedback tool, the survey process often provides an unusual opportunity for individual managers to receive feedback without the usual positive biases that append most upward organizational communication. As mentioned previously, it is one of the few formal upward communication vehicles that most organizations have. Also, a survey with proper acknowledgment by management sends a message to employees that concerns have at least reached top management. What is done about these issues is another matter altogether.

A survey of attitudes can also provide a broad portrait of organizational strengths and weaknesses at one point in time. Most firms have unique profiles that represent their history and culture. Such profiles highlight both opportunities and obstacles. These profiles allow top management to compare perceptions across the organization in a systematic manner. Because all organizational units are being measured the same way, comparisons can be made across business units and across job groups (e.g., managers, clerical, professional, and hourly). Key differences across units and job groups can be noted for corrective action.

A note of caution is in order, however. Comparisons of attitudes across homogeneous business units can provide feedback regarding problems or concerns in certain pockets. However, unless these units have identical histories, caution should be exercised in drawing too many conclusions about unit differences. Too often management is immediately blamed for such differences. The differences should be a cause for investigation; causes should not be assumed. Businesses often have different internal histories (e.g., labor issues, skill differences, and operational problems). Some of these may well be due to management. But it is important to find out root causes before attributing all problems to the management team. Moreover, other differences may be caused by external forces: different labor markets, pay rates, competition, and geographical culture.

In comparing differences across job groups, it should also be noted that different job groups can have different norms. For example, managers are usually more positive than professionals, who in turn are more favorable than hourly employees. These differences are not as dramatic today as they were several decades ago. More important, comparisons of the same groups over time or with reasonably comparable groups are *most* useful. Knowledge of job group differences can also be helpful in comparisons across different business units, which may otherwise result in misleading conclusions. A recent client had compared the data from two acquisitions and drawn some severe conclusions about management style and leadership. A more complete analysis of the findings, however, clearly showed that most of the differences were due to the higher concentration of hourly employees in one workforce.

The most important feature in evaluating unit and total firm profiles is understanding what caused the differences. At the conclusion of the analysis, management should have a firm understanding of the causes of major differences. Causes may be quite apparent in some cases (e.g., new incentive plan in unit A or recent strike in unit B). In other cases, additional information may need to be gathered. Here is where focus groups can be an asset. If they have already been conducted, reasons for the differences may be in these data. Or targeted focus groups can be conducted after the survey to identify these causes. A structured feedback and action planning process can also illuminate root causes.

As this process is unfolding, the ownership of line managers is essential. Line managers should have access to the information first and the opportunity to study and interpret the data. It is through this process that line commitment is secured and managers learn how to use attitude survey feedback as a management tool. Thus, the solution to the corporate puzzle should not come from an audit team, but from line managers seeking to understand the issues from their respective employees. And this is the point where survey feedback can become the catalyst for important organizational corrections and action planning.

Survey Feedback: A Catalyst for Action

Moving a survey from the feedback stage to the action planning stage is probably the most difficult phase—more difficult than actually implementing plans once formulated. Several factors are key:

- Management involvement, commitment, and understanding
- Manager training
- Action planning process
- Disciplined follow-up strategy
- Communication of results and actions

Management Involvement, Commitment, and Understanding

Without senior management involvement early in the process, it is unlikely that the survey will serve as a strong catalyst for change. Management is likely to have an agenda that is independent of the process, the survey will not have been a prominent activity (low profile), and it will not be viewed as a key component in goal attainment. The survey can become a political football to be used by those with positions to gain.

Line managers, especially at senior levels, need to know the process parameters, understand what the survey or other assessment tool can do for them, participate in its development (thereby assuring a level of ownership and commitment), and see the survey as a tool to help them reach their objectives. This early involvement also helps to focus the assessment so that information will naturally flow into decisions.

Manager Training

A common cause of unsuccessful follow-up is a lack of manager feedback, action planning, and communication skills. Many organizations decide to save money and time at this stage, assume that managers know how to use the information, take this inappropriate opportunity to delegate authority (budgets have already been spent or the staff coordinating department has run out of time and people), or assume that other training has already prepared them for the process. All of these reasons are sure signals of impending failure.

Because they are not trained in this process, most managers are likely to go about this in a totally inappropriate and sometimes destructive way. The positive essence of a survey can be lost at this point. Not surprisingly, managers with the best interpersonal and communications skills do far better, and managers most in need of a sound feedback and action planning session with their subordinates are most likely to fail when left to their own devices. For the latter group, training is not only desirable, but essential. Many managers read through a cookbook approach or are given a limited training session, conduct a mediocre to poor action planning session with their subordinates, and become extremely frustrated or embarrassed. They then blame the survey process when in fact it was their preparedness that failed. Furthermore, their subordinates are also frustrated that little action resulted from the survey process.

A major contributing factor is the "management macho" syndrome. Most managers will not ask for help because it demonstrates weakness. Most are not sure what help they need. Many do not know where to start and certainly won't ask. Others will not devote the time needed to carry the process to completion, an outcome that is worse than not starting at all (because expectations have been raised and then dashed). If the firm is committed to this process, then it must be prepared to train managers how to conduct effective feedback and action planning sessions. These sessions and the activities that follow are the real bread and butter of change.

Managers should be led through a reasonably structured process that covers not only the analysis, interpretation, and prioritization of their data, but also the mechanics of conducting feedback sessions, the process issues that are so important, and the products or outcomes that can be obtained. Successful training efforts include instruction in how to do the following:

- Analyze unit data
- Develop themes or issues
- Prioritize issues
- Prepare for an action planning session
- Conduct the session(s)
- Develop specific action plans
- Mobilize plans
- Communicate and follow-up with employees

This may look like a formidable task that is well beyond most organizations. In reality, the training time is one to two days; the analysis, preparation, and feedback time is one to three days, depending on the complexity of the unit.

The Action Planning Process

After training, managers feel more comfortable about using survey data as a source of information about company, unit, and supervisory issues. A key step in utilization is a disciplined action planning process. This begins with the feedback and action planning meeting, but doesn't end there. During the feedback and action planning meeting, an overview of the survey findings should be fed back to employees and key issues discussed in depth. Additional meetings may be needed to cover difficult or complex subjects. The successful meeting will yield not only greater depth of understanding about key issues, but also information about the relative priority of different issues, probable causes of problems, and potential solutions. Not all issues will be resolved, but a serious step toward solution will have begun.

Solutions are impossible or inappropriate if problems are not clearly defined and causes identified. Furthermore, a particular issue may be moot if other issues supersede it in importance. Therefore, the first goal of the action planning meeting is the clarification and listing of major issues. The second goal is the prioritization of these issues. An often fatal error for many managers and organizations is tackling too many issues at once and accomplishing little change on any. Over the years, I have met many proud managers who have announced their attack on forty or fifty issues. The usual result a year or two later is a disappointed manager who has accomplished little on any of the issues and a frustrated workforce that has been led to expect too many changes.

It is usually more effective to address a manageable number of high-priority areas that will bring about the greatest improvement for the time invested. This may represent more issues for some managers than others, but the important feature is to set realistic objectives.

The next objective from the action planning session is a better understanding of the root causes underlying high-priority issues. Some of these causes become clear during the discussion, whereas others will require further investigation. Some solutions to these issues will be obvious, whereas others will require special effort, multiple individuals or departments, or external parties. Too often managers assume that they know best what the root cause is. Their hit rate is questionable from my experience. Attacking the wrong causes can derail a sound action planning strategy. It is both costly and time-consuming. More important, it can also destroy credibility.

A personnel director of a *Fortune* 100 firm recently declared to a survey consultant that the issues from a recent survey did not surprise him. In fact, to the consultant's surprise, he also had an immediate answer to each issue. Holding back his doubt, the consultant asked the director how he was so prepared and he replied that he had already been promoting solutions to these issues for several years without success. The detailed analysis of the issues by cross-functional teams subsequently discovered root causes that differed substantially from those identified by the director. One of the key solutions from the armchair analyst (changing a key employee benefit) would have been directly contrary to the actual solution, an attack on an information deficiency, not on the design of a highly valued benefit.

A Disciplined Follow-up Strategy

Another reason employee assessments may not achieve the type of change and improvement possible is a failure to follow through in a disciplined manner. This means complete follow-through at both the individual manager and organizational levels. A process should be established to facilitate the upward flow of information on issues, causes, and potential solutions. At one level this means simply reporting on action plans to higher management. This will be the case for issues that are totally within the control of individual managers. For example, if a given manager discovers that his employees do not receive enough communication from him on changes in administrative scheduling (under his control), then he is in a position to institute changes to improve this problem. Such plans can simply be reported to his management as part of the action planning reporting process.

At another level, this means constructing a uniform way to pass key issues that require higher levels of authority to managers who possess this level of control. This upward flow of issues should continue until all issues reach the appropriate level of authority or until they are bounced back as something that should be solved at a lower level. Each level of management must assimilate the issues from subordinates and go through the prioritization process. It is important that issues not be deleted along the way without proper feedback to those below who are waiting for a response to a problem.

For example, problems with the fringe benefit plan or the compensation system are candidates for resolution at more global organizational levels. Issues that require coordination across different departments or business units, policies issues, or business strategy may require senior level attention.

This strategy leads to actions at all levels in the organization, an unlikely outcome with many first-time survey users. Too many first-timers believe that all issues will somehow be resolved by the executive team. The executive team seldom has the time or the appropriate level of information to tackle the issues thoroughly. Moreover, this eliminates the input, involvement, and action that should take place at lower and middle management levels.

The other first-timer error is delegating all of the problems and solutions down the line. Usually these pile up at the first-line supervisory level with some frustrated supervisors without adequate authority or perspective to solve the issues. *It is essential to match issues with appropriate levels of authority to solve these concerns.* This is a key component to a successful change intervention.

Other Key Components to Change

Several other key components to a disciplined follow-through are as follows:

- Clear assignment of responsibility to an individual or a solution team
- Realistic, but firm timetable for change
- Identifiable milestones for more complex solutions
- Feedback on change process
- Formal evaluation of problem resolution

- Reward for successes
- Communication of results and actions

Each of these steps contributes to the completeness of an effective change effort.

Clear assignment of responsibility to an individual or a solution team. Responsibility for identifying solutions (or causes) should be clearly defined once issues have been agreed on. Too often solutions are left to chance or "everyone," and little changes. Typically, many issues at the individual manager level will be the responsibility of the manager (e.g., holding more frequent staff meetings or giving more complete performance feedback) or a direct report (e.g., gathering additional data on a particular issue or generating a report for the group). For more complex issues, however, a solution team should be identified that has the proper time to commit, the correct mix of skills needed, and adequate authority to accomplish their mission. Furthermore, their charge should be clearly identified. One of the most frequent occurrences in large bureaucracies today is the establishment of teams or task forces that spend three-quarters of their time trying to identify their purpose or "what the assignor wants."

Realistic, but firm timetable for change. Goals should be attached to aggressive but realistic timetables. A master plan should be constructed to ensure that key corporate efforts are not conflicting with one another in commitment time.

Identifiable milestones for more complex solutions. Many complex solutions will require greater time and will be staged in implementation. Some will require feedback points to establish that the proposed solution is having the intended effect. Furthermore, people working on such complex efforts need to have intermittent feedback that significant accomplishments have indeed occurred. By utilizing this step, many firms have averted further work on solutions that were not having the intended effect.

For example, two departments in a large financial institution had identified a new system of interdepartmental communication using new computer technology that would reduce serious conflict across these two units, resulting in poor customer service. This new approach seemed sure to work, but at the phase I review, it was clear that the two units were cooperating no better than before because of low trust, artificial numbers being entered into the system, and computer downtime that reduced customer response. Clearly, more work was needed, but a more serious disaster was averted before the costlier phases II and III were implemented.

Feedback on change process. Whether the solutions are simple or complex, a good feedback channel is needed to assess whether changes are on track. Because many of the issues were generated by employees in the survey and the subsequent action planning sessions, managers should meet again with these groups at periodic intervals to ascertain if the solutions are having the intended effect. This can be quite simple at the individual manager level. More complex methods (systems tracking, surveys, focus groups, or analysis of archival data) may be needed at broader organizational levels.

Formal evaluation of problem resolution. Regardless of the periodic implementation feedback or milestones identified, a formal, objective assessment of real change should be conducted after the target implementation schedule has been completed. This might be accomplished through a follow-up survey, focus groups, changes in key indices, or other factors that one would expect to change as a result of the solutions. This measurement should be discussed during the planning stage and agreed to *before* implementation.

Examples of such change might include higher attendance, fewer accidents, higher performance levels, more cooperation across units, better understanding of issues, policies, and procedures, greater satisfaction with key attitudinal areas, and lower turnover. It is important that measures be selected that reflect the intended improvement.

Reward for successes. For serious organizational improvement, a great deal of effort by many individuals and groups is required. This effort should be recognized by management and rewarded, or it is unlikely to be repeated in the future.

Communication of results and actions. Another area of frequent shortcoming in many firms is in communicating changes that result from the evaluation of employee opinions and attitudes. This step is important in validating the usefulness of the survey assessment process. It tells employees that their attitudes are important, that their ideas have contributed to organizational improvement, and that management listens. This greatly enhances the credibility of the process.

A mistake that many firms make is trying to "sell" employees on "all the changes" just before the next survey. This public relations approach usually backfires for several reasons. First, in these firms, too often few significant changes have really been implemented, and management is now worried that the "chickens have come home to roost." Second, a sales approach at the eleventh hour is usually viewed as exactly that—a sales approach. Most employees are sophisticated enough that they view such efforts as a substitution for real changes of which they should already be aware. Finally, most work attitudes change gradually over time and are unlikely to be affected by these last-minute efforts. It is more important to address issues gradually over time and then clearly communicate these changes to employees as they are implemented. This steady approach will have far better effect.

A Tracking System over Time

The most sophisticated utilization of employee attitudes is in tracking the cultural and behavioral profiles over time in harmony with the changing strategic and operational needs of the enterprise. This level of assessment enables managers to integrate current employees' (or for that matter any other stakeholder) profiles with the profiles that will be needed to meet future goals.

APPLYING SURVEY RESULTS TO SHAPE HR PROGRAMS

The HR function in the firm most often takes responsibility for coordinating these efforts. In many ways, a comprehensive survey program of the workforce can provide essential information regarding the organizational roadmap. Because current attitudes and values are inextricably intertwined with both current and future behaviors, the assessment of these attitudes provides HR managers and the entire senior executive team with an insight into not only today's, but also tomorrow's behavior.

With this increasing trend toward the strategic as well as the operational use of employee attitudes and values, there is a tremendous opportunity for the HR function to play a crucial role in strategy that has been heretofore absent in many firms. Because of the key role that surveys, focus groups, and other assessments can play, a sophisticated HR team using a combination of internal and external expertise can craft and manage a tool that provides continual feedback on organizational progress.

A number of key roles include developing the core measures (questionnaire scales, focus group formats, and key content areas) that will be used to track long- and short-term progress; developing a game plan for implementation of the assessments; ensuring that the data collection is confidential; ensuring that the analysis and interpretation are complete and unbiased; developing a follow-up action planning strategy that incorporates the elements described earlier in this chapter and serves as a coordinating point for the flow of information (manager reports and unit and company action plans) after the assessment; coordinating outside resources to assist in various phases of the work; monitoring action plans for common themes and developmental needs that should be coordinated on a companywide basis; communicating companywide plans and actions; serving as a resource to individual units in these efforts; and evaluating change.

Although many themes in a typical survey reflect specifically on unit management, a number of issues relate to HR policy and programs (e.g., benefits, training and development, and performance appraisal process). Survey feedback regarding these issues will be an important ingredient in assessing the effectiveness of these efforts and potential changes that might be needed in the future. For example, most broad-based surveys provide feedback regarding the effectiveness of training and development efforts. Problem areas are often identified along with areas of additional need. This feedback is one part of the information that HR managers need to justify the cost effectiveness of investing in particular training efforts.

In kind, such feedback can also identify areas in which programs may be eliminated—a safety program that is not working or manager training that is not delivering the intended effect. Information regarding compensation and benefits and their relation to individual and unit performance is always helpful in identifying how these reward systems are functioning.

Finally, in understanding the needs for tomorrow, the cultural profile of today's workforce, and the changing profile of the external labor pool, HR managers will be in a better position to select new hires for both current and future needs.

In sum, HR managers can use attitudinal and behavioral information from such assessments to fine tune, change, or develop key programs that support strategic objectives. The survey feedback can also provide a more strategic role for human resources in overall organizational planning.

Part III

Formulating Human Resource Strategies

The three chapters in this section focus on how human resource (HR) strategies are developed in response to organizational needs and information about internal and external labor force trends.

James Walker, a well-known author and consultant in the area of HR planning, writes about how companies are increasingly addressing HR issues as business issues. He outlines four steps for developing HR strategies, including defining HR issues, analyzing the issues, planning actions, and determining how results will be evaluated. Examples of people-related business issues and resulting HR strategies include introducing new technology, managing growth and change, achieving and maintaining low costs, improving service quality, and managing business units as profit centers ("divisionalizing"). Companies define critical HR issues by sorting through the many environmental trends and external conditions, such as those discussed in Part I, along with organizational changes. Walker recommends promoting "open thinking" about emerging issues by brainstorming and other ways to envision the future and generate action strategies. He also recommends obtaining input from a variety of sources, including managers, employees, and other constituents (customers and suppliers). Once action plans are developed, a plan is necessary for evaluating their impact. This should be more than determining whether the plans or programs have been implemented. Criteria need to be established for evaluating success, measurement strategies need to be identified or developed, and a tracking mechanism needs to be imposed, including plans for digesting and responding to the results.

James Sheridan, an independent consultant with many years of corporate experience in HR planning, addresses how to think about HR data. He emphasizes the importance of establishing the assumptions underlying data, such as specifying the time period for the forecast and the purpose of the forecast. In fact, the purpose of the forecast will dictate the type of data required. Sheridan suggests the development of HR indicators, such as head count, salary expenses, and money spent on training. One way to better understand these measures is to express them in ratios, such as the number of employees in the HR department to the total number of employees in the firm. These ratios can be examined historically and also used as a basis of comparison with other firms, especially competitors. In addition, forecasts of how these ratios will (or should) change in the future, given organizational changes such as a major growth or reduction in the workforce, must be tempered by assumptions about what is good and bad. That is, whether 1 HR employee for every 150 employees in the organization is a good ratio or a bad ratio will depend on the particular needs of the firm at the time. For instance, an organization that is experiencing major downsizing may need to maintain a large HR staff for a while to help with outplacement activities and to help surviving employees improve their morale. The goals of ratio analysis are to understand the relationship of HR data to other performance data in the company, to provide alternative HR solutions to business objectives, to identify possible business opportunities and/or threats, and to educate line management in the integration of human resources into strategic and operational planning. Some HR measures should become objectives. Other HR measures should remain indicators—ways to study and interpret events in the company and the environment, but not necessarily goals to attain. An important part of developing HR strategy is establishing which measures, and levels of these measures, are to be objectives and which should be indicators. Similar to Walker, Sheridan emphasizes the importance of evaluating HR programs with the proper measures to better understand human resources within the context of the organization.

Diana Kramer, a psychologist with extensive business background in HR forecasting and planning, offers basic tools for executive succession planning. As organizations become more global and face increasingly competitive environments, they must ensure that the right people are available when they are needed. This requires advance planning. Kramer provides step-by-step methods that can be used by HR professionals to help managers and executives recognize the need for planning to fill important positions before they become vacant. She describes a participative process that will ensure agreement about the evaluation of executives and managers and plans for their development.

Manuel London, an industrial and organizational psychologist who worked for AT&T for twelve years during a time of major organizational change, considers the role of the HR professional as change agent and strategist. The purpose of the chapter is to help HR professionals recognize how they influence organizational direction, and how they can use HR forecasts as one source of information to contribute to organizational strategy. He suggests that HR professionals are probably more effective change agents and strategists when they are at higher organizational levels and when they have a close relationship with key managers. Being knowledgeable about the firm's business operations is a critical element of developing such relationships. London reviews frustrations that HR professionals experience and barriers they encounter in trying to influence organizational strategy, such as a lack of business training and being at the mercy of executives who have limited commitment to HR initiatives. However, he argues that these frustrations and barriers can be overcome by several critical behaviors, such as being a good listener, being problem-focused, and developing partnership relationships with line managers. London outlines challenges for the HR professional and ways to be more effective in the future. For instance, one challenge is gaining support for new ideas, and one way to be a more effective strategist is to search for opportunities to influence organizational strategy. Developing "scenarios of the future" is a way to engage line managers in interpreting environmental trends and formulating strategic action plans. The case of Grumman Corporation demonstrates how HR programs, such as phased retirement, result from a recognition of demographic trends, in this case the aging workforce and the need to avoid age discrimination. London concludes by examining several probable HR problems for the 1990s, such as managing a corporation in a global, multicultural environment.

_____

CHAPTER 6

DEVELOPING HUMAN RESOURCE STRATEGIES

_____ JAMES W. WALKER

As companies rely on strategic planning as a fundamental process in managing business organizations, they are paying more attention to human resource (HR) planning. Today leading companies are developing explicit HR strategies as part of the overall strategic thrust. With increased emphasis being placed on productivity, quality, and service, executives are recognizing that attention to the financial and technological side of the business must be balanced with attention to planning for HR management.

Functional strategies for finance, marketing, technology, manufacturing, and information management are often developed in support of overall business strategies. HR strategies, however, have remained largely informal and operational. Often HR plans are prepared by the HR staff and presented as a separate functional or departmental plan to senior management. Even when the strategic planning process has been adapted to include a section on human resources, the emphasis typically remains on financial, marketing, and product concerns.

Planning for human resources itself often involves separate processes. Planning for management succession and organization has received wide attention, but typically as a process separate from strategic planning. Also, in many companies, major thrusts for total quality or productivity improvement have often been adopted independently of other HR plans.

FOCUSING ON ISSUES

To achieve improved integration in planning, leading companies today address HR issues as business issues and develop strategies to address them. They examine critical management issues and opportunities within the context of business strategies and operational plans, considering issues at each organizational level and perspectives of all constituents. By focusing on critical business concerns, any of the approaches for developing HR strategies can become more effective.

An issue represents a gap between the current situation and the state required for achievement of strategic business objectives. Although there may be many important HR issues, leading companies focus on a few important actionable concerns so as to develop a sense of urgency and commitment to action. In the planning process, they consider inherent conflicts and trade-offs among issues.

Leading companies plan specific management actions to address key issues. Their HR strategies involve multiple activities over a one- to three-year period. They assign clear responsibility, timing, and resources required to implement the strategy. Also, they consider how the strategy will be executed—how all parties will be informed and involved in implementing the strategies.

In this chapter, the process for developing HR strategies with an issues focus is described. Specifically, the following four steps are outlined, with examples provided from leading companies.

1. Define HR issues: What is the problem, gap, or opportunity identified as an implication of business change?
2. Analyze these issues: What are the dimensions of the issue?
3. Plan management actions: What courses of action will be implemented?
4. Determine how results will be evaluated: How will performance be measured and what will be the target levels?

These steps parallel the basic questions addressed in formulating strategies in other functional areas. However, an explicit planning process is more important for HR management because issues and strategies are often more ambiguous than financial, product, or other management concerns.

WHY DEVELOP HR STRATEGY?

Developing HR strategy allows management to address people-related business issues in achieving strategic business objectives—to enhance current and future performance and sustained competitive advantage.

HR strategy provides various benefits to a company. Specifically, the process of developing HR strategies accomplishes the following:

• Defines HR opportunities and barriers for achievement of business objectives
• Prompts new thinking about HR issues—orients and educates participants and provides a wider perspective

- Tests management commitment for actions—creates a process for allocating resources to specific programs and activities
- Develops a sense of urgency and commitment to action
- Focuses on selected long-term courses of action considered high priority over the next two to three years.
- Provides a strategic focus for managing the HR function and developing HR staff talents

HR strategy is required to address issues that arise from fundamental changes that occur in the business environment. Such changes include the following:

- More rapid rate of business change and high uncertainty
- Increasing competitive pressures on both revenues and costs
- Rapid technological change, resulting in new skill demands
- More complex, flatter, leaner, more flexible organizations
- Changing demographics and workforce availabilities
- Changing work-life patterns and employee expectations
- Changing external forces: governmental regulation, litigation, union relations, and so on.
- Increasing multinational competition and collaboration

In response to these changes, companies are defining and addressing specific HR issues, such as the following:

- Achieving and sustaining cost competitiveness—personnel costs, utilization, downsizing, eliminating unnecessary work
- Achieving competitive differentiation through total service and product quality—productivity, customer satisfaction, and other components of total quality
- Implementing organizational restructuring and mergers or acquisitions
- Increasing delegation of authority and responsibility—streamlined approval processes, increased employee involvement, risk/reward compensation, and empowerment to act
- Enhancing organizational effectiveness—team building, shared vision and values (culture), lateral relationships, and so on
- Developing leadership—staffing, appraisal, and development of managers
- Enhancing workforce capability and motivation—staffing, retention, motivation and rewards, development, communications and involvement, work life issues

The relevance of any of these changing conditions or HR issues is established in a company only by direct assessment of the HR implications of business issues. The following are several examples of business issues and HR issues being addressed by companies today.

EXAMPLES OF PEOPLE-RELATED BUSINESS ISSUES AND RESULTING HR STRATEGIES

There is, of course, only one primary HR issue in any company: How can the organization assure that it will have people of the right types and numbers, organized appropriately, managed effectively, and focused on customer satisfaction? It is necessary to define specific HR issues, however, as illustrated in the following examples.

Introducing New Technology

Leading manufacturing companies are focusing on the introduction of new products and technology. Business strategies require shifts toward shorter product cycles, simultaneous engineering, and use of new technology such as expert systems, artificial intelligence, fiber optics, computer-aided design and manufacturing, and robotics.

The HR issue defined here is one of strategic importance: re-skilling of the workforce. HR strategies address needs for changes in recruitment, education and training, teamwork and technology transfer, organizational and staffing changes, project management and cross-discipline integration, and assessment of individual skills and development needs.

In an automobile company, design and manufacturing engineering organizations are being merged to address new technological needs and an "engineering college" has been established to provide expanded technical training. Other strategies include assessment of skills, forecasting of staffing and skill needs, and improved program management and organizational effectiveness.

A computer manufacturer is emphasizing cross-training, teamwork, and collaboration across units to improve engineering and technology transfer. Retraining, transfers, and recruiting are needed to ensure that the required new skills are available as needed to sustain the company's technological competitive advantage.

Managing Growth and Change

Many companies are experiencing rapid business growth or change. Their business strategies call for development of entrepreneurial business units and transformation of business practices to anticipate competitive needs and respond to increasing business complexity.

The HR implications of these strategies often concentrate on staffing and changing the way staff are managed. Companies that experience these changes emphasize recruitment of needed talent (both in numbers and changing skills required) and replacement or retraining of those who do not match needs. Strategies also involve design of new compensation programs to attract and retain key talent and changes in the way the organization is managed to ensure a competitive, entrepreneurial spirit.

A leading commercial bank, for example, shifted away from traditional corporate and retail banking services and toward investment banking and corporate financial services. This resulted in shifts toward autonomous banking units, creation of many new incentive plans, widespread changes in staff, and new management planning and control processes. The bank evolved from a large, stable institution into a flexible, fast-paced, risk-oriented enterprise.

A retail food business with both company-operated and franchised stores has grown rapidly in recent years. As it has expanded, both domestically and internationally, strains on its management systems and its people became evident. The HR issue of strategic importance is to equip management with the capacity to sustain the targeted growth and profitability—to not let management talent or effectiveness be a barrier to continued expansion.

A fast-growing computer company is noted for its "family culture," its informality, youthful vigor, and creativity. As the company has expanded, nearly doubling in size every several years, the demands on recruiting, development, and effective integration of new talent into the culture have mounted. Additionally, pressures to become more businesslike are being balanced with the desire to retain the spirit of the company.

Achieving and Maintaining Low Costs

For many companies, becoming or remaining a low-cost producer is a key business objective. For them, lower direct product costs, minimized indirect and overhead expenses, and avoidance of future costs or extraordinary expenses are key concerns.

The HR implications are evident—reducing and managing personnel-related costs, rightsizing the organization, reducing benefits costs, adopting pay-for-performance programs, improving productivity and efficiency, and avoiding costs resulting from litigation and regulatory demands.

A major manufacturer is seeking continual improvements in product costs. An across-the-board reduction in staff of 25 percent is being followed by more selective changes in staffing and organization. A cooperative strategy process involving the unions focuses on opportunities for further productivity gains.

An office equipment company found itself a high-cost producer as it experienced increased foreign competition in its markets. It is gradually and steadily reducing its cost structure by identifying and addressing opportunities for improvements. Similarly, a steel company has reduced the scale of the organization by eliminating operations and downsizing the entire organization, while maintaining and strengthening the capabilities needed to achieve targeted profitability.

A fresh-poultry processor is facing an unusual business issue with significant HR implications. Carpel tunnel syndrome, caused by repetitive motion, is increasing in attention and cost potential (fines and litigation costs). The condition and competition for employee talent are also increasing wage rates at company locations. The preferred strategy—increased use of automation—is constrained by the state of technology: the capacity to handle chickens of various sizes efficiently and the capacity to control *Salmonella* contamination. In the absence of automation, strategies will emphasize rotation and retraining of employees to minimize the effect of the syndrome.

Improving Service and Quality

Enhancing the value or quality of products and services is a key objective in many companies for gaining competitive advantage, or at least parity with competitors. They are setting tougher performance requirements, seeking continual quality improvement in products and services, and strengthening the value chain involving vendors and distributors.

For these companies, the overriding HR issue is organizational effectiveness. Strategies include streamlining the work (structure, delegation, and activities), strengthening management for performance and service or quality, attracting and retaining needed talent, improving team effectiveness, and building employee involvement and commitment to changes supporting the company vision and values.

A national lodging and food service company seeks to continue its rapid growth while sustaining profitability and cash flow. However, the industry is overbuilt, and the economics are increasingly difficult to sustain. The available labor pool is diminishing (owing to changing demographics), and turnover is rising in some segments of the business. Accordingly, the company is implementing strategies to become a preferred employer, aimed at reducing turnover and improving employee capability and motivation to provide superior service.

To maintain its competitive superiority in business results, a pharmaceutical company seeks ways to sustain and improve performance in research, sales, manufacturing, and other functions. Until 1995, the company faces organizational blockages resulting from low turnover, flatter organization structures, age compression and postponed retirements, and an oversupply of promotable talent. Accordingly, HR strategies address needs for tougher performance and productivity goals, increased employee understanding and support, and strengthened overall organization.

A leading computer manufacturer recognizes that to maintain its competitiveness in a rapidly changing market, it needs to improve its focus on the customer. Effective customer service requires quicker responses, more effective information support, and lower overhead costs. Strategies address opportunities to redeploy and retrain talent, streamline internal communications and decision processes, and more directly support customer needs.

An electronics company includes quality and productivity improvement as a strategic requirement to remain competitive on a global basis. Each year, each business reviews its strategy, structure, management processes, and performance and identifies ways to improve organizational effectiveness. Over five years, each has planned and implemented a series of unique projects aimed at achieving breakthrough steps in these areas. Priorities have included competitive benchmarking, achieving total customer satisfaction, and reducing total cycle time. The organization effectiveness process itself is part of the strategy because it is a shared learning experience that involves a large number of managers and employees.

Divisionalizing

Some companies are seeking to increase business unit competitiveness in diverse markets by managing business units as profit centers. At the same time, they are seeking to maintain enterprise value added.

The primary HR challenge is to make flexibility work. Typical strategies include developing customized or flexible compensation and benefit programs, clarifying management philosophy and policy, strengthening management capabilities or capacity to act, and building teamwork and organizational effectiveness.

A large insurance company encourages initiatives in its diverse financial services and investment business units. Each business unit defines its own competitive requirements and priorities, including HR issues. However, the overall enterprise monitors these priorities, provides coordination and integration on common concerns, and imposes issues of overriding corporate concern (e.g., affirmative action and management succession and management incentive plan design).

A leading retailer is seeking to increase its competitiveness by organizing the business along product lines and then expanding its network of stores within each, rather than as integrated, full-service stores. HR issues arise regarding the ways employees are to be recruited, compensated, and managed differently in each business segment, according to its competitive environment.

A leading food products company acquired several unrelated businesses in recent years, but continued to manage them from the food products perspective. Now it is further decentralizing management processes and the HR function itself to respond to different subsidiary needs and bring accountability for HR management within the businesses.

Unregulated subsidiaries of a telephone operating company are developing

HR strategies to address their unique HR issues, such as technical staffing, sales effectiveness, and international staffing. At the same time, these strategies are formulated within the context of the far larger telephone company, which has different issues and concerns. The balancing of subsidiary and enterprise strategies is itself an issue being addressed by the corporate and subsidiary executives.

HOW TO DEFINE HR ISSUES

In formulating HR strategy, it is important, first of all, to know what the "real problems" are and understand their relation to the business strategy. What are the gaps or "sources of pain" in managing human resources? Leading companies address HR issues as business issues. A HR issue is important when management of people can make or break achievement of business strategies.

To define the critical HR issues, companies sort through the many environmental, organizational, and strategic changes that have HR implications. The issues that survive the screening process should have a direct business impact and should be issues that can be acted on. The following activities may be used to help identify issues:

- Identify HR implications of key business strategies and objectives, considering key success factors (e.g., low cost, service or quality, and differentiation), stage of business maturity, and critical changes occurring in the business.

- Identify implications of significant external conditions and internal organizational conditions, such as labor availability, labor mobility and turnover, union relations, employee attitudes and productivity, and substance abuse.

- Consider perspectives of all relevant constituents, such as managers at different levels, employees, vendors and suppliers, and customers.

- Assess people-related business issues in each business unit or situation and chart them on a companywide basis—overlay company and business unit issues using a common framework.

- Consider inherent conflicts and trade-offs among issues (e.g., low cost and high service, union avoidance and productivity).

- Focus on a few important actionable concerns, recognizing the need to be selective and to concentrate management attention and limited resources.

Rarely are HR issues or strategies explicit in business plans. Accordingly, they must be interpreted from business changes or issues such as those described above. An understanding of the nature and structure of the business, competitive strengths and vulnerabilities, and key business success factors provides the best possible foundation for HR planning.

HOW TO ANALYZE HR ISSUES

Once key issues are identified in broad terms, the next step is to assess these possible HR issues and conduct focused data collection and analysis of specific issues of concern:

- *Conduct open thinking about issues and options.* Conduct brainstorming, "visioning," or Delphi analyses of the possible future HR issues and strategies that might address them.
- *Assess business plans and situations.* Examine information pertinent to HR issues from business plans and other relevant sources.
- *Obtain perceptions from managers.* Conduct interviews, focus groups, or surveys with key managers, or include HR questions in the planning process itself.
- *Obtain perceptions of employees.* Examine available attitude or climate survey data; conduct interviews or focus groups to help define issues and alternative strategies.
- *Obtain perceptions from other constituents.* Interview or survey customers, contractors, and business partners regarding HR issues to be addressed.
- *Examine external data.* Identify and assess external environmental factors that influence HR issues in the business.
- *Assess parity of HR management.* Assess relative HR strengths and vulnerabilities of the company and its key competitors; assess the company's talent, management practices, and HR systems and programs relative to other companies.
- *Conduct focused data analysis.* Obtain and assess evidence on each issue and define its scope, timing, and applicability and coverage in the organization; examine employee productivity issues, service quality, staffing surpluses or shortfalls, succession needs, skill requirements, turnover and retention patterns, employee attitudes, and so on.

HOW TO DEVELOP MANAGEMENT ACTION PLANS

Here is where companies typically concentrate their efforts in HR planning. They consider the alternative actions that could be taken—HR programs or practices that are applicable to perceived needs. Leading companies first prioritize the issues and then develop management action plans by selecting the actions that will address the key issues most effectively.

To prioritize issues, consider the importance of each issue, the organization's capacity to address it, the urgency or timing of the issue, resource constraints, management perceptions, and current work in progress. One leading company screens issues by assessing (a) the probability of the issue occurring, (b) the impact on the business if it occurs, and (c) the company's ability to influence, manage, or control the issue. In that company's view, the first two factors represent importance to the business.

Management action plans should address the issues. Strategies typically define a series of actions planned over a one- to three-year period. The actual time frame usually parallels the time frame of other functional planning in a company. These strategies call for multiple activities and programs as required. Within the strategies, responsibility and timing should be specified. Also, financial and staff requirements should be described, to the extent they are known.

Strategies that address issues common to different business units should be presented as part of business plans, both business unit and integrated company plans, as appropriate. Also, the key issues and strategies should be presented in the context of both business plans and functional HR plans (departmental plans) at each appropriate level of the organization. Management concurrence on strategies should be achieved in the same manner as for other functional plans.

Management action plans should also address how the strategies will be communicated and executed. HR strategies should include plans for assuring effectiveness of managers in implementing plans (e.g., communication, training, performance objectives, and incentives). They should also address needs for modifying HR processes and operations of the HR staff function to lead and support the implementation.

HOW TO EVALUATE RESULTS

Most companies evaluate the results of HR strategy implementation in terms of the actual completion of planned programs, projects, or other actions. This is consistent with the typical process of translating broad plans into specific operational plans, objectives, and activities. Accomplishment of the operational objectives is the measure of results attained.

It is possible, however, to define measures of achievements in terms of the ultimate impact on the issues defined. This requires definition of the specific measures to be used—the evidence required to determine the impact of the actions on the issue (e.g., turnover rates, personnel cost ratios, employee attitude indices, productivity improvement, service quality, or skill development). These should be stated quantitatively, if possible, and preferably in financial terms.

Target levels of impact should be defined for these measures (e.g., improvement in the turnover rate, reduction of costs, and improvement of service). The timing and accountability for these results should be specified, as for any management performance objective. The evaluation process is often most effective when it is integrated with the normal business planning and review process.

Evaluation of results maintains the focus on the original issues defined as important, rather than on the activities that are deemed relevant and practical. To develop effective HR strategies in today's increasingly demanding business environment requires a focus on the end results—resolution of issues, not merely the means. Measurement of results in terms of issues, however, requires a more diligent and comprehensive process of defining issues and developing management action plans. Developing HR strategies becomes a more demanding task of management.

CHAPTER 7

FORECASTS AND PROJECTIONS: DRAWING IMPLICATIONS FROM CHANGES IN EMPLOYEE CHARACTERISTICS

JAMES A. SHERIDAN

The development of employee forecasts in many businesses has been based primarily on the need to prepare their budgets. Clearly, the focus question in the past has been: How many employees will it take, and what will the employee costs be if we are to accomplish our financial targets *next year*? Every manager has had to answer this question when budget time rolls around, and one can safely say that most business managers are not naive when it comes to preparing an answer for that question. In the real-world budgeting process there is the tendency, and in many companies the practice, of overstating personnel requirements at the beginning of the budget and then adjusting the figures downward as the year unfolds. Valid reasons for the overstatement exist. The most valid reason is that the manager doesn't know what the future will hold, nor does he fully understand the relation between people and revenue. This chapter focuses on a few simple quick-look forecasting and projection approaches that should provide managers with some easy analyses that in turn will assist them in detecting key changes in their human resource (HR) requirements and in planning for those changes. Although high-level math is not required, the reader is encouraged to think about the implications of the information to be used. In thinking through the implications, the reader should discover a new level of understanding about his or her own company. The power of this thought process cannot be underestimated. Selected examples of interpretative clues are provided in the chapter for the reader to evaluate and to provide a starting point for thinking when analyzing HR data. It is my intention to create a process for thinking about these problems that will allow the reader to solve many problems; therefore, the emphasis is more on how to think about the issues than on providing specific answers to and examples of the many issues that exist.

FORECASTS AND PROJECTIONS

For those readers with little or no experience in HR forecasting, there is a difference between a forecast and a projection. A *projection* is an extrapolation of historical data. For example, in creating a projection, you would plot five years of data and then draw a straight line through the points. The creation of this line is sometimes "eyeballed" and sometimes "fitted" statistically. In either case, the line is extended beyond the five years of data for, say, another five years. Such a projection has many limitations. First of all, it assumes that history accurately predicts the future, and we all know that such an assumption is foolhardy in today's business environment. A projection does not take into consideration known internal facts about the business. Equally important, it does not take into consideration external facts that could impact the business positively or negatively. Projections are simple to do, quick, and inexpensive, and they can be enlightening when carried out with meaningful data. They can have serious negative consequences when used beyond the limitations of data and the assumptions.

A *forecast* is based on the mathematical relations between sets of data elements that can be both internal and external, either or both simultaneously. The key difference between a projection and a forecast is that a forecast specifies the assumptions under which the forecast is made. The future can be a straight-line forecast, but it can also be a nonlinear prediction (e.g., cyclical). Forecasts can be simple or complex, but, as with projections, they rely on *meaningful* data and the proper construction and statement of the assumptions. All forecasts are restricted to the limits of their assumptions.

When discussing forecasting, we should be aware that the mere mention of a forecast doesn't necessarily mean a change from the past. It could very well mean the status quo. Although that isn't likely in today's business environment, it still could be possible from year to year but not probable over longer periods of time. Therefore, in any forecast, the time period or "forecasting horizon" is a major consideration. In budget planning, the emphasis is usually on the current year, next year, and, in some cases, a preliminary for the second year (usually called the going-forward year). For strategic planning, the forecasting horizon is usually beyond the budget-planning years. Thus, a strategic planning forecast should be at least three years, and most are between three and five years into the future. The budget forecasts and the strategic planning forecasts should be synchronized. Quite often the budgeting cycle and the strategic planning cycle are different, resulting in different sets of numbers for the two forecasts. Depending on how far apart the cycles are in the year, the forecasts could be significantly different because of the later forecast having more current information, and the business environment is *dynamic*. The basic problem of off-cycle forecast generation leads to many disagreements in the ranks between planning staff and operations management. For operational managers, the budget is the key to success. A strategic plan out into the future for five years doesn't play a major role in the day-to-day management decisions. Consequently, a key factor in any forecast or analysis of HR data is *the purpose*. The purpose of the forecast dictates the level of required data, the assumptions, the effort to be expended, and the justifiable cost. Assumptions are the backbone of the forecast, and a great deal of time and effort should be expended in determining their parameters. Remember, in business, you cannot stop the world, get off, and start all over again. What is, *is*! There is momentum in a business, and this momentum is the history of the company's performance. Performance is a complex index of the total company and the environment in which it exists—marketplace, economic trends, technology, and employee body, all playing a role in the history and in the continuity into the future.

FORECASTING MODELS

Various types of forecasting models are utilized in HR forecasting. Most of these models or techniques are complex, requiring significant amounts of historical data and overlaid with statistical routines. Some of the most common modeling techniques are regression models, correlational models, econometric models, relationship models (elasticity models), and simulation models. By far, simulation models provide the most useful data for making business decisions, but each modeling technique can play a role and provide input to management regarding the direction of the business. All of the models except the simulation model approach should be used to determine the relation between the parameters that are used in the simulation model and to validate those relations with some degree of statistical probability. In other words, I see their primary value as being building blocks for simulation models, not as direct modeling techniques for making *business decisions*.

Forecasts should be evaluated on the basis of their value-added. That is to say, generating forecasts and numbers for managers to look at can be interesting, but they should *add value* to the overall knowledge base of the business managers. When I refer to value-added, I am using the term within the following context and definition: The net increased value to a product, raw material, or service as the result of adding labor, capital or other products, or production processes. Simply translated, this definition indicates that almost any operation performed, regardless of the cost, that results in a new value of the product or service that is greater than the sum total of the original value and the cost of the operation results in a positive new value. Thus, when you add your HR *knowledge* to the forecast and the interpretation of the results, you are adding value. The following interpretations of forecasts are clearly value-added results:

- The cost of employees will be reduced.
- Output of the workforce will be increased.
- The number of employees will be reduced, or the growth rate will be slowed with the same output of product or service (increased productivity).
- The quality of the product produced by the workforce will be increased, resulting in a higher-valued product in the marketplace.

The forecaster must be cognizant of a number of variables that pertain to the business that are not people numbers. Many HR professionals are not fully aware, or in some cases are remotely aware, of other key aspects of their company's business. HR professionals should understand their companies' business in detail if they are to be effective in staffing the organizations to meet their financial goals and be competitive in the market. Some of the business areas that HR professionals should be totally knowledgeable about are production, service, market share, financial, and strategic plans. Where appropriate, HR professionals should understand how each of these areas of company performance is measured, what the performance measures mean, what the history of the performance measures has been, and where and how these measures are expected to change in the future. That is a tall order for HR professionals, considering that they, in many instances, are already overworked with day-to-day personnel matters. Regardless of the work load, if HR professionals do not integrate themselves into the business, the obvious will happen: they will continue to be an expense with little "value-added" to the company.

THE PROCESS

To be effective, the HR forecaster must be totally familiar with measurements of the company's performance. Additionally, it is important that the forecaster take the time to evaluate the relations between these measures and the workforce's characteristics. One way to develop these relations is through the development of ratios. Keep in mind that the ratio needs to be interpreted; therefore, it is important to think through the ratio before spending a lot of time and energy doing calculations. Some of the key HR measures that should be considered in developing ratios with other company measures are head count, direct expense, indirect expense, productivity (quality of the workforce and employee mobility), and training. Without getting into complex measures, we can establish a relation between these areas and the financial performance of the company. These relations can be established both historically and into the future. Thus, a continuity of company performance can be established for sets of company measures. Each of the areas above can be related to the financial picture and performance of the company.

Through the use and understanding of the ratios and their projections, HR professionals can make an impact on the company. Understanding of these measures allows HR professionals to plan programs and implement procedures that will affect the bottom line of the company. Interestingly, many of the opportunities for impact are interrelated, and when one area of opportunity is expedited or improved, another area of the business can also be positively or negatively affected. For example, a company can reduce its total workforce (head count) and almost always there will be a concomitant decrease in direct expense. However, there might also be a decrease in productivity. A decrease in productivity can be interpreted negatively or positively. Head count is one aspect of the company for which HR department management has a direct responsibility to management to understand and a key role in advising on every aspect of workforce management. Just looking at the historical past of the size of the workforce can tell us many things about the potential of the workforce to obtain corporate goals.

Let's do a little logical analysis of workforce size. First of all, we know that workforce size, when graphed, is likely to show that the workforce is growing, declining, or stable (flat). There can be cyclical trends during the year, over a number of years, and even within a month; however, these are easily spotted if you have plotted more than ten years of data. Five or fewer years of end-of-year data will not show major cyclical trends in head count data. Monthly or weekly data are required to show cyclical trends within a year. If head count data are related to historical marketing measures through the use of a ratio, then we can project this ratio forward to determine if marketing objectives proposed in the strategic plan pass a reality test of the proposed future. Interpreting such a simple ratio of widgets sold over head count, or vice versa, is straightforward. If the widgets sold per employee is going up, then we can immediately infer that there is an assumption of increased productivity on the part of the employee population that is selling the widgets. This would tell us to look at the number of employees selling widgets and see if this number is growing. If it is, is the number growing in the same ratio of employees to widgets to be sold the same as it was in the past? Only one of two answers is possible: yes or no. If the answer is yes, then we are not assuming any increase in productivity of the widget sellers. Now that finding has some real implications for the business. For example, does the business plan call for an increase in marketing and advertising costs? Does it mean that if we add more widget sellers, we can sell an unlimited number of widgets? Was there a capital improvement program that made it easier for the widget sellers to sell more widgets (automation)? All of these questions are aimed at determining the people requirements, given that the strategic plan is to *make* the marketing and sales objective.

Taking this logic a step further, HR professionals know that wages increase over time owing to a variety of factors. Consequently, they need to know how this increased wage factor fits into the total picture with the strategic marketing objectives. Such questions as, Is the profit margin in the widgets being maintained in light of the increase in wage costs and as that relates to the current or proposed workforce needed to sell the widgets? Many questions come to mind when we put these two important sets of data together—head count and marketing and sales objectives. You can further complicate this by suggesting that if additional people are needed and new people have to be hired and trained, then there will be a drop in overall productivity, making the profit margins shrink to some degree. But asking questions is not the main purpose of ratio analysis. The real purposes are to (a)understand the relation of HR data to other performance data of the company; (b) provide alternative HR solutions to business plans in order to achieve corporate objectives; (c) identify possible business opportunities and threats; and (d) educate management in the integration of human resources into operational and strategic planning.

Most HR departments don't control the head count of the company; however, there is always opportunity for exerting an influence on the size of the workforce. This is especially true if the head count data have been sufficiently analyzed. If control is not exercised by the HR department, there are alternatives to achieving the same goals through various HR programs. Increased productivity can be achieved through training programs, hiring, selection, and placement, as well as through supervision and support materials. Reorganization can be a tool in increasing productivity. HR personnel are normally responsible for all of these functions in a corporation. For example, HR planning and forecasting are responsible for providing estimates of staffing requirements. These staffing requirements can be linked to estimates of sales volume, revenues, market share, and a host of other business plan objectives. As a result of HR evaluating the forecasted staffing level, alternatives to achieving the corporate goals and objectives can be determined while keeping in mind that cost and future needs are important. A simple flashback to the head count analysis above would suggest that we can hire more widget salespeople and increase our revenues. *Maybe*! More widget salespeople will require more supervisors or managers, more clerical support, more space, and so on.

The previous example used a familiar index of HR information, head count. Let's look at a measure that isn't quite as popular, but is a surrogate for head count and, in many ways, even a better way of looking at the cost of human resources. This measure is *direct expense*. Most companies have a well-defined category of expense called direct expense. In general, direct expense equals salaries, with indirect expense used to define benefit costs. Using total direct expense, many ratios can be constructed from historical and planning data. When such data are plotted, three basic trends are evident: level, increasing, and decreasing. The interpretation of the trends depends on the ratio that has been plotted. For example, a typical analysis might reveal a trend of decreasing net revenue dollars per direct expense dollar expended. Some of the reasons for such a trend are

- compensation rates are rising faster than product profit margins;
- compensation rates are holding steady, with a shift in the marketing strategy (discounts) eroding the profit margins;
- compensation rates are competitive, but total revenues dropped owing to a loss of market share; and
- the total market has shrunk even though the company's share of the marketplace has remained constant.

As can be seen from above, the trend is not always the direct result of growing compensation costs. Regardless of the reason for the decline, there is a problem to be resolved, and HR professionals are obligated to not only detect the problem, but also develop alternative solutions. By doing so, HR professionals who do basic forecasting as part of their functional work have the opportunity to show the added value of their function. It also behooves the HR professional to point out to management those aspects of the problem that are not driven by the human resources of the company. Without performing some of the rudimentry forecasts, the HR professional will never know where the problem lies.

The actions that the HR organization might take to offset a decline in revenues trend will be quite different, depending on the reason for the decline. The following are a few selected remedies for problems that may be encountered:

Compensation Rates Rising Too Fast

- Reevaluation of jobs
- Change compensation practice
- Introduce performance appraisal system
- Set productivity standards
- Reduce hiring
- Increase or decrease spans of control

Decrease in Profit Margin

- Use sales incentive compensation plan
- Training for volume selling
- Reduce staff
- Flatten organizational structure
- Slow compensation rate growth

Loss of Market Share and Market Downsizing

- Forecast HR requirements
- Downsize through attrition
- Slow hiring
- Increase training
- Set productivity goals for everyone
- Weed out nonperformers
- Employee communications program emphasis on marketing and sales

The value-added calculations for direct expense actions take two forms. The first is similar to the head count analysis, which uses numbers of employees multiplied by an average wage to estimate a cost savings. The second method starts with the wage rates and focuses on the modification of those rates to reduce the overall direct expense line of the budget. The results of the two approaches are basically the same, in that the total direct expense will decrease. This might be accomplished through pay-for-performance programs or resetting the comparative baseline for determining wages paid for a particular job set. Resetting the comparative baseline is best accomplished using wage surveys or job evaluation procedures. Some firms have responded with more innovative multiple compensation plans that are market driven rather than the standard blanket compensation plans. Such plans are more responsive to the needs of the company for specific skills. Keep in mind that a combination of structural change of the workforce such as organization and skill mix, when combined with adjustments of the compensation rate structure, will produce longer-term positive effects for the company than a straight reduction in force. The major point to keep in mind is that an effective HR compensation plan can lead to significant cost savings without additional HR personnel costs or capital outlay!

In this chapter I have selected just a couple of key measures that can be used in forecasting and planning for human resources. This has not been an exhaustive exercise, but rather an exercise that should lead readers to think through their own situations and come up with ways of utilizing existing data to add value to their HR function, regardless of that function. And although the focus has been on head count and direct expense as a means of analyzing HR data, a number of other ratios can be constructed that will allow the HR professional to better understand human resources within the context of the business. Some of the other areas that should be evaluated are indirect expense, productivity, training, and employee attitudes. Each area holds fertile information for the HR professional and can be a major contributor to the understanding of the business as well as play a vital role in the development of alternative strategies for maximizing company assets.

CHAPTER 8

EXECUTIVE SUCCESSION AND DEVELOPMENT SYSTEMS: A PRACTICAL APPROACH

DIANA KRAMER

Executive development, executive education, high potential, replacement planning, and succession planning—these topics are widely discussed, yet we know little about their successful implementation. Many companies are widely acknowledged for successfully implementing parts of these systems, for instance, General Electric, General Motors, Exxon, IBM, and ITT. Still there is fragmented information on the use of these executive processes (Friedman 1985; Vancil 1987).

This chapter discusses executive succession and development planning systems that I have worked with over the years. The chapter is designed to be practical and to illustrate techniques and applications.

There are many versions of executive succession and development planning systems. The types focused on here have three integrated phases:

1. *Potential planning*: To identify exceptional people to fill divisional, corporate, and worldwide staffing needs; to develop these people and plan for their successors

2. *Succession planning*: To plan for all higher-level and key positions; to identify, prioritize, and develop successors

3. *Promotions management*: To identify all employees who are promotable to the next level

GUIDING PRINCIPLES AND PHILOSOPHY

A few principles and a well-articulated philosophy guide the development of any executive succession and development program. These principles and philosophies need to be actively discussed by the line and the human resource

(HR) professional early in the process and reworked throughout the development of the system. Some of these guiding principles are discussed below.

Determine line and HR responsibilities for the program. In order for an executive program to be successful, the line needs to accept responsibility and hold itself accountable for the development and implementation of the system (Desatnick 1983; Walker 1980). Additionally, the line has to agree to be evaluated on how well the system works.

The role of the HR professional needs to be that of a facilitator and of a consultant to the line (English and Marchione 1977).

Ensure that the program meets the needs of the line. This is said all too often; yet I continue to see programs and systems that are masterfully designed but not used. These well-designed systems are often in binders on the shelves of line managers. Often they are viewed as obstacles to overcome. Usually these programs are associated with enormous amounts of paperwork and documentation. A well-planned needs analysis should determine the line's requirements and, in the process include the line as an active partner (Bright 1976; Levinson 1974; Walker 1980).

Establish common consistent approaches with other HR programs. Other HR systems need to be examined and thoroughly understood before any type of new system is established. This is to ensure that programs and procedures are complementary and do not conflict. Additionally, this step helps the HR department integrate all components into a logical framework (Mahler and Drotter 1986; Pitts 1977).

The following are some examples of system components that need to be delineated:

- How does performance appraisal tie into the career planning process?
- What is the training department's role in career planning? in succession planning? What parts of training can we use in pulling together our executive plan?
- How is employee selection related to the way we groom people for higher levels? Are we choosing people based on our division's needs.?
- Is recruiting related to the way we evaluate employee potential?

Ensure that the program is flexible. Many HR programs are so structured in design that they do not allow for organizational differences. A program such as executive succession needs to be consistent to apply, yet be flexible enough to meet the needs of different locations and departments (Desatnick 1983; Digman 1978; Walker 1980).

Agree on tough issues and philosophies for the system. Determine the issues that are hardest to face and get them on the table for discussion. For example, Should high-potential candidates know that they are in the program? What about staffing? Do we really want to move our people to other divisions? Who pays for training costs? What about moving managers to other departments for development internships? We're understaffed already. An executive succession program is totally dependent on the initiative and effort of the line. These are the types of issues that, if left unresolved, can become obstacles (Friedman 1985).

SETTING UP THE EXECUTIVE SUCCESSION AND DEVELOPMENT PROCESS

In developing succession planning and development systems, I've used a ten-step approach, based on suggestions from Mahler (Mahler and Drotter 1986; Mahler and Gaines 1983; Mahler and Wrightnour 1973).

Step 1: Conduct a needs analysis and ensure executives' awareness for executive succession. There are five major purposes of a needs analysis: (1) getting a broad understanding of the needs, concerns, and issues surrounding executive succession and development; (2) getting line managers to be partners in the development of the system; (3) gathering information about current HR practices and procedures to ensure complementary and consistent approaches in program design; (4) educating line managers about succession planning and executive development; and (5) selecting a target unit for a pilot (Burdick 1976; Gutteridge 1986; Mahler and Drotter 1986; Mahler and Wrightnour 1973).

Throughout this phase, there is a two-step approach that can be implemented concurrently. First, meet with the officers as a group and then individually. Next, meet with the top-level HR people in a group setting and then individually. During these meetings, some of the questions to ask are the following:

- What do you want an executive succession and development program to do for your organization? What are your objectives for such a program?
- What types of things are you doing in this area now?
- What are you doing in the area of strategic planning?
- What parts of your current system are meeting your needs?
- What parts are not meeting your needs?
- What needs to be improved? Changed?
- What problems are you having?

In later discussions, questions can become more specific. Also, during the second or third meeting, it is good to review definitions and ideas of succession planning and executive development programs. This is done in order to get more specific reactions for this area. It is important not to put this step too far ahead in the process, as it tends to focus attention to the particular area.

As a result of this phase, a decision is made as to where to test a system.

Testing a system in a major department and then extending the process as appropriate in a controlled manner helps to identify and correct possible problems as well as build on good design principles before broad implementation (Gutteridge 1986; Walker 1980).

Step 2: Focus needs analysis on a pilot group. Major purposes of this step are (a) focusing on the needs and issues for the pilot group and (b) continuing the buy-in and education process for the new system (Burack and Mathys 1980, 1987; Desatnick 1983). During this phase, the procedure is similar to that of the more general needs analysis; that is, conduct group and individual meetings with the top officials. The difference is that now the work is being done with a specific department in mind. Typically, open-ended questions are used in initial meetings. During the second and third meetings, a straw proposal can elicit more focused answers.

Step 3: Check the needs analysis and verify its accuracy. There are four purposes to this step: (1) continuing the process of needs analysis, (2) verifying information already obtained, (3) continuing to educate line managers, and (4) increasing ownership for process.

After documenting the findings, arrange sessions to check the analyses thus far. At these sessions, discuss the findings and ask for reactions, comments, and concerns. Typically, little revision is done; the major benefit is more in-depth discussion on topics that are causing problems. These can include the following:

- How can we hold key officers responsible for making sure candidates' developmental plans are acted on?
- What do you think of moving people out of the unit to other divisions? to corporate? to headquarters?
- What problems will we have with line managers coming together to discuss candidates? How much time will it take?
- Should we have formal review discussions once a year? twice a year?
- How are we staffed? Do we have enough people to allow development to happen and to get our work done?

Step 4: Integrate executive succession planning with other HR programs. Executive succession and development needs to be understood within the framework of other HR programs. During this phase, it is necessary to review other HR procedures and policies (e.g., recruiting, training, and career planning) and determine how the executive succession program should work in relation to programs that exist or are planned. Key decision points need to be defined with other HR program elements (Carnazza 1982; Tichy 1983). Also, relations need to be established with the corporation's strategic business planning process (Fombrun, Tichy, and Devanna 1984).

For example, the recruiting strategy and the way people are selected into the firm need to be tied to the business plans over the next year and for the next five to ten years. HR planning is very different for a business that expects to expand versus a business that plans to grow smaller and close down a few plants. Also, the qualities that are important for employees to have differ for firms that want to become more competitive versus those that want to become stabler over the next few years.

Step 5: Conduct job analysis. There are three major purposes for this step: (1) establish standards that will help to evaluate candidates in a consistent way across the firm's departments; (2) select a benchmark job or a target job as a standard against which candidates are evaluated and developed; and (3) determine the skills and knowledge required for successful performance in this benchmark job (Burack and Mathys 1987).

To identify the benchmark jobs, I have found it most effective to conduct meetings with groups of executives. After the benchmark jobs are selected, group meetings with supervisors and incumbents are useful to analyze the requirements for each job. During these meetings, rating the importance of job dimensions for each job family completes the process. In some cases, questionnaires can also be used to confirm information that has already been obtained from the meetings (Byham 1980; Hodgson, Levinson, and Zaleznik 1965; Levinson 1968).

Additionally, during this stage, it is helpful to document examples of behaviors that represent important job dimensions. These examples will be very useful to line managers as they identify and discuss candidates.

Step 6: Draft process and review with line managers. The purpose of this step is to check the accuracy of the information collected and to generate further buy-in for the system. Here the new system is outlined on paper and shared with others. The proposed system is then further refined based on the comments and discussions.

Step 7: Training on program procedures. The purpose of this step is to ensure that appropriate line managers have a good understanding of the program. Workshops on how to evaluate, develop, and discuss candidates reinforce major program areas. A typical workshop agenda might include the following:

- Program overview
- How to evaluate candidates
- Behavioral dimensions required for benchmark jobs
- Workshop on evaluating candidates
- How to create development plans
- Workshop on development planning
- Choosing successors for high-potential candidates
- Action planning
- Review discussion procedures for candidates

- Review of forms and administrative procedures
- Workshop on practice review session

Training sessions can last on the average of one to one and a half days. It's helpful to hold these sessions off premises, if possible.

Step 8: Implementation. The review session, which is where line managers nominate and discuss candidates for program inclusion, is the major implementation phase for the new system. (This review session is discussed in more detail below.).

Review sessions should be scheduled far enough in advance to allow time for line managers to prepare. Additionally, HR professionals should actively coach line managers during the first full review sessions.

Step 9: Administrative support for the system. During this phase, it is necessary to establish a system to track all information on each candidate and on each position. This helps to keep a status on the system, as well as monitor its effectiveness. For candidates, it is useful to manage information on background, evaluation statistics, development plans (including next assignments, targeted training, coaching steps, and other experiences). Also, it is helpful to monitor the rationale for each candidate's inclusion, as well as his or her major accomplishments.

For each job, it is useful to track job responsibilities, skills, and knowledge critical for effective job performance, and job challenges. Also, a system should track all possible successors, as well as biographical and position information on each. This should probably be a computerized system in large firms.

Step 10: Establish the evaluation system—a continuous process. Evaluation is typically a two-part process. First, all line managers should complete a questionnaire at the end of a review session. A typical questionnaire can ask (a) what is liked about the process, (b) what is not liked about the process, and (c) what changes should be made to the system. Second, interviews with line managers can be held to further refine the system. Evaluation should be continuous.

JUDGING MANAGERS' POTENTIAL

Usually there are three or four categories of potential that correspond to perceived candidate ability. These can be potential for president of a major division, vice president of a major division with operating or major functional responsibility, or director or general manager for a major division. Typically, there is one early identification category.

For potential programs, there are seven major program parts (see Figure 8.1).

Figure 8.1
Brief Outline of Succession Planning and Executive Development

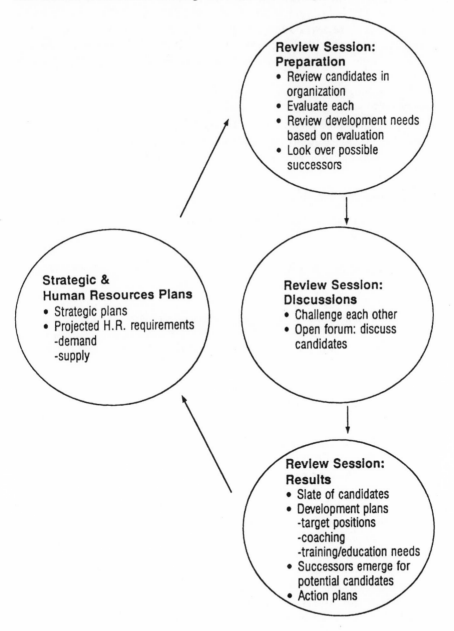

Reviewing Strategic and Business Plans

The succession planning and development program needs to be actively integrated with the strategic and business plan in order to be effective (Fombrun et al. 1984; London 1988; Tichy 1983; Walker 1980). Each organization needs to review its business plans before discussing individuals and positions. This provides a context and meaning for these subsequent discussions. Some major questions to be considered are:

• What are our plans for the next year? the next three to five years? What goals do we want to achieve during these times?
• What organizational changes do we anticipate?
• What businesses do we plan to be in? What areas do we want to grow? to focus less attention on? to research?

Discussing HR Needs

After this broad discussion, more focused discussion evolves around positions and individuals. For example:

• What types of people will we need in the future to achieve our strategies and goals?
• What will be our most important positions?
• What kinds of people do we have today? What are their strengths and weaknesses?

These questions and their answers become the framework for the rest of the processes.

Selecting High-Potential Candidates

Behavioral standards (dimensions) are used by line managers for evaluating candidates. These standards correspond to benchmark jobs associated with each potential category. All candidates are evaluated on their current level of proficiency on each behavioral dimension against the level required to effectively perform the benchmark job. This information is obtained as a result of the job analysis (Burack and Mathys 1987).

Guidelines need to be developed to help the line manager judge candidates. All candidates should have demonstrated excellent performance on their job, as evidenced by results on performance appraisals. Additionally, all candidates need to demonstrate the ability to progress in each of the behavioral dimensions. Also, it is suggested that all the candidates have demonstrated interest and skills reflective of global abilities. Alternatives to these global interests could be waived if candidates are targeted for highly specialized senior positions (e.g., finance and government relations).

The Review Process

The review process is the heart of any succession planning system (Friedman and Levino 1984; Mahler and Drotter 1986). It includes line managers who are peers meeting to discuss high-potential candidates. This session is normally chaired by the head of the particular department. At this meeting, candidates are nominated, their development plans are reviewed, and their next assignments are discussed. Also, successors for these people and action plans are reviewed.

These meetings move upward through higher levels in the organization. Candidates are added and deleted as talks progress. Development plans are often changed, as are next assignments. The objective is to ensure open, honest discussion.

Each review session needs to begin with a discussion of the group's or organization's strategic plan and HR needs and forecasts.

Developing People

All high-potential candidates need to have individual development plans. Line managers need to focus on those skills that are rated lower in proficiency than what is required for the benchmark job (Craig 1976; Walker 1980).

Typically, there are three major categories of developmental experience to discuss and recommend for candidates:

Work experiences and assignments

- Task force assignments
- Functional job moves and changes
- Starting a new business function
- Closing down a plant or facility
- Transfers to other divisions or to corporate
- International assignments

Coaching

- Focus on a specific area that needs improvement (e.g., how to delegate more effectively and how to motivate subordinates)

Educational courses and seminars

- Broadening experiences and general manager's curriculum
- Functional areas (e.g., finance and marketing)
- Self-awareness and assessment
- General leadership skills (e.g., motivating others and negotiation skills)

For each candidate, target dates need to be indicated for each developmental experience.

In order to be sure developmental plans are acted on, two actions are suggested. First, the line, not the HR department, should be held accountable to ensure that the person experiences the appropriate developmental assignment. The HR department should act as a consultant to line managers to guide and to help select the appropriate developmental mix. Second, this developmental responsibility needs to be placed high into the appropriate line organization. Responsibility should be no lower than at a director or vice-presidential level.

Staffing: Cross-Pollinization and Seeding

The department needs to decide how much inter-entity and intra-entity movement is desirable for high-potential candidates. For example, job moves within the same department for people who have potential for high levels would be low. However, job changes within the unit would be higher for people at lower levels of management who are in the early stages of their career and seen as having high potential (Borucki and Lafley 1984).

Procedures need to be documented to coordinate these job moves and changes. High-potential candidates need to always be considered for most job openings.

Successors for High-Potential Candidates

Successors need to be discussed at each level of the review sessions in light of (a) key challenges of the position, (b) candidate specifications critical to success, (c) priority order of nominees, and (d) strengths, weaknesses, and readiness (Mahler and Drotter 1986).

Action Plans

Action plans provide a summary of development activities that have occurred since the last review session, as well as next planned developmental actions and dates. These plans help to reinforce the line's accountability for the developmental assignments (Burack and Mathys 1987). Also, they provide an overall status check for the organization's needs in these areas. Action plans should be documented at each level of the review talks.

SUCCESSION PLANNING AND PROMOTIONS MANAGEMENT

The same program parts constituent of potential planning are parts of succession planning and promotion management. For succession planning,

Figure 8.2
Partial Succession Chart

Database: Succession Candidates
For Key Positions

ABC Corporation
Succession Plan

Incumbent/ Position	Division	Position Points	Possible Candidates	Present Position	Position Points	Ready Code	Performance	Potential
Samuel E. Benton President/CEO Executive Offices	Corp	7000	R. Jones G. Watson A. Hanson	President, Air Division President, Tires President, Rubber	5096 4026 3029	1990 1992 1993	1 1 1	1 1 1
John R. Jones President Air Division	Rubber	5096	E. Smith R. Smithy E. Edwards	VP-Finance VP-Logistics Director-Traffic	4050 4019 3800	1990 1992 1994	1 1 1	1 1 1
E. Smith VP-Finance	Corp	4050	E. Johnson G. Alston J. Kirkhorn	VP-Administration Director-Administration Director-Logistics	3950 3600 3500	1990 1993 1993	1 1 1	1 2 2
E. Johnson VP-Administration	Tires	3950	R. Bolter J. Haney J. Kirkhorn	VP-Operations Director-Finance Director-Logistics	3940 3700 3500	1990 1992 1993	1 1 1	2 1 2

Performance Code: 1 = performance — outstanding.

Potential Code: 1 = potential for president, CEO; 2 = potential for vice president.

the emphasis is on identifying people for executive level positions within the company. These people may or may not be identified as having high potential. For promotions management, line managers distinguish between employees who are promotable to the next level versus those who demonstrate potential for high levels in the organization. See Figure 8.2 for a sample of a partial succession planning chart.

In both processes, employees are identified using the same behavioral standards as are used for high-potential candidates. Also, identified successors and promotables have development plans.

RESULTS WHEN IMPLEMENTING SYSTEM

It takes about five to seven years to see and measure the effects of a succession planning and development process (Friedman and Levino 1984). However, two areas can show marked improvement early on in the process.

Identification of Candidates

Managers begin to use behavioral dimensions to evaluate candidate. Additionally, candidates are discussed and reviewed by several line managers in line with strengths and weaknesses. The line becomes more open to review new choices and more ready to hear and listen to alternative ways of thinking about their choices. Previously, candidates would be placed on listings with little or no systematic evaluation or review.

Development of Candidates

Because of responsibilities accepted by the line in this area, development plans begin to be acted on by the line. Although this is a slow process, managers begin to use the HR department to assist with development plans.

As the system matures, other areas begin to show some progress, such as job moves and changes. Also, as the process is used, it becomes more integrated with the organization's business plan and strategic goals.

REFERENCES

Borucki, C. C., and A. F. Lafley. 1984. Strategic staffing at Chase Manhattan Bank. In C. Fombrun, N. M. Tichy, and M. A. Devanna (eds.), *Strategic human resource management* (pp. 69–86). New York: John Wiley.

Bright, W. E. 1976, January–February. How one company manages its human resources. *Harvard Business Review, 54*, 81–93.

Burack, E. H., and N. J. Mathys. 1980. *Career management in organizations: A practical human resource planning approach.* Lake Forest, IL: Brace-Park.

Burack, E. H., and N. J. Mathys. 1987. *Human resource planning: A program approach to manpower staffing and development.* Lake Forest, IL: Brace-Park.

Burdick, W. 1976, July. A look at corporate and personnel philosophy. *Personnel Administrator, 21,* 21–26.

Byham, W. C. 1980. *Targeted selection: Dimension determination discussion.* Pittsburgh: Development Dimensions International.

Carnazza, J. 1982. *Succession/replacement planning: Programs and practices.* New York: Center for Research in Career Development, Columbia Business School.

Craig, R. L. 1976. *Training and development handbook* (2nd ed.). New York: McGraw-Hill.

Desatnick, R. L. 1983. *The business of human resource management: A guide for the results oriented executive.* New York: John Wiley.

Digman, L. A. 1978, Autumn. How well-managed organizations develop their executives. *Organizational Dynamics, 7,* 63–80.

English, J., and A. R. Marchione. 1977, June. Nine steps in management development. *Business Horizons, 20,* 88–94.

Fombrun, C., N. M. Tichy, and M. A. Devanna. 1984. A framework for strategic human resource management. In C. Fombrun, N. M. Tichy, and M. A. Devanna (eds.), *Strategic human resource management* (pp. 69–86). New York: John Wiley.

Friedman, S. D. 1985. *Career center research report: Leadership succession systems and corporate performance.* New York: Center for Career Research and Human Resource Management, Columbia Graduate School of Business.

Friedman, S. D., and T. P. Levino. 1984. Strategic appraisal and development at General Electric Company. In C. J. Fombrun, N. M. Tichy, and M. A. Devanna (eds.), *Strategic human resource management.* New York: John Wiley.

Gutteridge, T. G. 1986. Organizational career development systems: The state of the practice. In D. T. Hall and Associates (eds.), *Career development in organizations* (pp. 50–94). San Francisco: Jossey-Bass.

Hodgson, R. C., D. J. Levinson, and A. Zaleznik. 1965. *The executive role constellation.* Boston: Harvard Business School.

Levinson, H. 1968. *The exceptional executive.* Cambridge, MA: Harvard University Press.

Levinson, H. 1974, November–December. Don't choose your own successor. *Harvard Business Review, 52,* 53–62.

London, M. 1988. *Change agents.* San Francisco: Jossey-Bass.

Mahler, W. R., and S. J. Drotter. 1986. *The succession planning handbook for the chief executive.* Midland Park, NJ: Mahler.

Mahler, W. R., and F. Gaines, Jr. 1983. *Succession planning in leading companies.* Midland Park, NJ: Mahler.

Mahler, W. R., and W. F. Wrightnour. 1973. *Executive continuity.* Homewood, IL: Dow-Jones Irwin.

Pitts, R. A. 1977, May–June. Unshackle your "careers." *Harvard Business Review, 55,* 127–36.

Tichy, N. M. 1983. *Managing strategic change: Technical, political and cultural dynamics.* New York: John Wiley.

Vancil, R. F. 1987. *Passing the baton: Managing the process of CEO succession.* Boston: Harvard Business School Press.

Walker, J. W. 1980. *Human resources planning.* New York: McGraw-Hill.

THE HUMAN RESOURCE PROFESSIONAL AS STRATEGIST
_____ MANUEL LONDON

Human resource (HR) forecasting and planning is usually the responsibility of the HR department, either to aid line managers in conducting their own forecasting and planning efforts or to spearhead forcasting and planning in the organization.[1] As many of the chapters in this book have indicated, HR forecasting and planning is a strategic activity, in that it should be done jointly with formulating the organization's operations strategy. That is, the goals of the organization drive the type of skills, knowledge, and abilities that the organization must have in the future. HR planners, then, must determine what must be done to ensure that the right people are available when they are needed. In addition, as HR planners examine labor force demographics in the organization and in the labor force population at large, they can use this information to inform and guide organizational strategy.

This chapter considers the role that HR professionals have as change agents and strategists in organizations. The goal is to help HR professionals improve their effectiveness by understanding how they influence organizational direction and, thus, how they can use HR forecasts as one source of information to contribute to organizational strategy.

To a great extent, the HR profession is about change. HR professionals design methods for selecting employees for new assignments, and they help employees develop their skills and take advantage of job opportunities throughout their careers. They help employees adjust to their jobs and cope with work demands and organizational changes. They measure employees' behaviors and attitudes and encourage employees to use the information to improve their performance. They help leaders adjust their behavior to accomplish organizational objectives.

HR professionals are change agents and strategists. A change agent envisions, communicates, designs, plans, directs, champions, and facilitates change. This includes refining the direction for change as well as evaluating the success of a change. A strategist is a change agent who focuses on long-term direction. The strategist envisions the direction, sets the course, communicates the plans, establishes an implementation strategy, and then guides the implementation.

One factor determining role is position—as a member of a support staff in the firm's corporate headquarters, as a personnel manager for a line department, or as an outside consultant. The HR professional's role is likely to depend on his or her level in the organization, prior experiences and reputation, and personal relationships with key managers. Often the HR professional will be part of a team charged with addressing a particular issue or designing a particular program. The issue or program may center on a basically HR task, such as a new compensation system or an upward appraisal process. The other members of the team will probably not be HR professionals or managers with a HR background. This will require the HR professional to educate and guide the team leader and the members, while recognizing their concerns and vested interests.

HR professionals will probably be more effective change agents and have a more substantial impact on organizational strategy the higher the level they are in the organization, the more they adopt a leadership and champion role, and the closer the relationship between the HR professional and key managers. Also, HR professionals will have more influential roles the earlier they are brought into the project. External HR consultants will be more influential than internal HR professionals because external consultants have less to lose by being outspoken, have reputations (often mythical in quality) that are difficult to confirm, and are hired by higher level managers, and hence develop close relationships with executives who are above the level of internal HR managers. In addition, I hypothesize that HR professionals are more effective when they have a high level of general managerial skills and are knowledgeable about the organization's business.

FRUSTRATIONS AND BARRIERS

Although there are many ways that HR professionals help organizations adapt and be effective in the changing environment, consider some of the frustrations and barriers they face in their work.

Lack of business training. HR professionals lack training in such fields as accounting, finance, and marketing, which makes it difficult to break down organizational barriers. For instance, understanding accounting principles and how to write a business plan could help HR professionals make more effective arguments for why certain HR programs are beneficial. Overall, HR professionals in industry are beginning to understand that it is critical to learn the business of their employer and to identify with and express commitment to this business.

Marginal influence in organizations. HR professionals are often not at a level to influence executive decisions. Certainly there are some exceptions to this. Nevertheless, many of us wish we had more influence in the corporations in which we work.

The corporate HR staff that is responsible for HR forecasting and planning may be perceived as generating busy work and as imposing unnecessary requests and deadlines on the field. Certainly HR professionals on a corporate staff should think about whether this is fact or perception and, in either case, what can be done to change it.

Another difficulty is that as an internal or external consultant, the HR professional's point of entry into an organization is usually as a "weak sister." Functions such as human resources, training, safety, and quality are not mainstreams in the organization—they do not drive the business. Therefore, sometimes expenditures in these areas are viewed as drains on corporate resources. We often wish that our skills were better known by managers and that our clients were more willing to jump on the bandwagon of our recommendations.

At the mercy of organizational politics and limited commitment to HR programs. Organizational politics seem to play a major role in the success or failure of a HR program. Many good ideas fail because of timing, not because the idea is bad. Often a member of the HR staff will put tremendous effort into a proposal or an idea and then have it rejected. The tendency at that point may be to give up and work on something else. Moreover, HR professionals complain that organizations fail to make a full commitment to the programs they do adopt. As a result, the programs never achieve all the positive benefits that were anticipated.

Frequently, the political arena seems to dictate over common sense. HR staff members often complain that external consultants are called on to do work that could be done more effectively or cheaper internally. Internal HR professionals may complain that there is no ready forum in which to present new ideas. They also may complain that managers fail to take action on clear issues, at least issues that seem clear to HR professionals. In other cases, the managers fall in love with a program or process that may not have much evidence for its true benefit to the organization. HR professionals may be asked to provide a trendy workshop rather than to analyze organizational needs and suggest alternative performance improvement strategies. We also face managers who give continuous lip service to the importance of human resources but don't practice what they preach. Another problem is that many managers focus on immediate return. They emphasize the micro and tactical as opposed to the macro and strategic point of view when it comes to human resources.

Change is a sensitive and fickle process. Just when a project seems to be going well, support may be lost. Implementing a change may require the buy-in of numerous managers, and the more people you ask, the more likely it is that someone will say no. Also, change is evolutionary. It progresses from one generation to another. However, backsliding and failure are highly likely.

Everyone's an expert in personnel. Although HR professionals understand diverse phenomena from organizational to individual dynamics, the tasks they are called on to perform are not unique to the profession. Managers often believe that anyone can do HR work and that there is no special place for the HR professional, perhaps except when legal requirements are involved, such as in personnel testing.

A related frustration is that managers may believe that being a good manager is more important than being a top-notch professional, which could be true in some circumstances. However, the implication is that professional skills are not really essential, and that good managers who are not professionals can do a better job than most professionals. The ideal is probably an outstanding professional who is also a good manager.

CRITICAL BEHAVIORS

Fortunately, HR professionals can reverse many of these barriers and frustrations by becoming more effective change agents and strategists. They should be responsive to the needs of the organization. This requires that they be good listeners, and not be in such a hurry to cite a study or theory. HR professionals should be problem-focused, trying to develop a reputation for problem-solving, not problem-creating. The HR staff should develop a partnership with managers as co-researchers and as sponsors or mentors. HR professionals need to find a way to educate managers without being self-serving, to communicate in a professional language that is technically correct but not obscured by jargon or esoteric studies. This is especially important in reporting the results of labor force analyses and demographic trends that are the foundation for HR plans.

HR professionals should get their hands dirty by not only designing methods, procedures, and interventions, but taking part in them as well. For instance, the HR staff should conduct its own forecast of HR needs and formulate its own plans for the future, given the predicted needs of the corporation. In this sense, the HR department should be a model for the rest of the organization.

HR professionals need to be able and willing to make macro and micro contributions. This means working with top managers on strategic issues as well as with other employees on nuts-and-bolts programs. Furthermore, HR professionals must stay abreast of current trends, research, and, in general, what's happening in business as well as in the HR profession.

HR professionals should learn how to support the mavericks and champions in the organization—people who are out on the cutting edge expressing new and radical ideas and trying to bring about change to enhance organizational effectiveness. Moreover, some HR professionals should be mavericks themselves by expressing their views even when they do not coincide with the status quo, engendering a sense of urgency for change, trying new programs, and influencing and creating new policies.

CHALLENGES

These new behaviors raise a number of interesting questions that pose challenges for the future. For example:

- How do you champion new ideas and gain acceptance for them and for you personally, that is, ensure that both you and the ideas survive?
- How do you manage the risks of being on or in front of the cutting edge of the field as a maverick and champion of new ideas?
- How do you express and gain support for new ideas in an organizational setting that is wary of change?
- How do you establish and foster sources of power? Is it better to be a respected expert or a power broker...or is there a difference?
- How do you become a player in the firm's strategy-setting team, that is, become a partner with key managers and executives in strategy development?
- How do you balance the multiple and often conflicting roles of scientist, practitioner, and organizational leader and manager?

These questions pose a number of challenges for the HR professional. For example, growing organizations will be concerned about hiring and retraining the right people. Organizational start-ups will need to attract creative, talented, and skilled people. Organizations that are restructuring or merging will need to evaluate their current workforce against new skill requirements and provide retraining, redeployment, and outplacement as needed. Organizations in decline should be concerned about reversing the trend by using employees' ideas. Other organizational events such as employee ownership, union-management cooperative efforts, and increased globalization present continuing opportunities for HR professionals to help organizations enhance their performance.

In the future, the HR professional can look forward to taking a broader role, one beyond that of the functional expert. The HR professional needs to be a personnel specialist, a manager, a consultant, a team builder, and a career counselor.

Consider how HR professionals can be more effective in the future:

- We should search for opportunities to influence organizational strategy by understanding organizational and environmental changes and trends.

- We should help executives to understand the values they promulgate through their decisions and actions, and how HR programs might be used to communicate existing values and focus attention on new values when necessary.
- We need to be proactive in "redesigning" the future of our profession as well as the businesses in which we work. We should constantly be thinking about what the next generation of our HR products and services will be like, given our forecasts of future HR requirements.
- We should stick with our vision of the future as long as it makes sense to us and not give up because the timing is wrong. This may mean taking risks, speaking our minds, and taking a stand. Most managers respect this kind of behavior.

LINKING HR PLANS TO BUSINESS PLANS

Too often HR policies and programs are developed in a vacuum, apart from the needs of the corporation. For instance, a career development program may be implemented without providing employees with information about current and anticipated career opportunities in the firm. HR plans should be an extension of the organization's business plans (London 1988). HR departments should avoid any semblance of stand-alone personnel systems and programs with goals or criteria that are not obviously associated with organizational needs (Manzini and Gridley 1986).

Developing Scenarios as an Aid to Planning

One way to highlight the relation between business and HR plans is to generate scenarios of possible future events. A scenario is "a documented narrative of anticipated conditions that the organization expects to deal with at some time in the future" (Manzini and Gridley 1986, p. 94). Scenarios encourage the organization to generate strategies to deal with these contingencies. The scenario combines analysis of environmental trends, organizational objectives, and HR demand and availability. Scenarios suggest the need for HR policy changes (e.g., regarding hiring, promotion, compensation, and retirements) based on changes in employee values and workforce indicators (e.g., the age, sex, and education mix). A good scenario influences intelligent action by framing the issues and developing the capability to respond. Moreover, the development of the scenario should involve managers who need to develop and implement business and HR plans. Developing the scenario can be an engaging process that helps business and HR managers work together to forecast personnel requirements and formulate plans.

THE ROLE OF THE CORPORATE HR STAFF

Companies vary in their degree of centralization. Some firms have strong corporate HR departments that dictate HR policy through the organization's business units and supply HR programs to all units. Other organizations have weak or no central HR staff, and allow each business unit to handle its own HR activities and policies. One reason for a decentralized approach may be that the business units are highly diverse. With little in common, they may need to guide their own HR function to ensure that it meets their requirements. In other cases, a central HR department allows the firm to benefit from economies of scale, for instance, developing a certain program once and then sharing it in every business unit, perhaps adapting the program to local needs.

A central HR department should be able to advise and support line organizations and business units in collecting labor force data, doing internal audits of employees' skills and demographics, and using this information to plan HR strategies. However, each unit should be able to answer the following questions (London 1988, p. 205):

- What human resource plans are not in place?
- What business developments are anticipated?
- What business developments influence human resource needs?
- What support is needed from the corporate headquarters human resource department for personnel selection, executive succession, development, and the like?
- How does the business plan translate into employee roles and behaviors?
- What kinds of people are needed to achieve the business strategy (education, management style, competency, values)?
- What needs to be done to identify these people?
- What types of people are available in the work force?
- How should these people be recruited?
- What companies are trying to recruit the same people we are?
- How do we develop our employees once they are hired?
- How do we motivate and retain our employees?

HR PROGRAMS TO ADDRESS CHANGING DEMOGRAPHICS: THE CASE OF GRUMMAN CORPORATION

Grumman, a major aerospace corporation, is an excellent example of a company that recognized the trend of an aging workforce, understood the need to avoid age discrimination in employment, and implemented several HR programs to address the needs of the older worker (Daniel E. Knowles, vice president HR Planning, Grumman Corporation, personal communication, May 23, 1989; Knowles 1984). Grumman conducts annual workforce utilization analyses to examine age demographics of the U.S. labor force using data from the U.S. Department of Labor. It then compares the age distribution of its own workforce with that of the U.S. labor force. For instance, Grumman's 1987 analysis shows that the average age of Grumman's employees exceeded the national average. Further analyses broke the data out by job categories (officials and managers, professional, clerical, blue-collar, and service—categories defined by the Equal Opportunity Commission). Grumman also considered characteristics of local labor markets in which they operate. It next considered a sample of specific job skills within the company and examined the age distribution of these categories.

This HR audit led to a consideration of the firm's policies, programs, and procedures to determine that middle-aged and older workers have equal opportunity in all respects. For instance, they examined whether they are hiring a proportional share of middle-aged and older workers in all locations. At Grumman, the average hiring age is in the forties, which reflects the long-term impact of their demographic analysis. The company also considered whether they are training and promoting older workers and whether there are any age differences in terminations and participation in the company-sponsored sports activities and clubs. If the company finds a problem in a certain area, the issue is addressed directly. Because most organizations do not conduct such workforce utilization analyses, they are usually unaware that any discrimination has occurred.

This long-term concern about the utilization of older workers has led Grumman to institute several progressive HR programs. For instance, they frequently rehire retirees who are interested in returning to work part-time or full-time. Their mid-career training programs are designed to update basic engineering, management, and mechanical skills of workers whose formal education ended many years ago. A Professional Awareness Workshop is valuable to women who are trying to redefine career goals and career paths after absence from the workforce for some years. The company's Women's Responsibility Training Center provides an opportunity for on-the-job training through job rotation. The company participates in job fairs conducted by local government agencies to help people fifty-five or older who are seeking work. A phased retirement program allows employees who are sixty years of age or older to request a reduction of their work week to prepare for retirement. Pre-retirement planning seminars assist employees over fifty in planning how to manage their resources and set personal goals. Grumman eliminated the mandatory retirement age one year before legislation abolishing mandatory retirement took effect.

Grumman's HR department continuously audits company policies and programs to ensure equal employee opportunity. Employees' perceptions, derived from regular attitude surveys, are carefully analyzed as the basis for new programs to enhance employee development. The company views older workers as a source of expertise and stability. Thus, the HR programs targeted to older workers are directly tied to the firm's commitment to excellence in the design and manufacture of quality products. The programs that encourage part-time employment for older workers and rehiring retirees when people are needed produce a somewhat flexible workforce. This has been valuable in times of retrenchment, for instance, when government defense strategies change, affecting aircraft orders and the need for personnel cutbacks at Grumman.

PROBLEMS OF THE 1990s

To conclude, let us suggest some of the problems that organizations will be facing in the 1990s and how the HR professional can help solve these problems. Topics for theoretical and research development in the 1990s include aging, career and life transitions, adult learning, communications, cross-cultural experiences, and labor force migration, to name a few. Problems will include the immigrant experience, as more immigrants enter this country. We will also be concerned with cultural assimilation and valuing differences. Moreover, we need to think about the experience of expatriation, that is, U.S. citizens leaving for temporary, developmental job assignments or permanent assignments in another culture. We need more partnerships with researchers and practitioners in other countries to create a more global HR profession.

Career and organizational changes suggest the importance of understanding transitions of all types. Moreover, they suggest the importance of communications in a global multi-cultural environment. We should consider the meaning of employee education and development in different cultures and across cultures. Given the aging of the workforce, we should study the experience of older workers and some of the stresses they face.

Cutting edge HR programs for the 1990s will include helping people to value differences and to work with people from different cultures as well as to work within different cultures. There will be a host of new technologies for doing this, for instance, computer-based, video-disk simulations of work settings in different cultures and in multi-cultural environments.

We should consider work in nontraditional settings (e.g., work-at-home) and in a diversity of organizations (small entrepreneurial enterprises as well as large organizations). Also, HR programs will have to deal with problems that relate to individual welfare as well as productivity. A prime example is ways to reduce and prevent substance abuse.

Comprehensive analyses will be required to guide HR policies. HR professionals can contribute by partnering with economists, psychologists, demographers, and other social and behavioral scientists to analyze the gap between current HR needs and labor force participation and project what will happen to this gap during the 1990s. The data will suggest trends and provide warning signals that should guide public and private programs and policies in such areas as child and elder care support and job training for displaced workers, the hard-core unemployed, and other new entrants to the workforce, such as immigrants.

CONCLUSION

This chapter has examined some of the frustrations and barriers that may limit the effectiveness of HR professionals. To a large extent, these frustrations and barriers can be overcome by recognizing the roles that the HR professional plays as a change agent and as a strategist. HR professionals of the future will be attentive to ways they can influence change and be proactive in helping managers design programs that maximize organization effectiveness. This will be furthered by a better understanding of labor force issues in the 1990s. We must think about strategies for change not only for society at large and for the organizations in which we work, but also for our profession. The HR professional will be expected to know more and to do more than he or she does today. This poses a challenge for training HR professionals for the future as well as for the continuous development and, in some cases, retraining of those currently in the profession. We should all be thinking of ways to enhance our effectiveness by making a contribution both to the organizations in which we work and to the HR profession.

NOTE

1. This chapter is largely based on London and Moses' (1989) paper on the role of the industrial and organizational psychologist as change agent and strategist. The current chapter broadens their discussion to apply to the role of the HR professional.

REFERENCES

Knowles, D. E. 1984. Middle aged and older workers—an industry perspective. In S. F. Yolles, L. W. Krinsky, S. N. Kieffer, and P. A. Carone (eds.), *The aging employee* (pp. 49–83). New York: Human Sciences Press.

London, M. 1988. *Change agents: New roles and innovation strategies for human resource professionals.* San Francisco: Jossey-Bass.

London, M., and J. L. Moses. The role of the industrial/organizational psychologist as change agent and strategist. Presented by M. London in an invited address at the Annual Meeting of the American Psychological Association, New Orleans, August 11, 1989.

Manzini, A. O., and J. D. Gridley . 1986. *Integrating human resources and strategic business planning.* New York: AMACOM.

Part IV

Human Resource Implications of Organizational Change

This section describes major organizational change efforts, the effects of these efforts on employees, and the implementation of new human resource (HR) policies and programs. These change efforts result from a combination of the organization's needs (for instance, to respond to a new market or to merge with another organization) and environmental trends, such as changing workforce demographics.

Carrie Leana and Daniel Feldman, professors of management, have studied the various ways organizations help employees who must be laid off because industries are losing business, as in the case of the steel industry in the United States, or because of mergers and acquisitions. Their chapter addresses the consequences of job loss to laid-off employees and how employees cope with job loss. They also report practical ways that organizations can help displaced workers find re-employment and how organizations can work effectively with government agencies and unions to help the unemployed. The authors report that often the stress of being unemployed gets in the way of people's searching for a new job or applying for available governmental financial assistance and retraining. Corporations help laid-off employees by advanced notification of the layoff, severance pay and extended benefits, retraining programs, and job search assistance (outplacement). Organizations should establish explicit strategies for dealing with displaced workers, such as determining and communicating criteria for layoffs (i.e., the basis for deciding who stays and who leaves), the role of performance evaluations in layoff decisions, treating laid-off workers with dignity and social support, fair recommendations to potential new employers, recognizing the stress felt by "survivors," and finding alternatives to layoffs, such as redeployment of personnel to different job functions. For-

tunately, there are a number of governmental programs that support displaced employees, and Leana and Feldman cite several examples. Also,
unions have cooperated with management to identify ways to save jobs or
prepare employees for new jobs. Employee ownership programs is one type
of solution. The chapter concludes by emphasizing that there are a number
of actions that organizations can take to mitigate the social and economic
impact of "downsizing," and that the support of other institutions (unions,
local and state governments, and federal agencies) can be invaluable in
ensuring fair and positive treatment of affected employees.

The next chapter describes a merger of two large corporations in the
hospital supply industry: Baxter Travenol and American Hospital Supply
to form the Baxter Healthcare Corporation. Anthony Rucci, senior vice
president of HR for Baxter Healthcare, Frank LaFasto, manager of HR for
Baxter, and David Ulrich, a professor of management at the University of
Michigan, report their experiences in staffing the newly merged organization
and ensuring employee cooperation and morale. The chapter begins with
an overview of the number and types of mergers that have occurred during
the past decade. Clearly, mergers and acquisitions are almost common occurrences these days. The authors argue that HR activities must play a
central role in accomplishing successful mergers and acquisitions. Training,
staffing, compensation, and organization design allow the change to happen.
In addition, HR programs can create a strategic unity within the firm,
increasing employees' identification with and commitment to the new organization. By the same token, if not handled right, HR programs can
hamper the merger effort by maintaining lingering loyalties to the old organizations and the way things were. Rucci, LaFasto, and Ulrich show the
importance of involving employees in making HR decisions. In the Baxter-
American merger, a steering committee was formed of top officers to review
and approve all activities. A transition team and a top management task
force identified new operating structures and philosophies and made recommendations for selecting people for new positions. Placement centers
were established to provide information to employees on job opportunities.
Career Continuation Centers helped with outplacement for people who were
unable to find jobs within the firm. The chapter concludes with ideas for
general managers and HR executives involved in mergers and acquisitions.
For instance, the authors recommend that executives spend ample time on
people issues, communicate extensively, create a new vision for the merged
company, be decisive, and maintain individual dignity at all costs.

Mirian Graddick and Pamela Jones describe a method used within one
business unit to integrate HR planning and business planning. Their model
helps to ensure that human resources is an equal partner in the development
of business strategies and plans. Their model demonstrates that business
strategies may need to be modified, based on information about HR availability, training, and other employee-related factors. The case, which in-

volves a large marketing department, also shows that HR information and strategies can help the department accomplish its business goals. In short HR strategy and business strategy should be formed in tandem and be mutually supporting. The model is a multi-step iterative process that begins with external analysis (e.g., a scan of the competition and the labor market) and continues to develop a statement of mission and strategy, an HR vision of excellence (e.g., a definition of organizational capabilities for marketplace success), data on the internal environment (e.g., employee competencies), and then, based on the gap between the current environment and the vision, a set of programs and interventions for successfully implementing the vision. This truly integrative approach encompasses many of the topics covered elsewhere in this book, such as strategy development, environmental scanning, internal force analysis, and HR program design.

James Shillaber's chapter examines a department's recognition for change and how executives in the department considered the need for new and different types of people. The department is responsible for regulatory and consumer affairs for a large corporation in the information movement and management business. As the industry was deregulated during the early 1980s, the department's responsibilities changed from lobbying state and federal regulatory agencies to dealing with the firm's reputation in the community. Shillaber describes the evolution from no HR planning to a reactive, non-strategic approach to HR planning, and finally to a strategic approach to human resources. Whereas employees had been selected for their experience with legislative and regulatory bodies, and they tended to be older employees, the department recognized a need for new talent to meet its future HR needs. A task force identified key jobs and training curricula. In addition, the task force conducted an analysis of the current environment and the likely future environment faced by the corporation as a whole and the department in particular. This led to developing employee selection and development strategies that recognized the need for people who understood what consumer affairs and regulatory issues meant in a highly competitive, market-driven environment. Shillaber concludes by outlining challenges faced by a corporation or a department within it for recognizing the need for strategic HR planning and taking actions to develop and implement plans.

CHAPTER 10 _____

JOB LOSS AND EMPLOYEE
ASSISTANCE: JOINT EFFORTS TO
HELP DISPLACED WORKERS
_____ CARRIE R. LEANA AND DANIEL C. FELDMAN

Although the national unemployment rate between 1986 and 1989 has been relatively low, the difficulties of handling displaced workers remain very high. Today 6 percent of the U.S. work population—or seven million persons—are unemployed. Three key trends are expected to keep unemployment as an important human resource (HR) issue throughout the next decade, even if the current prosperity sustains itself.

First, many "rust belt industries" are dying, flooding the labor market with thousands of workers who do not have readily transferrable skills. As just one example, in 1978, U.S. Steel had six operating facilities and employed 42,000 in the greater Pittsburgh area. By 1986, all but two of these plants had been closed and employment was down to just over 6,700, a loss of more than 35,000 jobs. In the Pittsburgh area alone, more than 120,000 manufacturing jobs have been eliminated since 1980 (Leana and Feldman 1989b).

Second, the increase of mergers and acquisitions activity is having some noticeably negative consequences on staffing; these corporate restructurings have forced companies to eliminate duplicate staff and unprofitable divisions. For instance, between 1980 and 1986, General Electric spent 11.1 billion dollars to buy 338 business; during the same time period, GE sold off 232 business worth 5.9 billion dollars and closed 73 plants and offices. Moreover, even when corporations are able to fight off takeover bids, they are often forced to buy back large blocks of stock, creating high levels of debt that are unacceptable to shareholders. For instance, IT&T, in the wake of fighting off Irwin Jacobs' takeover bid in 1985, cut its labor force by 44 percent, including 66 percent of its headquarters staff (Leana and Feldman 1989a; Russell 1987).

Third, as corporations have turned to labor reductions as a means of increasing profitability, there has been a shift in which categories of workers are being let go. Although historically workers on routine production jobs were targeted for layoffs, today while-collar employees and managers are likely to be as hard hit as blue-collar workers. Between 1984 and 1989, General Motors reduced the number of its managers and salaried workers by 25 percent; between 1982 and 1987, close to one million middle-and upper-level executives with annual salaries over $40,000 lost their jobs (Bennett 1986; Leana and Feldman 1989a).

Over the past few years, we have been conducting research on unemployed workers, especially those who have been laid off because of business reverses. We have collected data from more than 500 employees about their reactions to job loss, how they coped with unemployment, and the availability and helpfulness of corporate and governmental assistance programs. Our sample comes from two very different environments—professional, technical, and managerial workers in Florida who were laid off from the National Aeronautics and Space Administration and the defense industry in the wake of the Challenger disaster and the blue-collar workers who lost their jobs in Pittsburgh as a result of the death of the steel industry. These samples, taken together, give a broad-based picture of the dynamics of job loss, from both the individual and corporate points of view.

In this chapter, we focus on four important HR management questions regarding job loss: (1) What are the consequences of job loss to laid-off employees, and how can employees effectively cope with job loss? (2) What can corporations do to help displaced workers find reemployment? (3) What are the key elements of a corporate strategy in dealing with workers who are being terminated? (4) How can corporations work effectively with governmental agencies and unions to help the unemployed?

CONSEQUENCES OF JOB LOSS

The initial reaction to job loss is overwhelmingly negative. Three-quarters of the participants in our study reported heightened feeling of sadness and fear of the future; more than two-thirds of our sample reported greater feelings of boredom, apathy, and nervousness as well. All in all, workers who have lost their jobs are depressed and anxious (Leana and Feldman 1988a).

Layoffs also have substantial negative consequences on employees' physical health. More than half our respondents, both in Florida and Pennsylvania, reported difficulties sleeping and overeating; more than a quarter reported significantly more drinking, more headaches, more stomachaches, and more days off not feeling well; 10 percent reported taking more pills to calm themselves. Seven percent reported distress levels high enough to severely curtail their ability to function in normal activities. These respondents reported that they were incapable of making decisions, concentrating on day-to-day activities, and enjoying their regular pastimes (Leana and Feldman 1988b).

Another issue that repeatedly emerged was a strong sense of anger—anger at being left without employment through little fault of their own and anger at management for the poor business decisions that led to layoffs. As one worker expressed it: "When they've cost you your livelihood because someone high on the corporate ladder—who doesn't even know your name—was too slow to get new business, you feel angry, bitter, empty." Many of the workers also felt that selection procedures for layoffs were arbitrary, politically motivated, and often discriminatory toward older workers. As one employee noted: "Age and salary had a great deal to do with my job loss. My job was not eliminated—myself along with several others were replaced by people half our age. It was simple economics."

Historically, the predominant approach that has guided research on job loss has been the "deprivation model"; most researchers have viewed the unemployed as inactive and passive (Jahoda 1982). Two of the major tasks of our research were to examine how people cope with job loss and how effective various strategies are in obtaining reemployment. After the initial reaction to job loss, our research suggests that most employees are much more active than is frequently assumed.

The most frequent strategy laid-off workers used to obtain reemployment was self-initiated job search; 86 percent of those we surveyed answered help wanted notices or used job placement services. Forty percent engaged in some type of education or training program, and two-thirds looked for opportunities for employment in a different geographical location. Less than a quarter of our respondents applied for governmental financial assistance, joined a support group, sought counseling, or became involved in community activities to aid the unemployed or stop further unemployment in the area (Leana and Feldman 1989b).

How successful were these coping efforts of the unemployed workers? Clearly, willingness to retrain and to geographically relocate were the most effective strategies for obtaining reemployment. With large-scale layoffs, often whole occupations, industries, and geographical regions are decimated. Thus, continued attempts to find scarcer and scarcer jobs with greater and greater competition for those jobs are exercises in frustration. Finding a new job often depends on getting out of the current job and home setting and getting retrained or resettled in a more economically prosperous community. Indeed, one-sixth of the people we studied were employed in better jobs than the ones from which they had been let go; as one blue-collar worker noted: "The layoff was the push I need to go back to school again and work toward established goals" (Leana and Feldman 1989b).

Unfortunately, the stress of being unemployed often gets in the way of people's pursuing some strategies that could ultimately relieve them of pressure. For example, many workers were embarrassed or intimidated by the prospect of getting more education, even though they intellectually knew such training might help. For example, one of our participants noted: "I feel I need further education to get anywhere, but I'm *very afraid* of failing; that would be like a final crushing blow. I think I would just give up then. So I have not enrolled in any courses."

Similarly, many workers were also intimidated by the prospects of applying for needed governmental financial assistance; repeatedly, we heard comments that echoed the feelings of a laid-off clerical worker: "The people in these government offices make you feel like you are the scum of the earth for trying to get help; they can really knock your self-esteem down." We also found that if workers did not get rehired in six months, the chances of getting rehired at comparable pay drop dramatically. After six months of receiving, in some cases, more than 100 rejections, workers become too discouraged to look further (Leana and Feldman 1988b).

INSTITUTIONAL INTERVENTIONS

Although laid-off workers may be able to cope with job loss on their own, our research suggests that corporations can facilitate employees' job search efforts and adjustment to unemployment through well-designed interventions. In our research, we focused on four corporate assistance programs in particular: advance notification, severance pay and extended benefits, retraining programs, and outplacement policies.

Advance Notification

As Leana and Ivancevich (1987) note, management has traditionally been disinclined to provide employees with advance notice of layoffs. In Kaufman's 1982 study, he reports that 80 percent of employers provide less than four weeks' notice of impending termination, and cites instances of less than a few hours' prenotification for some groups of professional workers. Management has historically been opposed to advance notification before layoffs because they fear productivity losses owing to work slowdowns or intentional sabotage, or that employees will seek employment elsewhere before the organization is ready to terminate them (Harrison 1984; Weber and Taylor 1963). Indeed, management's opposition to new federal legislation requiring sixty days' advance notice has brought this issue back to the public forefront.

In our study, only one-third of the laid-off workers received more than one week of advance notice; another third received only *one day's notice*. However, for those fortunate employees who were given substantial advance notice of layoffs, the consequences of job loss were much less severe. They had shorter periods of unemployment, suffered less financial distress, and had less need to move geographically to find reemployment. In one instance, the company's failure to provide advance notice even led to needless hardship. As one employee noted: "I feel top management did not keep us informed enough about current conditions that might end up with a layoff. In my case, I had just turned down a job two weeks before my layoff. I had no indication it was coming" (Leana and Feldman 1989b).

Moreover, other empirical research on advance notification suggests that there are few adverse consequences of advance notification. Weber and Taylor (1963) found that the announcement of impending plant shutdowns does not result in perceptible decreases in productivity; in a few cases, productivity actually increased as workers tried to persuade management to reverse their decisions to keep plants open. "Early quit" rates are low because alternative job opportunities are usually limited in small, depressed labor markets (Fedrau 1984). Furthermore, companies like American Hospital Supply have carefully scheduled layoffs that keep jobs open in other facilities for the "skeleton crews" that remain. Lastly, there may be some positive goodwill advantages of advance layoff notification. "Slash and burn" terminations create ill will in the business community and society at large; companies like Atari and E. F. Hutton (who laid off 1,500 employees in one day, with no advance notice) have received substantial negative publicity for such actions (Sutton, Eisenhardt and Jucker 1986).

Severance Pay and Extended Benefits

Like advance notification, severance pay and extended benefits allow employees whose jobs have been eliminated to buffer the financial losses of unemployment. Employees who received such benefits frequently commented that such financial aid reduced marital friction, reduced the need for spouses to increase hours of work, and reduced the need to grab any job that came along simply to obtain cash (Leana and Feldman 1988a, 1988b).

In general, companies have been much more concerned with giving financial assistance to white-collar workers than to blue-collar workers. Partly out of guilt and partly out of fear from an increasingly litigious workforce, top executives are showering many laid-off managers with generous severance packages (Bennett 1987; Deutsch 1988). On the other hand, it has been mainly at the blue-collar level that companies have held the line on generous severance pay and extended benefits—and ironically, it is these employees who are most in need of assistance. Companies often count on the government and the union to help blue-collar workers (Leana and Feldman 1989a).

Our results showed that only 16 percent of the blue-collar workers in Pittsburgh received severance pay, as opposed to 38 percent of the white-collar workers in Florida. In contrast, 42 percent of the Pittsburgh sample received extended benefits, as opposed to 33 percent of the Florida sample.

Thus, we see that even for white-collar workers, the percentage of employees receiving financial assistance is relatively small. In addition, the amount they received was sufficient to hold them for one to three months; after that, they were on their own. Moreover, even in the Pittsburgh sample, where extended benefits were more common because of union contracts, not all workers were eligible for such assistance. For example, steelworkers with less than two years' experience (and thus the most likely to be laid off) were not eligible, by union contract, for Supplemental Unemployment Benefits. Forty percent of the Pittsburgh steelworkers had been without health insurance at some time (Blotzer 1985).

The severest problem arises, as Latack and Dozier (1986) point out, when the terminations are related to financial difficulties; those employees who need economic support do not receive it because the organization lacks sufficient resources. The authors suggest that in profitable times, companies should commit funds for severance benefits, particularly firms in volatile sectors of the economy, such as high-tech manufacturing and steel.

Retraining Programs

Particularly for firms in declining industries, occupations, or geographical locations, simply encouraging workers to go out and find new jobs misses the mark. These workers will need to get considerably retooled in order to obtain satisfactory reemployment. Moreover, these retraining efforts can help employees reduce the amount of time spent unemployed between jobs (Kaufman 1982). There are also some secondary positive consequences of retraining programs (Leana and Ivancevich 1987). Enrollment in training programs can give unemployed workers some structure to the day, provide them a regular activity and some work-related identity, and mitigate the feelings of reduced self-esteem and control often associated with involuntary job loss.

In our study, few workers (less than 10 percent) were given any type of retraining by their corporations. In general, the private sector has relied on the public sector to meet this need of displaced workers. A notable exception to this pattern has been Ford Motor Company. Ford instituted a National Development and Training Center at an annual cost of fifteen million dollars. This program is unique because it does not offer sets of formal courses, but tailors its program to each individual employee's needs and interests. IBM has developed retraining programs for professional workers, more with an eye to helping them relocate within the corporation than for the external labor market (Bolt 1983). These programs are especially appreciated by workers because they may be intimidated by initiating retraining or re-education on their own, as noted above.

Outplacement Programs

Perhaps no set of company interventions has attracted as much public attention as outplacement. Outplacement is not a specific program or service, but encompasses a whole variety of services such as résumé-writing workshops, career counseling sessions, and direct placement assistance (Scherba 1973). Because the content and length of these programs vary so greatly from corporation to corporation, hard empirical evidence on their effectiveness has, by and large, lagged their favorable publicity (Leana and Feldman 1988a, 1989a).

There has been tremendous variability in the quality of outplacement activities. At the top end, AT&T has provided its laid-off workers generous financial severance pay as well as a full-service package of outplacement services, from individual career counseling to printing of business cards (Langley 1984). Wang, likewise, provided its laid-off employees with office space, telephones, personal computers, job search workshops, and other auxiliary services for up to six months after termination.

At the mid-point in terms of quality of outplacement activities are programs that are well-intentioned but perhaps too meager in scope or poorly executed (Langley 1984; Leana and Feldman 1989b). For instance, NBC ran résumé-writing workshops for its laid-off employees, but workers felt that these workshops "were conducted by a youngster in the personnel department who didn't realize that seasoned professionals don't get jobs by sending out résumés." Lehman Brothers did provide a base of operations for laid-off stockbrokers, but the office had only one phone per every three or four persons, so employees couldn't seriously make or take calls.

At the low end of the quality dimension are outplacement programs that have the veneer of helpfulness but are often seen as manipulative or punitive. Probably the most visible of these programs has been General Motors' Mainstream Program. Several GM employees are currently in litigation after their experiences in Mainstream. A draftsman who didn't "volunteer" to leave claims that for his defiance, he has been put at a desk in front of his boss's office where he has been filing product description manuals in binders; an engineer who didn't "volunteer" to leave has been assigned to wiping grease off oil drums (Naj 1987).

Only about 20 percent of our sample received outplacement assistance, but our research suggests that outplacement activities can be quite beneficial to laid-off workers. Several respondents noted that outplacement activities gave them the added stimulus to seek further education, get into a more suitable occupation, or to move to a more economically prosperous location. Outplacement also provides workers with some companionship and social support, and serves as a signal from the company that it is behind employee efforts to obtain reemployment (Leana and Feldman 1989b).

Our research on outplacement suggests two other points. First, a valuable outplacement activity is providing laid-off workers with a temporary base of operations from which to job hunt, as well as some clerical and technical support for résumé writing and contacting potential employers. Second, it appears that counseling and career planning activities are better implemented *after* the layoffs are finalized, and are best done at that time on a one-to-one basis.

CORPORATE STRATEGIES FOR DEALING WITH DISPLACED WORKERS

Our research, as well as the research of others (e.g., Schweiger, Ivancevich, and Power 1987), suggests that there are six key elements of an effective corporate strategy for dealing with laid-off workers: (1) explanations of criteria for layoffs; (2) the role of performance evaluations in layoff decisions; (3) treatment of laid-off workers with dignity and social support; (4) fair recommendations to potential new employers; (5) attention to the stress and discomfort of the "survivors" who remain; and (6) finding as many alternatives to layoffs for cost reduction as possible. Each of these is discussed in more detail below.

Explanations of Criteria for Layoffs

As noted above, many laid-off employees attributed their layoffs to age bias or other forms of arbitrariness. Another common perception about layoff procedures was that top management spared average middle managers from cuts while greatly slashing the number of lower-level workers, even those who were especially competent. In some companies, perceptions of sex bias are also an issue when layoffs occur. At NBC, for instance, a female associate producer was laid off from her job—and then discovered that all but one of the people laid off in her unit were women (Langley 1984).

Thus, when business reverses or corporate restructurings force layoffs, it is important for managers, first, to construct fair criteria for the order of terminations (e.g., seniority, merit, and job category) and, second, to make those criteria clear to all employees. Otherwise, management leaves itself open to legal action from those who are laid off, ill will from the public, and justified distrust from those employees who remain (Leana and Feldman 1989a).

Performance Evaluations

One of the major reasons employees view their layoffs as arbitrary and capricious is that they see little connection between their formal performance evaluations and the layoff lists. In our study, 75 percent of the displaced workers received ratings of outstanding or excellent on the last performance appraisal, and yet they had still been let go. Some respondents also noted that ratings had been distorted to justify layoff decisions: "Inaccurate and untrue performance appraisals were used in support of company layoff goals—a very cavalier attitude toward dedicated, long-term employees. The human aspects were gruesome" (Leana and Feldman 1989b). Other research has also documented that managers deflate performance appraisals to speed up a termination process (Longenecker, Gioia, and Sims 1987).

When layoffs occur, all the political games used to justify the performance results become open for inspection. The negative spin-off effects for top management can prove to be embarrassing or costly if employees file suit. Even if the layoffs occur as a result of corporate restructuring, managers from the acquiring firm will look closely and critically at personnel files before making layoff decisions. Corporations need to make sure that performance evaluations accurately reflect true employee abilities (Leana and Feldman 1989a; Longenecker, Gioia, and Sims 1987).

Treatment of Employees with Dignity and Social Support

Schweiger et al. (1987) write that one of the most important executive actions for managing human resources during terminations is the treatment of laid-off employees with dignity and social support. Executive actions that they cite as particularly helpful are giving employees accurate and honest information about time frames of layoffs so they could make plans, and talking extensively with employees to give them a chance to vent their anger and frustration.

In contrast, there have been some unpleasant episodes involving laid-off employees being mistreated. Sutton et al. (1986), for instance, document the problems that occurred at Atari in 1982 and 1983, just before Atari was sold by Warner Communications. Production workers were herded into a public high school; security personnel took away their identification badges and escorted them off the property. Top management spoke disparagingly of the departed workers, causing morale to decline even further. Instead, Sutton and his colleagues suggest that laid-off employees be given the bad news in person and by people they know. Moreover, allowing departing employees an opportunity to say good-bye to co-workers and to express their sorrow is psychologically better for both the laid-off workers and the workers who remain.

Fair Recommendations to Potential Employers

Increasingly, terminated employees who think that they are not fairly recommended for employment in other corporations are suing; suits filed by discharged employees against their former bosses now account for about a third of all defamation actions (Striarchuk 1986). It is extremely important for executives to be sensitive to the legal implications of negative recommendations for employees (Leana and Feldman 1989a, 1989b).

Indeed, counseling companies on large-scale layoffs in order to avoid class action discrimination suits has become a growing specialty in labor law (Langley 1984). Because of the many legal ramifications of layoffs (e.g., recommendations, renegotiated contracts, and pension distributions), many corporations are employing the services of "undertaker" firms like the The Directorate to advise them on the legal technicalities of laying employees off (Putnam 1987).

Handling "Survivors" of Layoffs

Corporations dealing with the HR problems resulting from layoffs have more recently been paying attention to the flip side of this issue: that the people who survive the layoff are often upset and angry as well (Brockner, Davy, and Carter 1985; Greenhalgh and Rosenblatt 1984). Survivors frequently miss the social support and companionship of their departed co-workers and often are angry with management either for having caused the layoff or for treating the laid-off workers poorly (Leana and Feldman 1988a). The productivity of survivors is also likely to decrease, as employees lose time complaining about their jobs, speculating on whether more layoffs will be forthcoming, and looking for new jobs of their own (Naj 1987; Reibstein 1985).

Because of these problems, firms have taken some positive, concrete actions to lift the morale and instill trust in the survivors of layoffs (Reibstein 1985). For instance, consulting firms such as Eclecon and Goodmeasure advise corporations to give employees relatively easy work the first week or so after the layoffs, followed by new, challenging assignments to distract them. When layoffs occur as a result of corporate restructurings, Schweiger et al. (1987) recommend integrating surviving personnel with the personnel from the acquiring firm through such actions as giving survivors accurate information about the culture and reward systems of the other firm. Reibstein (1985) suggests that in order to keep survivor morale up, management should not dribble layoffs over a long period. At Amax, Inc., unfortunately, a series of layoffs occurred over a four-year period, each accompanied by management's claim that the company was now "lean and mean." Such action only further demoralized workers (Reibstein 1985).

Finding Alternatives to Layoffs

Because of all the problems associated with layoffs, several writers have urged corporations to consider alternatives to layoffs when faced with adverse business conditions (Carroll 1984; Lawrence 1985; Perry 1986).

The case of IBM is particularly instructive because even though IBM has a high commitment to preserving job security, it still was forced to deal with the need to redeploy personnel. First, IBM reduced new hiring, and temporary and overtime work was stopped. Next, IBM set up financial incentives for older workers to retire, did not replace retiring employees, and encouraged voluntary relocations to other plants. IBM also established an open-door policy and a hot line for employees so that they could get quick and accurate information about IBM's plans (Greenhalgh, McKersie, and Gilkey 1986).

A variety of innovative practices have also been attempted as means of reducing personnel costs (Leana and Feldman 1989a, 1989b). One alternative that has received considerable attention is "short-time pay"; instead of laying off employees, companies voluntarily split reduced work among existing staffers by cutting the working hours and paychecks of all (Feinstein 1987). Polaroid experimented with job-sharing, in which two employees cut back their hours to half time to share a job. Pacific Northwest Bell implemented a leave of absence policy, in which workers could take unpaid leaves of absence but were guaranteed jobs on return; Mountain Bell saved substantial money by reducing paid vacation time and decreasing the number of long weekends (Perry 1986). In general, research suggests that innovative corporate actions seem to elicit more volunteers than originally expected—and that these volunteers, when considered together, really allow corporations to make less drastic cuts than they would have to otherwise (Greenhalgh et al. 1986).

COOPERATIVE VENTURES AMONG CORPORATIONS, UNIONS, AND THE GOVERNMENT

Because the magnitude of the displaced worker problem is so severe and the ripple effects so wide, more and more corporations are motivated to join other institutions in their efforts to help the unemployed.

For instance, in terms of providing training, corporations can take advantage of federal government financial incentives to assist laid-off workers. The National Alliance of Business, established in 1980, provides governmental subsidies to businesses for hiring and training the hard-to-employ. More recently, the Title III Dislocated Workers Program (1982) was enacted to provide governmental assistance to employers who are directly involved in efforts to re-employ laid-off workers (Leana and Ivancevich 1987).

Another area in which the government and private industry have cooperated is outplacement. In Florida, for example, the federal government funded an outplacement center at Brevard Community College for workers laid off at the Space Coast. At the height of the layoffs, sixty persons a night showed up for advice on résumé writing, interviewing, and changing careers (Kelley 1986; Leana and Feldman 1989b).

As unions have become increasingly hard hit by plant closings, they have become more willing to engage in cooperative ventures with management to stem layoffs (Leana and Feldman 1989b). In the area of collective bargaining, unions have been willing to give concessions in wages, benefits, and work rules in an attempt to help the company become more profitable and survive. They have also been willing to exchange wage demands for increased job security, more advance notice of layoffs, and increased severance pay for workers (McKersie and McKersie 1982).

In the area of political action, some unions and employers have joined forces to seek legislation aimed at protecting their industry from foreign competition and to oppose environmental regulations that may have negative effects on profitability. For example, the United Steelworkers, on several occasions, have supported industry efforts to weaken or postpone implementation of emissions standards (Lawrence 1985). There have even been cases in which unions have worked with management in developing new uses for plants faced with declining product demand or obsolete technology (e.g., the United Electrical Workers and General Electric).

Obviously, hostile labor-management relations are unlikely to take a positive turn overnight. Nevertheless, in many cases, management's willingness to work with unions can reduce the number of workers who need to be laid off, or can vastly ameliorate the negative consequences for the unemployed.

A third avenue for corporate cooperation is company-community relations (Carroll 1984). Corporations can take a series of socially responsible steps to avert layoffs, reduce their sizes, or mitigate their effects on their communities.

For instance, before shutting down a plant or division, Carroll (1984) urges companies to consider selling off the unit as an ongoing enterprise, an option likely to reduce the need for layoffs; when Viner Brothers Shoes was going out of business, its sale to Wolverine Manufacturing saved 90 percent of the workers' jobs. The National Center for Employee Ownership has documented some cases (e.g., Ruth Packaging Company) in which companies have sold plants or divisions to the employees themselves, and the new companies have survived.

Even after the decision to close a plant or division is made, there are a variety of actions that corporations can take to mitigate the social and economic impact of their actions on employees and their communities (Leana and Feldman 1989b). For example, Tate and Lyle (United Kingdom), when it was closing its sugar refineries, invested capital in firms that were willing to expand their workforce by offering jobs to former Tate and Lyle workers. Olin, in its departure from Saltville, Virginia, gave that town 3,500 acres of property, mineral rights, the plant, and all remaining tangible property as well as more than a half-million dollars in cash subsidies (Carroll 1984).

The issue of how to assist displaced workers is becoming increasingly complex; even well-intentioned corporations operate in broader environments that are not without constraints. For corporations to effectively handle layoffs and terminations, they need the cooperation and support of other important institutions involved with this important HR management issue—the unions, local and state governments, and federal agencies.

REFERENCES

Bennett, A. 1987. After the merger, more CEO's left in uneasy spot: Looking for work. *The Wall Street Journal*, February 3, p. 35.

Blotzer, J. 1985. Jobless adrift, cling to hope. *Pittsburgh Post Gazette*, December 30, pp. 33–36.

Bolt, J. F. 1983. Job security: Its time has come. *Harvard Business Review*, 16, 115–23.

Brockner, J., J. Davy, and C. Carter. 1985. Layoffs, self-esteem, and survivor guilt: Motivational, affective, and attitudinal consequences. *Organizational Behavior and Human Decision Processes*, 36, 229–44.

Carroll, A. B. 1984. When business closes down: Social responsibilities and management action. *California Management Review*, 26, 125–39.

Deutsch, C. H. 1988. Why being fired is losing its taint. *The New York Times*, January 24, pp. 3–11.

Fedrau, J. 1984. Easing the worker's transition from job loss to employment. *Monthly Labor Review*, 107, 38–40.

Feinstein, S. 1987. Short-time pay fails to catch on as a way to hold down layoffs. *The Wall Street Journal*, February 3, p. 35.

Greenhalgh, L., R. B. McKersie, and R. W. Gilkey. 1986. Rebalancing the workforce at IBM: A case study of redeployment and revitalization. *Organizational Dynamics*, 14, 30–47.

Greenhalgh, L., and Z. Rosenblatt. 1984. Job insecurity: Toward conceptual clarity. *Academy of Management Review*, 9, 438–48.

Harrison, B. 1984. Plant closures: Efforts to cushion the blow. *Monthly Labor Review*, 107, 41–43.

Jahoda, M. 1982. *Employment and unemployment*. London: Cambridge University Press.

Kaufman, H. G. 1982. *Professionals in search of work: Coping with the stress of job loss and unemployment*. New York: John Wiley.

Kelley, J. 1986. Jobless workers feel lost in space. *USA Today*, October 2, p. 1.

Langley, M. 1984. Many middle managers fight back as more firms trim workforces. *The Wall Street Journal*, November 29, p. 55.

Latack, J. C., and J. B. Dozier. 1986. After the ax falls: Job loss as a career transition. *Academy of Management Review*, 11, 375–92.

Lawrence, A. T. 1985. *Plant closing and technological change provisions in California collective bargaining agreements*. San Francisco: Division of Labor Statistics and Research, California Department of Industrial Relations.

Leana, C. R., and D. C. Feldman. 1988a. Individual responses to job loss: Perceptions, reactions, and coping behaviors. *Journal of Management*, 14, 375–90.

Leana, C. R., and D. C. Feldman. 1988b. Job loss: How employees react to layoffs. *Personnel Journal*, September, pp. 31–34.

Leana, C. R., and D. C. Feldman. 1989a. When mergers force layoffs: Some lessons about managing the human resource problems. *Human Resource Planning*, *12*, 123–40.

Leana, C. R., and D. C. Feldman. 1989b. *Individual and institutional responses to job loss.* Lexington, MA.: Lexington Books.

Leana, C. R., and J. M. Ivancevich. 1987. Involuntary job loss: Institutional interventions and a research agenda. *Academy of Management Review*, *12*, 301–12.

Longenecker, C. O., D. A. Gioia, and H. P. Sims. 1987. Behind the mask: The politics of employee appraisal. *Academy of Management Review*, *12*, 301–12.

McKersie, R. B., and W. S. McKersie. 1982. *Plant closings: What can be learned from best practice?* Washington, D.C.: U.S. Department of Labor.

Naj, A. K. 1987. GM now is plagued with drop in morale as payrolls are cut. *The Wall Street Journal*, May 26, pp. 1, 18.

Perry, L. T. 1986. Least-cost alternatives to layoffs in declining industries. *Organizational Dynamics*, *14*, 48–61.

Putnam, W. C. 1987. Undertaker helps businesses close down. *Gainesville Sun*, April 27, p. 8C.

Reibstein, L. 1985. Survivors of layoffs receive help to lift morale and reinstill trust. *The Wall Street Journal*, December 5, p. 33.

Russell, G. 1987. Rebuilding to survive. *Time*, February 16, pp. 44–45.

Scherba, J. 1973. Outplacement as a personnel responsibility. *Personnel*, *50*, 40–44.

Schweiger, D. M., J. M. Ivancevich, and F. R. Power. 1987. Executive actions for managing human resources before and after acquisition. *Academy of Management Executive*, *1*, 127–38.

Striarchuk, G. 1986. Fired employees turn the reason for dismissal into a legal weapon. *The Wall Street Journal*, October 2, p. 33.

Sutton, R. I., K. M. Eisenhardt, and J. V. Jucker. 1986. Managing organizational decline: Lessons from Atari. *Organizational Dynamics*, *14*, 17–29.

Weber, A. R., and D. P. Taylor. 1963. Procedures for employee displacement: Advance notice of plant shutdown. *Journal of Business*, *36*, 312–15.

CHAPTER 11

MANAGING ORGANIZATIONAL CHANGE: A MERGER CASE STUDY

Anthony J. Rucci, Frank M. J. LaFasto, and David Ulrich

The 1980s may be characterized as a decade of turbulence and change in organizations (Drucker 1980; Ulrich and Wiersema 1988). Technological change, globalization, changing demographics, and changing capital market structures have led firms to modify their strategies. One increasingly common strategy is for firms to undertake mergers or acquisitions.

Pressures for mergers and acquisitions come from many sources. They come in part from increased competition and the need for increased efficiency, or lower operating costs. They also come from changes in the capital market structure, where more resources are allocated to pension funds and institutional investors. Capital markets have encouraged more of a short-term perspective and increased the relative power of investment bankers who control increasingly large blocks of capital. Institutional shareholders increasingly recognize the power of their ownership, and find that they are able to influence a firm's managers to make decisions that are designed to increase the value of their stock. Mergers and acquisitions offer shareholders and large capital fund managers an immediate return as the price of the stock increases for the merger or acquisition.

The net result of these increased pressures is reflected in the enormous growth in merger and acquisition activity from 1980 through 1987 (Power and Maremont 1988). The number of acquisitions has grown from 1,500 in 1980 to more than 3,000 in 1987, and the total dollar volume has more than quadrupled from 30 billion dollars to more than 140 billion dollars. And non-U.S. investors are increasingly interested in merger and acquisition activity in the United States.

CHALLENGES TO MAKING MERGERS OR ACQUISITIONS WORK

Only when a merger or acquisition is financially completed does the real challenge begin (Richmond 1984). Managers have the task of integrating diverse strategies, cultures, and employees (Schweiger, Ivancevich, and Power 1987; Siehl, Ledford, Silverman, and Fay 1988) into a new and unique company. We propose that one of the greatest challenges to *successful* mergers rests with how organizational systems and people are incorporated into one (Marks 1982; Ivanevich, Schweiger, and Power 1988; Ulrich, Cody, LaFasto, and Rucci 1989), and how that change process is managed.

Human resource (HR) activities must play a central role in accomplishing successful mergers and acquisitions for three reasons (Schuler and Mac-Millan 1985). First, HR activities allow change to occur for the newly merged company (Ulrich 1986). Through training, staffing, incentives, and organizational design employees come to accept changes that may affect them in the new organization. Second, HR practices may be used to create a strategic unity within the new company (Perry 1986; Ulrich and Brockbank 1989). The strategic unity occurs as people inside and outside the organization come to share core values, assumptions, and beliefs (Schein 1985). Third, HR activities allow strategies for the newly merged companies to work (Schuler and MacMillan 1985; Ulrich 1987). No strategy is accomplished without involvement and participation of people. By designing reward, staffing, communication, and training programs that cause members of an organization to behave in particular ways, strategies are accomplished (Ivancevich, Schweiger, and Power 1987).

To demonstrate the importance of and choices for HR practices in successful mergers or acquisitions, we report on a major merger in the hospital supply industry: Baxter Travenol's 1985 acquisition of American Hospital Supply Corporation for 3.7 billion dollars, which affected more than 60,000 employees. The intent of this case is to illustrate how HR practices became central to the development of a successful "new" corporation. It also highlights the role of senior managers and HR professionals in making mergers work. We conclude with learnings and implications for general managers and HR professionals involved in major organization change.

BUSINESS SETTING FOR BAXTER-AMERICAN MERGER

Several factors combined to make the Baxter-American merger unique. First, both were historically strong and successful companies by all market, management, and financial measures. Despite shocks to the health system brought about by legislative changes and cost-containment efforts, the market remained large, attractive, and dynamic, not a shrinking market frequently seen in large mergers and acquisitions. Instead, it required that

Baxter and American quickly and effectively integrate strategies to maintain market presence.

Second, the interwoven history and competition between Baxter and American spanned forty-five years. The two companies had been closely associated since the early 1930s. Both were striving to become the dominant supplier to health care providers. American, the older and larger of the two, had become Baxter's sole distributor for intravenous solutions when Baxter was just getting started in Glendale, California. The distribution agreement, despite contractual disagreements, continued into the 1960s, when it was terminated for each company to pursue its separate track with explosive growth by the Medicare and Medicaid legislation of the mid-1960s. Before that, however, American in fact bought the modern Baxter's predecessor company, Don Baxter Intravenous Products of Glendale, California, and in 1950 sought to acquire Baxter itself. This long and often combative history produced residual attitudes in both organizations that had to be understood and dealt with in the 1985 merger.

Third, this merger was unique because of the speed with which decisions about guiding philosophy, organization, staffing, compensation, and benefits were made, while business strategy necessarily evolved more slowly. All the initial basic organization and HR decisions were made between July 15 (the date of the merger agreement) and November 25, 1985 (the merger closing date). The thesis was that everything should be ready for implementation by the time of merger closing and that additional time would not produce additional quality, but only prolong uncertainty. This time pressure meant that executives and other managers faced extremely demanding work loads during this four-month period. More important, it required that management processes be as close to error-proof as possible.

These background factors highlight that the Baxter-American combination was conceived as a *strategic* merger, first by Baxter but progressively agreed to by American's executives. A cooperative, "equal partner" approach was established to assure that the new organization's strategy would be based on the best thinking and experience of both companies. Expectations and objectives had to be *jointly* established. Understandably, many employees even at management levels had difficulty grasping and accepting the approach. Some interpreted it as merely "getting along together" and others found it difficult to concentrate on the development of a new, forward-looking strategy at a time when so many organizational routines and certainties were disrupted. A number of employees expressed impatience for all the change to be over "so that they could get back to work."

MERGER INTEGRATION PROCESS AND HR PRACTICES

The merger integration process focused on three major initiatives: (1) defining the operating philosophy for the new (merged) organization; (2)

designing an organizational structure consistent with that philosophy; and (3) executing the people-related aspects of the merger: employee communications, executive and corporate staff selection, employee severance, and career continuation assistance. Senior HR executives from both organizations were involved in all three of these initiatives, not just the third. This ensured that the people aspects of the merger were not just grafted on to the organization after the fact.

Before discussing the process used in each initiative, it is worth noting a superordinate step: identifying the values and philosophy that would drive the new organization. Admittedly intangible, these values have profoundly influenced the landscape of the merged company. From the outset, an explicit position was taken regarding *how* the merger would proceed, and the process issues below have found their way into the culture of the new company. The key philosophical objectives of the merger were as follows:

- Participative—The design and integration of the two companies would be undertaken with broad participation from executives of *both* companies.

- Strategic—any activities in merging the companies would be consistent with the strategic direction of the merger, not expedient.

- High standards—An explicit decision was made to conduct the merger integration in an unprecedented way; to avoid the traumatic impact on people as much as possible, and to select into the new organization the best people from the prior two companies.

- Dignity—*All* employees (Baxter and American, retained and outplaced) were treated in an open and honest manner, and with a sense of dignity and respect at an individual level.

We cannot overstate the impact and importance of this values infrastructure on the integration process. It established a tone from the chief executive officer (CEO) level throughout the organization.

Operationally, the merger integration process was managed by four major task forces, as shown in Figure 11.1. The Merger Steering Committee comprised the CEO and chief operating officer (COO) of Baxter and the chairman and CEO and COO of American Hospital. These four persons conducted frequent reviews of the integration process. The Transition Team comprised eight senior executives—four from Baxter and four from American. All the tactical task forces (fourteen in all) reported to this group, including the Top Management Organization Structure task force and the Corporate Staff Integration task force. These two task forces were the primary groups involved in actually putting together the operating structure and the integration of the two corporate staff groups. Combined, these four task forces were responsible for managing the three major initiatives related to integrating the companies.

Figure 11.1
Building the New Organization: Four Major Support Groups

Merger Steering Committee	Transition Team	Top Management Org. Structure Task Force	Corporate Staff Integration Task Force
·Office of the Chief Executive ·Baxter/AHS Balance	·Full Time Group ·Baxter/AHS Balance	·Human Resource VP's ·Planning VP's ·Baxter/AHS Balance	·Human Resources Execs. ·Planning Executives ·Baxter/AHS Balance

Role

Merger Steering Committee	Transition Team	Top Management Org. Structure Task Force	Corporate Staff Integration Task Force

·Review/Approve ALL Activities (e.g.)
  – Org. Design
  – Executive Selection
	·All Task Forces Reported to This Group (e.g.)
	  – Corp. Staff Design
	  – Culture
	  – Manufacturing
		·Identify Operating Structure and Philosophy
		·Design Staff and Line Configuration
		·Corp. Officers Selected
			·Formal Organization Design Process
			·Formal People Selection Process

Identifying the Operating Philosophy

The first step was to define the philosophy under which the new organization would operate. Before the merger, each company was characterized by a substantially different operating philosophy. American Hospital Supply Corporation was characterized by a decentralized operating structure that included multiple operating units with a fully integrated operating philosophy. By contrast, the pre-merger Baxter organization was a much more centralized and functional operating style with few autonomous operating units and functional responsibilities such as human resources and finance reporting directly to the corporate headquarters. It should be noted that each of these philosophies was consistent with the historical operations of the two companies. A key question, therefore, before proceeding with the integration of the two companies was to determine what type of operating philosophy would characterize the new, merged organization.

It became common practice to use the dichotomy of centralized versus decentralized philosophy in discussing where the new company was headed. Most employees were told that the new company would have an operating philosophy somewhere between the two. Ultimately, the top management task force determined that a hybrid concept was most appropriate. In short, the intention was to decentralize decisionmaking authority to the level closest to the customer, thereby decentralizing those decisions that had a substantive impact on the customer. For those areas not seen as critical to customer interface, however, centralization and consolidation to realize economies of scale became a critical variable. This hybrid approach represented a change to all employees and had significant implications for the resulting organizational structure.

Designing the New Organizational Structure

Consolidation of Operating Units

Once the decision was made to effect a decentralized customer decisionmaking style, the organizational structure task force turned its attention to the consolidation of operating units. In preparation for that process, extensive profiling was done to document the product lines, customers, and market segmentation of the existing divisions within each of the premerger companies. Based on that information, the organizational structure task force identified ten rational groupings of operating units. Each of the resulting ten operating groups then had multiple operating divisions reporting to them.

Corporate Staff Organization Design Process

The next major decision to be made in connection with organizational structure and design had to do with the corporate staff organizations. In a merger the size of Baxter-American, one of three approaches can be taken in attempting to integrate the companies. The first approach can be characterized as a holding company wherein each of the existing corporate staffs remains intact and no integration of personnel or functions occurs. Under that configuration, each premerger company continues to operate as a wholly owned subsidiary of a parent company. The second option is to do what is usually done in merger or acquisition situations. That is, the corporate staff structure of the acquiring company stays intact and selected staff members of the acquired company are fit into that structure where openings or management discretion allows. The third approach is to attempt to integrate the two corporate staff groups and design a totally new structure. In the case of Baxter and American Hospital Supply Corporation's merger, the decision was made to effect a true integration. Once again, this philosophical objective had profound implications for the process required to create a new corporate staff structure.

The organizational structure task force determined that there would be ten corporate staff functions. Once that decision was made, the officers to head each of the operating groups and staff functions were selected through a candidate slating process, which is described later. The next step was for the corporate staff integration task force to execute the formal design and people selection phase of the integration. Among the staff groups, consistent with all other aspects of the merger, task forces were formed in each functional area that maintained equal Baxter and American representation.

In order to take an objective approach to the evaluation of the new corporate staff areas, a formal organizational design process was established. First, each staff executive evaluated the strategic mission or charter of his or her function in the newly merged organization. There was no assumption that the way either company had staffed its corporate groups before the merger would necessarily be followed after the merger. Once the strategic mission for the new function was identified, each executive was asked to identify all the functions, programs, and systems that would be needed to meet that strategic charter. Next, each executive was asked to evaluate whether a centralized or decentralized operating approach would be most appropriate. Then, the executives were asked to estimate what resources, both dollars and staffing levels, would be needed to accomplish the strategic mission. Next, the executives were asked to recommend an organizational structure consistent with the strategic mission and centralized or decentralized philosophy that was to be adopted.

Finally, and only *after* all the steps above had been completed, the people selection phase of the merger was implemented. This fact is noteworthy in that executives who were involved on the task forces to design the new staff structures did not know at the time of their participation whether they personally would be selected for a role in the new organization. This uncertainty created a climate of interdependence and cooperativeness among some executives, a climate of competitiveness among others.

People-related Aspects of Merger

The people selection process at the corporate staff level created some unique challenges. First, the magnitude of the task was significant: before the merger both companies had a combined total of nearly 3,000 persons on their corporate staffs. With a more decentralized operating philosophy, the task was to reduce that number by nearly one-third, to 2,000. Not all 1,000 reductions would result in job loss, however. Many of those positions would be decentralized to operating units. Second, from the outset of the merger, the CEO of the acquiring Baxter organization (Vernon R. Loucks, Jr.) had maintained that a true integration would be implemented and that the best person would be selected for any given job regardless of prior company affiliation. That philosophy is a dramatic departure from the usual practice in acquisitions, in which, typically, employees of the acquired company are given little chance of securing a role with the new organization.

In order to meet the unique aspects of this merger, the people selection process was formal and rather elaborate. It can be characterized by the following points:

- Select the best person regardless of company
- Full-time staffing transition team appointed
- Slate-making teams established for each functional area
- Formal placement centers established
- Career continuation assistance offered
- External hiring freeze in all operating units
- Review and appeals board established

The mandate to select the best person required a set of criteria for what defined best. It also posed the issue of how managers from either of the given companies could make an intelligent decision without having knowledge of people from the other company. Also, the sequence of events and flow of the people selection process were significant issues to deal with.

To effect an orderly process, a full-time staffing transition team was appointed, reporting to the corporate staff integration task force. As in all other phases of the merger, the staffing transition team comprised executives from both the premerger Baxter and premerger American organizations. It was the responsibility of the staffing team to outline the process and sequence of events for people selection decisions.

Candidate Slate-making Process

At the heart of the people selection stage was a candidate slate process. It was also the slate-making process that assured the integrity of data collection and consideration of *every* current employee. The first step was to establish slate-making teams within each functional staff, with representation and HR executives from each of the prior companies. These slate-making teams effected a systematic process of matching current employees to newly designed organizational roles. In order to further emphasize the importance of the slate-making and people selection process, the merger steering committee indicated its desire to be directly involved in the selection of the top 100 executives in the new company. Figure 11.2 is a graphic representation of how the candidate slating process proceeded.

The first step was the selection of the top twenty officers: the ten new corporate staff executives and the ten new operating group executives. Each of those twenty jobs had a candidate slate prepared for consideration by the merger steering committee. An all-day meeting was convened with the merger steering committee along with the two senior HR executives, devoted solely to making candidate choices for the top twenty positions. For instance, the candidate slate for the staff position of general counsel and senior vice president may have included the names of the general counsels from each of the prior two companies, and perhaps even a third or fourth name of another senior-ranking legal executive in one of the prior companies. At the meeting, the experience and executive capability of each of these candidates were openly discussed by the committee members and a final decision was made.

The twenty newly selected officers then began the candidate slating process for positions that would report directly to them. The same slating process was followed: slate-making teams met, considered the requirements of each direct report position, and built candidate slates that had representation from the prior Baxter and prior American companies in nearly every case. Once again, the merger steering committee met in yet another full-day session devoted to people selection. The committee heard presentations from each of the new corporate staff officers regarding their organizational structure and the candidate slates they had constructed for their direct reports. At that meeting, the newly appointed staff officers indicated their preference of candidates to be selected in each case, but the merger steering committee was able to give their input, and in many cases influenced the final decision as to who would hold the top 100 executive roles. Once completed, each of the next level of newly selected managers were notified, and they then began slating, interviewing, and selecting candidates for jobs

Figure 11.2
Staffing Process: Corporate and Group Staff

Process

- **Merger Steering Committee**
- **Candidate Slates**
- **Selection Decision**

- **Candidate Slates**
- **Merger Steering Committee
  and Functional VP Selection Decision**

- **Candidate Slates**
- **Interviews**
- **Hiring Manager Selection Decision**
- **Functional VP Approval**

- **Job Posting/Slating**
- **HR Screens Posting List**
- **Interviews as Necessary**
- **Hiring Manager Selection Decision**
- **One-Over-One Approval**

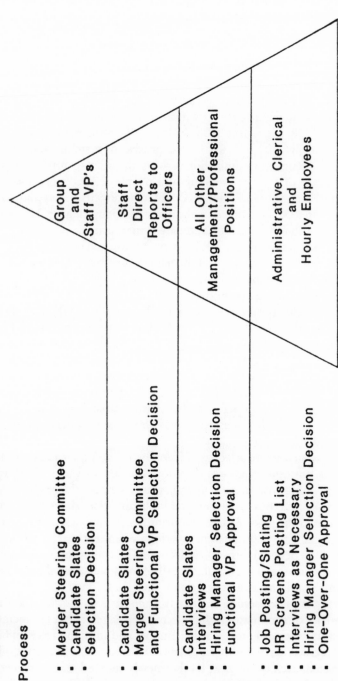

Group
and
Staff VP's

Staff
Direct
Reports to
Officers

All Other
Management/Professional
Positions

Administrative, Clerical
and
Hourly Employees

reporting to them. The process proceeded until *all* positions on the corporate staff had been slated and filled.

The unique feature about this process was its zero-based organizational design and staffing approach. No assumptions were made about the new staff structures; no assumptions were made about who would be in any of those roles. A second critical factor was the inclusion of executives from both premerger companies, so that employees within the organization felt that someone who knew them personally was representing their interests in the selection stage. Lastly, as a safeguard to ensure that every employee had been given due process, a senior officer Review and Appeals Board was established.

The role of the Review and Appeals Board was to individually review the files of any employee who would be affected and removed from the payroll *before that occurred*, to ensure that each employee had received due process consideration in securing a job in the new organization. It was not a role of the Review and Appeals Board to second-guess the actual selection decision of any given manager. Rather, the Board simply verified that any given employee had been slated for one or more jobs, had been given an opportunity to interview for one or more jobs, and that some rationale existed for why this particular person was not as good a fit for the new role as the candidate who may have been selected. It was only after due process review by the Review and Appeals Board that an employee was notified that he or she had not been selected, and would be eligible for outplacement and career continuation assistance.

Assistance to Affected Employees

Formal placement centers were established within the company where affected employees could go and get full information about all open positions within Baxter operating units. Placement center personnel would then put an affected employee in touch with an operating unit for consideration and an interview. A hiring freeze had been implemented throughout both companies nearly three months in advance of the merger closing in anticipation of corporate staff reductions. This hiring freeze and internal placement effort resulted in placement of more than 150 employees from the corporate staff who would otherwise have lost their positions.

Finally, if an individual employee was not selected into the new corporate staff or was unable to find placement within one of the operating units, he or she was then referred to the Career Continuation Centers. These centers were staffed with HR professionals and were equipped to accommodate full job search efforts on the part of affected employees. In addition to an enhanced severance package designed for the merger integration process, each affected employee was given full use of the center, which included office space, telephone coverage, secretarial coverage for résumé preparation, a job search bank listing open positions with other employers in the immediate geographical area, a reference library, and, most important, professionally conducted career continuation workshops and job search counseling. By offering such extensive outplacement assistance, the organization made a clear statement about its people values. It sent a message to those who remained that it intended to be equally concerned about people issues in the future.

LEARNING AND IMPLICATIONS FOR GENERAL MANAGERS AND HR EXECUTIVES

As anticipated, the complexities of the Baxter-American merger presented numerous opportunities for observing some of the intricacies of merger practices. The following general observations command particular attention for general managers and HR executives in making mergers work through people.

1. *Spend time on people issues.* In the rush and pressure of merger or acquisition activity, executives' time may be easily focused on quantifiable, objective indicators (e.g., financial mergers). In the Baxter merger, executives from both companies paid attention to people issues and activities. Spending time on those issues not only ensures that people are considered during merger, but also sets a tone for the values of the new company's culture after the merger.

2. *Communicate extensively.* Communication internally with employees at all levels is a critical element of success. Rather than allow rumors to run rampant and overstate expected outcomes of the merger, managers who share honest information with employees build commitment to the new merger. At times, the information shared may only be a "we-don't-know-yet" answer, but people appreciate honest information, even when it is bad news. It is imperative to overcommunicate with employees. In addition to sharing information internally, communications to outside constituencies is equally critical. During the Baxter merger, information was shared with customers, suppliers, financial holders, and the communities in which Baxter employees resided. Such information helped those outside the company be comfortable with the internal transitions. These communication programs both before and after the merger helped to build commitment to the merger.

3. *Create a new vision for the merged company.* After companies merge, it is critical for executives to send a message of confidence and future success to employees. The new vision of the merged Baxter included a new company name, a new mission statement, new advertising, and numerous efforts to create a new vision for the company. The guiding principles and philosophy were the core of this vision for the new company. Ensuring that these principles were understood, accepted, and practiced was a primary role of the general managers.

4. *Move boldly.* In cases of mergers or acquisitions, financial, strategic, and HR decisions must be made quickly. But boldness must not occur without reason. Reason comes when decisions can be assessed systematically and with thorough, reliable data. Gathering good data requires that professionals know the details

of HR practices and work with line managers to eliminate job security uncertainty as quickly as possible.

5. *Individual dignity must be maintained at all costs.* Although a merger is accompanied by many potential career opportunities, it is also accompanied by potentially shattered career and personal dreams. Traditional friendships and working relationships are radically modified. These new employment contracts often create a loss of identity. The uncertainty surrounding the merger creates emotional stress and possibly depression. It is within this framework that each "person" decision must be made. Respect for employees is unequivocally in the best interest of all constituencies: the organization, the remaining employees, and, most of all, the affected people.

CONCLUSION

The merger integration and people selection process in the Baxter-American merger was a tremendous investment of resources and effort, but an excellent investment. In the three full fiscal years since the merger, sales have increased at a compounded annual growth rate of 10.2 percent and net income has increased at a compounded rate of 21.2 percent. Equally important, the care and effort taken to ensure the dignified treatment of people have set a tone that will influence the landscape of the organization for years to come. Mergers or acquisitions need not be unilaterally traumatic to employees; they can be done right.

REFERENCES

Drucker, P. F. 1980. *Managing in turbulent times.* New York: Harper & Row.

Ivancevich, J. M., D. M. Schweiger, and F. R. Power. 1988. Strategies for managing human resources during mergers and acquisitions. *Human Resource Planning, 10,* 19–35.

Marks, M. L. 1982, Summer. Merging human resources: A review of current research. *Mergers and Acquisitions,* 38–44.

Perry, L. T. 1986, Spring. Merging successfully: Sending the "right" signals. *Sloan Management Review,* 47–57.

Power, C., and M. Maremont. 1988, April 15. The top 200 deals. *Business Week,* 47–83.

Richmond, J. D. 1984, Fall. Acquisition decision making: An ethical analysis and recommendation. *California Management Review,* 177–84.

Schien, E. G. 1985. *Organizational culture and leadership.* San Francisco: Jossey-Bass.

Schuler, R., and I. MacMillan. 1985. Gaining competitive advantage through human resource management practices. *Human Resource Management, 23,* 241–55.

Schweiger, D., I. W. Ivancevich, and F. R. Power. 1987. Executive actions for managing human resources before and after acquisition. *Academy of Management Executive, 1,* 127–38.

Siehl, C., G. Ledford, R. Silverman, and P. Fay. 1988. *Managing cultural differences in mergers and acquisitions: The role of the HR function.* Working paper, Center for Effective Organizations, University of Southern California.

Ulrich, D. 1986. Human resource planning as a competitive edge. *Human Resource Planning, 9,* 1–15.

Ulrich, D. 1987. Strategic human resource management: Why and how? *Human Resource Planning, 10.*

Ulrich, D., and J. W. Brockbank. 1989. *Institutional antecedents of shared organizational cognitions.* Working paper, University of Michigan.

Ulrich, D., and M. Wiersema. Gaining strategic and organizational capability in a decade of turbulence. 1989. *Academy of Management Executive, 3,* 115–22.

Ulrich, D., T. Cody, F. LaFasto, and A. Rucci. 1989. Human resources at Baxter Healthcare Corporation merger: A strategic partner role. *Human Resource Planning, 12,* 87–103.

CHAPTER 12 ——————————————————————

HUMAN RESOURCE PLANNING AND BUSINESS PLANNING: A CASE ANALYSIS AND FRAMEWORK FOR FULL INTREGRATION
—————— MIRIAN M. GRADDICK AND PAMELA C. JONES

An absence of sound human resource (HR) planning can ultimately translate into missed opportunities or failures in the marketplace. These mistakes can in turn result in lost revenues, market share, and customer satisfaction as well as increased costs. Some rather startling cases have recently been cited highlighting the costly hitches attributable to firms that lack a business-focused people plan. One firm, for example, assumed the ability to transfer a specific technology from the United States to Brazil without adequately researching whether or not it could find or train the computer technicians and service people needed to run a facility that used this kind of technology. The facility later had to be adapted to the realities of the local labor force at considerable cost to the firm, both in terms of dollars and lost time.

Numerous articles have stressed the importance of more closely integrating HR planning and business planning. More recent articles have focused on identifying the critical success factors required to develop a fully integrated approach. The truth is that few firms have positioned human resources as a full partner at the business planning table. In addition, most published articles offer little in the way of practical examples and strategies for leveraging human resources to gain and maintain a competitive edge in the marketplace.

This chapter describes a case analysis of a methodology used by AT&T within one of its business units to integrate HR planning and business planning. A model is also explored that summarizes the major learnings and ensures that human resources is an equal partner at the table during the development of business strategies and plans. In summary, our initial experience focused on developing HR strategies and interventions in response to finalized business strategies. The emphasis has now shifted to diagnosing and even modifying proposed business strategies based on the various HR implications that are identified while strategies are being formulated.

CASE ANALYSIS: THE BUSINESS MARKETS GROUP

AT&T's Business Markets Group (BMG) launched a major effort in 1987 aimed at integrating HR planning and business planning. The major goal was to develop a set of HR strategies and programs that would help the BMG achieve its business objectives. The BMG's primary mission was to sell premise or network solutions to large domestic and international business customers. With more than 20,000 employees, the BMG was virtually a self-contained business unit that encompassed a variety of functions, including market planning, product management, sales, and sales support.

The following assumptions guided the initial efforts to build a HR agenda that was directly linked to the business plan:

- The business plan for 1987–88 had already been established; therefore, the first step was to develop a set of HR objectives to achieve this plan. A long-term goal was to ensure that HR issues were generated during the business planning process.

- The approach used was clearly deductive. Because a model or framework fitting our unique context did not exist, we decided to build one at the end of the project. This provided the flexibility to modify the approach along the way based on what we learned.

- An accurate data base providing critical data, such as the skill mix of employees, was not available. Given the initial time constraints, we identified areas in which more internal data were needed. Rather than stop the process and spend several months gathering this information, we decided to include these data requirements as action items tied to specific HR objectives.

- A key strategy was to involve all the relevant stakeholders throughout the process and to decide at what points to involve various groups.

An Overview of the Process

Led by the executive support group within the BMG, the process began in March of 1987. The head of this group reported directly to the president of the BMG. The group's primary role was to provide HR planning and support to the various BMG organizations.

A core group was established with members from the BMG strategy group, the BMG sales development and education group, and several people from corporate human resources. Because the heads of various departments within the BMG were anxious to implement the business plan, the core team set a time frame of two months to propose a 1987–88 HR plan. Each

Figure 12.1
Process Used by the Business Marketing Group for Linking Business Plans and HR Planning

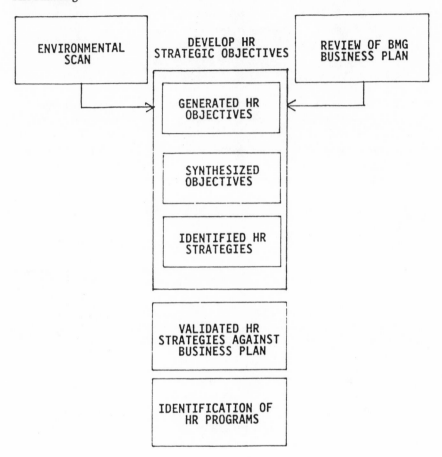

core team member worked almost full time on the project during these two months.

Another group of key stakeholders included a subset of directors within the BMG. This group served as a sounding board for periodically reviewing ideas and soliciting input. Finally, the BMG officer team was kept apprised of the core group activities and outputs at key milestones throughout the process.

The core team used the approach depicted in Figure 12.1 to develop an HR strategy. First, the core team examined trends in the internal and external environment and assessed how these trends might impact human resources over the next five years. They then thoroughly reviewed the BMG business

Table 12.1
Demographic and Social Trends That Impact Human Resources

TREND	STRUCTURE	SELECTION
WORKFORCE DEMOGRAPHIC AND SOCIAL TRENDS:		
● DECREASING 16-24 YR OLD POPULATION; BULK OF LABOR FORCE IN PRIME 25-54 AGE BRACKET BY 1995	● PART-TIME PERMANENT JOBS ● JOB SHARING ● FLEXIBLE HOURS	● INVESTIGATE NEW MARKETS FOR ENTRY-LEVEL JOBS - PERMANENT PART-TIME WORKERS, JOB SHARING - PART-TIME WORK FROM WITHIN ORGANIZATION ● MAKE COMPANY MORE ATTRACTIVE TO PROSPECTIVE EMPLOYEES (e.g., BY PROVIDING ON SITE DAY CARE, FLEXIBLE BENEFITS, FLEXIBLE WORK HOURS, TRAINING)

plan. This information was subsequently used to generate a list of HR strategic objectives, which were validated by evaluating the extent to which each one supported the business plan. Finally, the process was further operationalized by identifying HR programs that were needed to implement the HR strategic objectives.

Each of the steps above is described in more detail below.

Environmental Scan and Assessment of HR Implications

A key step in the process was to identify external influences that could impact human resources over the next several years. The initial source used to identify external trends was a document by Coates (1986) titled "Future of Work and Workers in the American Corporation." This document, produced by the Environmental Scanning Association, is one of the most comprehensive sources available for identifying environmental trends.

The core team categorized the trends into the following four major areas: (1) technological innovation, (2) legal and regulatory, (3) demographic and social, and (4) globalization. Several team members were assigned to each

Table 12.1
(continued)

DEVELOPMENT	COMPENSATION	LABOR/EMPLOYEE RELATIONS
=======================	=======================	=======================

DEVELOPMENT	COMPENSATION	LABOR/EMPLOYEE RELATIONS
● MAKE TRAINING/ RETRAINING AVAILABLE TO EMPLOYEES ON COMPUTERS, NEW TECHNOLOGY, TECHNICAL JOBS, BASIC	● NEED TO INVESTIGATE ALTERNATE MEANS OF COMPENSATION AND REWARDS, OTHER THAN SALARY AND PROMOTIONS (e.g., EXTRA VACATION TIME, AWARDS, PUBLICITY)	● JOINT UNION- MANAGEMENT PROGRAMS FOR RETRAINING OLDER WORKERS
● INNOVATE WAYS TO KEEP UP EMPLOYEE MOTIVATION	● ATTENTION TO EARLY RETIREMENT PROGRAMS	● RISING PRESSURES
- ROTATIONAL ASSIGNMENTS		
- TEMPORARY JOB SWAP		
- LEARNING EXPERIENCES		
- LATERAL CAREER PATHING		

major area and were responsible for extracting as many relevant trends as possible using the Coates document. In addition to thoroughly reviewing this document, each team member generated internal trends by interviewing people within the company who were experts in one of the four major areas. This phase resulted in a comprehensive list of internal and external trends associated with the four categories.

The next step was to determine the impact each trend could have on key HR systems, including organizational structure, selection, development, compensation and rewards, and employee relations. Table 12.1 provides a few examples of the HR impact statements identified for the workforce demographic and social trend.

Once an exhaustive list of trends was identified and their impact on the HR systems articulated, the team had several meetings with the director group. The purpose of each meeting was to demonstrate the value of examining external trends and how they might impact AT&T's ability to attract and retain talented employees. It also gave the directors an opportunity to assess the importance of various trends to the BMG. After these meetings, the core team drafted a final list of trends and HR implications.

Review of the BMG Business Plan

Once the team had assessed how internal and external events were likely to impact human resources, the next step was to examine the business plan. Each team member reviewed the entire business plan, totally familiarizing themselves with the BMG's four strategic thrusts: (1) integration of sales and services for transport; (2) establish core business profitability; (3) achieve lessened regulation for tariffed services; and (4) establish position in new markets (i.e., data networking and triad countries). The team members who represented the BMG strategy also reviewed the strategy in more detail with the core team and answered questions that arose.

Development of HR Strategic Objectives

Using the insights that surfaced from analyzing the internal and external trends and the knowledge gained from reviewing the business plans, the team scheduled a "blue sky" meeting designed to begin identifying the HR strategic objectives. On completion, the team had identified more than forty HR strategic objectives, which were then logically clustered into areas of similarity. This process resulted in a list of eight HR strategies designed to support the business plan and reflect major internal and external events that were likely to impact the BMG during the next several years. Several examples of HR strategies include ensuring talent is available to meet business needs and developing global support systems.

Validation of HR Strategic Objectives

Once a set of HR strategies and objectives was established, an additional step was taken to further ensure that each HR strategy related to some aspect of the business plan. To accomplish this, each team member independently reviewed the eight HR strategies to ensure that each supported the business plan. Having documented these relations, the team convened to discuss and resolve any issues. Even if a strategy had intuitive appeal, the consensus was to drop it unless a direct linkage could be established. The output of this process resulted in a refined list of HR strategies and objectives as well as a document showing how each HR strategy supported the business plan. The head of the executive support group reviewed this list with the directors and officer team, and the core team subsequently generated specific HR programs designed to implement the HR strategies. Ultimately, the executive support group and the BMG officers agreed on a set of HR priorities for 1987–88.

AT&T CORPORATEWIDE HR PLANNING

Before the BMG approach was expanded corporatewide, a group of HR planners in corporate human resources reviewed the business plans of all AT&T business units. They quickly discovered that most business plans needed a stronger focus on the HR requirements for marketplace success. It also became evident that top management and the business planning community needed to be specifically educated on the importance of understanding the HR implications of strategies and business plans. Additionally, the HR planners needed to provide a more comprehensive model or tool for diagnosing the HR requirements for success, as well as provide individual consulting to interested business units to apply it.

As a result of these learnings, corporate human resources undertook a variety of interventions with the top officers of the company as well as with the HR community within AT&T to begin the education process. For example, internal and external trends were reviewed, emphasizing the HR implications for various business units. Concurrently, the HR planners developed a model or tool for use as each unit began a systematic process for integrating HR planning and business planning. Highlights of this model are described below.

AT&T's Model for Fully Integrating HR Planning and Business Planning

The model was specifically designed to identify the HR ingredients required to create and sustain organizational capability, which is defined as

- the specific organizational structures and HR policies, practices, and systems needed to create and sustain competitive advantage in the marketplace;
- people with the right skills, knowledge, attitudes, behaviors, experiences, and leadership attributes in the right place; and
- the ability to quickly adapt to changes in the environment and strategic direction.

Figure 12.2 provides an overview of this generic model. The basic steps are described below as actions to be taken. Some steps may be taken simultaneously and others may need to be repeated to gather additional data.

Step 1: External Environmental Assessment

To fully take HR considerations into account, this step should ideally include HR components (e.g., workforce trends and values and labor market conditions) as well as the areas generally covered in the environmental analysis (e.g., legal and regulatory, economic, technological, and competitors). An assessment of competitors from an HR standpoint should also be

Figure 12.2
Framework for Fully Integrating HR and Business Strategy Development

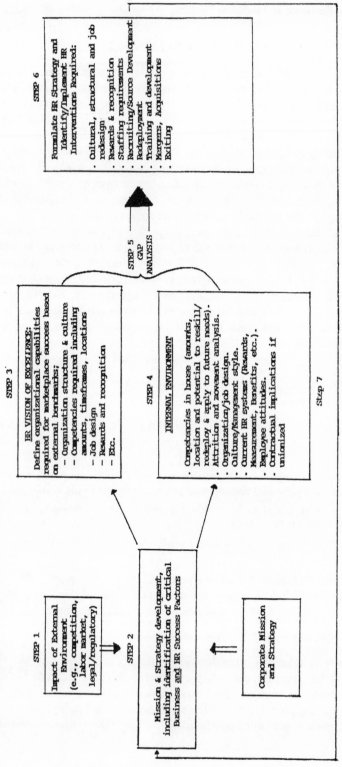

included at the same time they are evaluated from marketing, technological, and financial perspectives.

Because many of the external trends change over time, it is necessary to routinely perform environmental scans. Competitive conditions also need to be reviewed fairly frequently.

Step 2: Diagnose Business Strategy and Identify Critical Business and HR Imperatives for Success

After the external assessment, the business strategy should be diagnosed to identify critical success factors. To do this, it is critical to articulate how the business strategy will be operationalized from a variety of standpoints— business scope, customers served, products or services offered, distribution channels, and use of technology. Other considerations include finances, geographic locations, organizational structure, organizational culture, and management style. By raising a series of questions associated with each of these aspects, the team charged with strategic planning can begin to visualize how the business strategy will be executed and to identify critical business and HR success factors (e.g., organizational redesign and acquisition required).

When diagnosing business strategies from an HR standpoint, it is helpful to frame a series of questions such as: What is the rate of technological change? Does the strategy lead to any acquisitions, mergers, or divestitures? What are the customers' incentives for a long-term relationship? Are the current values and cultural characteristics' supportive of the strategy? Once these kinds of questions have been raised, it is easy to see why a team of individuals with different perspectives is mandatory. The HR planner or professional can begin to demonstrate contributions at this stage in the following three ways: (1) identifying the HR issues and requirements of the strategy chosen; (2) highlighting the difficulties that may arise during execution and the HR interventions that will be required (e.g., need for labor market studies in site selection of new facilities and lack of specific competencies in-house); and (3) suggesting modifications to the business strategy that may be necessary owing to HR issues.

Step 3: Defining HR Excellence

In short, the purpose of this step is to develop a "vision of excellence" from an HR standpoint to successfully execute the strategy. The input to this process is primarily based on external measures such as customer expectations, competitor standards, and "best in class" companies. Data used in this step should include benchmarking "best in class" companies in specific HR systems that are deemed critical to market success, as well as the results of pilots or trials done both internally and externally. This HR vision for success, or statement of organizational capabilities required, should also encompass the entire spectrum of HR systems, including organizational structure and culture, employee competencies, job design, employee source development and staffing plans, rewards and recognition, and employee measurement and evaluations.

Step 4: Assessing the Internal Environment

Once the organizational capabilities have been defined, an inventory or assessment of the current condition needs to be taken. It should include three basic areas: (1) employees (e.g., competencies, locations, ability to redeploy against new or changed business needs, attrition or movement trends, and attitudes or morale); (2) the organization (e.g., structure, culture, management style, and job design); and (3) the state of current HR systems (e.g., rewards and labor agreements).

Steps 5 and 6: Gap Analysis and Identification of Required HR Strategy and Interventions

A gap analysis or comparison between the HR vision for market success and the current HR condition is done next. This step helps to formulate an HR strategy and make informed decisions regarding the HR interventions required to operationalize the business strategy. The HR strategy and interventions must recognize the relations between HR systems and the fact that they should be driving consistent outputs. Additionally, it may not be possible to immediately move directly to "excellence" in one or more of the HR systems (e.g., rewards) based on the current condition of each. As a result, targets should be set for each system, taking the organizational context into account and the degree to which rapid or incremental progress can be made. It is particularly critical to ensure consistency across various HR systems.

Step 7: Monitor, Evaluate, and Adjust Based on Key Business Indicators

Business performance must be routinely monitored and the results used, where appropriate, to do the following: reassess the business mission and strategy; redefine the HR vision of excellence or organizational capabilities required for success; and revise the HR strategy and systems based on the current condition and redefined vision of excellence.

Critical Success Factors for Implementation

Based on the BMG approach and more recent AT&T experiences, we identified the following critical success factors.

High-level commitment and belief in the investment in people. Top officers in the company must believe that employees are a key factor in gaining and maintaining a competitive advantage, and must act on this belief by ensuring that

- HR is at the table when strategies and business plans are formulated;
- HR interventions required for success are endorsed and supported; and
- the culture of the organization supports and rewards stated beliefs in people.

In short, it is not sufficient to include HR components in planning processes. The beliefs and actions of top managers must demonstrate their commitment to people.

Formation of an HR and business planning team. One step top officers can take is to establish and become involved with a planning team composed of the right people to develop the business and HR strategies and plans. People from human resources, the line organization, and business planning should tackle this kind of project as a team. The business planning people can ensure that team members fully understand the strategy. People from human resources can articulate the HR implications of the proposed strategy and also help to translate these implications into programs or systems needed to execute the strategy. And line managers can bring the implementation perspective to the table, both from a business and an HR management standpoint. In summary, it is important during the start-up of strategy development to establish a team of line and staff managers who are dedicated to this effort, and who work with direct endorsement and input from the top. It is also critical that these managers have a good understanding of the business, especially the HR managers selected to participate.

Gathering and analyzing internal and external trends. The external influences that could impact an organization from an HR standpoint must be incorporated into the planning process. Issues such as changing demographics, technological advancements, and changing worker values can have a tremendous impact on the kinds of HR systems and programs that must be implemented to achieve business goals. For the BMG, the trend data proved invaluable in helping them better understand the characteristics of the applicant pool over the next several years. Analyzing different scenarios clarified the actions required to maintain a competitive advantage. Translating the environmental trend data into the unique HR implications that fit an organization is key, since some will obviously have more relevance than others.

In addition to doing an external environmental scan, it is important to routinely review profiles of the organization by age, sex, skill mix, performance, education, service, and so on to understand the existing available resources. Mapping these against future needs will provide information on the critical gaps that may exist where HR interventions are required. Having this data mechanized not only makes this task easier and timelier, but also enables more "what if" analyses for strategy development and contingency planning.

Another pertinent activity is the analysis of the corporate infrastructure, including organizational design, culture, climate, shared values, policies and practices, and labor issues to understand how the organization operates today and where it has to move to achieve excellence.

Competitive analogs. In a competitive marketplace, integration of HR planning and business planning is never fully complete without analyzing a firm's own strategies against those of competitors. Currently, these kinds of analyses do not typically include HR, but are performed from industry, marketing, technological, and financial standpoints. It is equally important, however, to analyze the HR systems of competitors and "best in class" companies to determine how HR systems can be leveraged for competitive advantage in the marketplace.

SUMMARY AND CURRENT STATUS

Developing and implementing sound HR plans can play a significant role in helping a firm gain and maintain a competitive edge. The BMG trial served to highlight strategic and implementation issues critical to fully integrating business planning and HR planning. While we do not advocate that companies (or even departments within the same firm) use a uniform approach, a diagnostic framework such as the one illustrated in this chapter is useful for proceeding in a systematic way and focusing on critical success factors.

AT&T had to undergo a major transition, resulting in more customer and market-focused strategic business units. To successfully accomplish this, a number of structural changes have been made to realign people and work. A significant change within human resources was to staff each business unit and major division with an HR professional. These people are accountable to both their business unit head and the head of corporate human resources. Aligned closely to the business unit head, the goal is to have the HR leaders actively participate in strategy development. They will be responsible for capturing critical HR implications and subsequently laying out a proposed HR agenda. With these structural changes, along with various diagnostic tools, we have taken some important steps toward fully integrating HR planning and business planning.

CHAPTER 13

MAKING PEOPLE DEVELOPMENT MEET STRATEGIC NEEDS: A CASE STUDY

JAMES B. SHILLABER

Fundamental changes in the way organizations approach basic business activities such as human resource (HR) planning and development are difficult to initiate and tend to come about slowly. Such shifts usually are motivated by an organization's internal "anxiety," its recognition, from various measures, indicators, or constituents, that the current way of doing things is not working.

A number of factors are provoking organizational anxiety and prompting the evolution of HR planning and development in the late twentieth century. The decreasing availability of labor, changing corporate structures through downsizing and mergers, regulatory and legal forces, workforce values, internal demographics, and the need to sharpen one's competitive advantage (through people) have all sparked HR management innovations in industry. These have contributed, since the 1970s, to a building momentum for a new way of thinking about employee development and its associated activities. Although businesses typically think of achieving their competitive advantage from their capital and technological resources, market position, distribution channels, and purchasing, there is increasing recognition that a company's ability to attract, develop, and retain the right human resources will give it a decided edge over competitors. It is no longer sufficient to implement HR plans and initiatives because you have to, or even because you want to. HR planning and development must be done to further a company's business goals today, prepare the company for tomorrow's business needs, and contribute to the company's overall competitive advantage.

Figure 13.1 shows the differences between strategic and non-strategic HR planning and development. Typically, HR "planning" consists of head count and budget allocation after business strategy is set. Business goals are established independently of their HR implications, and HR managers are then asked to get the skills, knowledge, and experience needed. In labor markets with high unemployment or in times of slow-moving business and technological developments, this approach often works. Organizations can acquire needed skills relatively easily. But when labor is in short supply, when specific skills or experience are needed, or when business and technology demands change rapidly, this tactic can result in inadequate resources and failed business objectives.

The following case study is about an organization that has undergone extensive change in its HR planning and development processes during a five year period. When the group was formed, they focused on simply getting organized and getting the work done; there was no HR planning and development. Within two years initiatives began to roll out on a reactive basis as the corporate headquarters issued HR policy guidelines and departmental managers requested assistance. Finally, a couple of years later, an attempt to integrate HR initiatives resulted in the development of a blueprint for a strategic assessment and realignment of the entire HR planning and development process. The department is now adjusting its thinking about people development activities to see them as a strategic partner to business planning and as an important part of competitive success. This study focuses on how the department made the shift from reactive to strategic HR planning and development. It looks at what the cues were that signaled the need for change, and how the organization went about integrating and coordinating its HR planning and development activities around the department's business needs.

HR PLANNING AND DEVELOPMENT IN REGULATORY AND CONSUMER AFFAIRS

A few years ago, coming to work for the Regulatory and Consumer Affairs (R&CA) department at a major information movement and management corporation was a bewildering experience. The department was established in 1984 to manage the company's growing external legislative, regulatory, and consumer interests. As a new department, R&CA had few HR programs or initiatives in place to select, orient, train, and develop employees. HR management and "development" was at the discretion of each individual manager and, as is typical in such situations, varied widely in quality and consistency. Attitude survey results for this department were poor. Employees questioned the value of the department to the rest of the company. They thought that their mission and goals were not clear, and indicated that HR initiatives for performance appraisal and feedback, career development, group and individual incentive compensation, and communication were nonexistent or ineffective. Not surprisingly, morale was correspondingly poor.

Figure 13.1
HR Planning and Development and Business Strategy

	Non-strategic	Strategic
HR Planning	Headcount report, force mapping & projections. Budget based.	Done in conjunction with business plan: What skills, etc. are needed to meet business objectives?
HR Development	Ad Hoc, discretion of the manager, perhaps linked to promotion or advancement.	Done strategically: in conjunction with business strategy & HR planning. Develop critical skills and knowledge.

Within the first two years, a reactive and non-strategic approach to HR planning and development evolved. The HR manager was given head count and budget projections for the various groups within the department and was told when to post jobs. She processed paperwork when new employees were hired but had only a consultative role in recruiting, selecting, or orienting them. Once in the department, their development was up to their individual managers. Specific job skills training was done ad hoc, and development, if done at all, was initiated by the employee and his or her supervisor. In this environment, small HR initiatives did develop, but they were based on local needs and individual manager requests. Desiring a more comprehensive approach to planning and development, the department established a director-level Personnel Steering Committee with representatives from each of the department's six geographical regions. This committee was charged with overseeing and coordinating R&CA's personnel development activities, but it found itself initially developing *individual* initiatives for career development, compensation, and training. No data was available for developing an approach to HR planning and development.

In this situation, HR planning and development are *reacting* to business plans and needs. Once skill or experience needs are identified, the HR department starts its work in conjunction with the company's recruiters and local management. If the appropriate resources are readily available, this strategy works fine. If not, the company stands poised with an aggressive business strategy that it cannot implement. R&CA initially was able to get the people it needed without much difficulty. When R&CA first was formed, there were many employees in the larger corporation with the skills and experience needed to perform successfully, and selection was merely a matter of choosing among them. A few years later, however, the situation had changed dramatically.

THE MOVE TO STRATEGIC PLANNING AND
DEVELOPMENT IN R&CA

While R&CA was busy building up its legislative, regulatory, and consumer activities in a separate department, the competition had been busy hiring many of the people from R&CA's parent company who had similar skills, and building up their own departments. The external environment had become increasingly complex. The company now found itself in both customer and supplier relationships with many of its competitors. The government had been quick to regulate many of the company's activities in response. Building up staff to meet these challenges was becoming more and more difficult.

Internally, something else was happening that would influence the department's need to recruit as well. The employees who originally staffed R&CA were chosen for their extensive experience with the parent company's legislative and regulatory constituents, and were older than employees at the same level in the rest of the corporation. Aware of this fact, the department HR manager analyzed and presented the age, sex, race, and retirement eligibility profiles of the department for R&CA's senior management. Looking at the preponderance of older white men nearing retirement generated some of the internal anxiety needed to motivate change. Questions arose about who would fill the department's key jobs when the current group of managers started to retire. The absence of coordinated HR development left the department vulnerable to future skills and experience shortages in analysis jobs that required specific knowledge bases and in contact jobs that required the development and cultivation of long-term relationships with key external constituents.

Increasing competition, a changing and increasingly complex external environment, a smaller labor pool, and the aging of the internal workforce all contributed to provide some pressure to review the department's HR planning and development procedures. The Personnel Steering Committee was the logical body to intervene at this point, but it was faced with the question of where to focus its energy: which initiatives should be developed first and what method should be used to do it? The committee decided to address the issue of skills development in R&CA to ensure that training and development were focused on the appropriate areas and developing the right skills. The first area to be tackled was the coordination of the educational opportunities offered by the department and company, and the development of a formal curriculum for R&CA jobs.

FROM CURRICULUM TO STRATEGIC HR DEVELOPMENT

The first question to arise was what to train? Training had always been done locally by each region in the department. Further, jobs with the same job titles were organized differently in the six regions, making it impossible to agree on what skills and knowledge were required for successful performance in each job. The first product needed was a map of the competencies required to accomplish the work in the department today.

The second question came rapidly after the first: why identify just the competencies required for successful performance *today*? It was clear that the environment in which the department was operating was changing rapidly, and to be truly strategic, training and development needed to focus on the skills required for successful performance *tomorrow*. The second output would be a revision of the first in light of the strategic direction of the department and major environmental forces likely to influence its HR needs.

Assessing the Current Environment

Most organizations have some inventory of the skills required to perform in their major jobs, usually in the form of a job description or job development aid. R&CA chose to break down the work performed by the department into sixteen distinct functions, such as regulatory relations, industry constituent relations, legislative analysis, and consumer affairs. Because the functions were relatively discrete, it was then possible to evaluate the competencies for successful performance within each function. A task force composed of regional representatives conducted an iterative survey within each regional job group to identify the skills, knowledge, and key developmental experiences required for each function. Function profiles were developed that listed these competencies in rank order at three job levels across the department.

Assessing the Future Environment

Concurrent with the development of the function profiles was an effort to explore what factors might influence departmental HR planning and development needs in the next three to five years. This task was not as discrete as the former. To do this, a Future Environment Survey was conducted of relevant internal and external experts in the information movement and management industry. Academics, competitors, key legislative and regulatory constituents, and consumer groups were surveyed, along with internal high-level managers and visionaries, to get their views on the factors that were likely to shape the HR planning and development needs of the department over the planning period. The output was not intended to be a definitive prediction of the future, but an exploration of the likely or possible forces that could influence HR needs.

Respondents listed such forces as a need for greater responsiveness to customers, more emphasis on market-driven instead of technology-driven business, and increased competition as likely influences on the department and company within five years. The results from the survey were reported to the department's top management as well as to each manager who had contributed to a function profile during the first-stage survey described above. Managers were asked to re-evaluate their profiles in light of the new information. If these forces came to bear on the business environment, what skills, knowledge, or experience would job incumbents need to be competitive? Each function profile was modified so that the skills being developed were as future-oriented as possible. In light of the information about the future, it became clear that some functions would increase in importance over the planning period, and some would become less important or cease to exist.

USES FOR THE FUNCTION PROFILE DATA

The project to identify the competencies required for successful performance in the R&CA department of both today and tomorrow was dubbed the Framework for the Future project because the information learned would form the foundation for *all* HR planning and development activities as the department moved into the future. A data base of competencies required for success was developed that could drive planning and development: each HR system would be operating from the same data, with internally consistent, future-oriented goals.

HR Planning

Through the assessment of its current environment, R&CA learned what skills and knowledge resources it had deployed in all of its locations. In addition, demographic information was available for each area that indicated the age and retirement eligibility of employees within the different functions. From this information, it was not difficult to profile skills within the department and project how rapidly they would leave the company through workforce retirement alone.

Likewise, the assessment of the future environment provided top management with a sense of the skills, knowledge, and experience that would be needed in the next three to five years. It was then relatively easy to evaluate the gap between existing resources and future needs. HR planning becomes strategic by recognizing and addressing that gap before it becomes a resource shortfall. Outcomes may involve researching new avenues for recruitment of talent or, preferably, providing the training and experiences for current employees to shift their focus and be prepared with the right skills at the right time.

R&CA recognized that the need for a greater market focus in its group had implications for both selection and development. It chose to focus its internal recruiting efforts on the marketing department, and provided marketing and customer-oriented training for existing personnel. Employees in an area that was likely to be downsized during the period began cross-training in another area in order to develop skills that would be useful to the department should the downsizing occur. This approach benefits the company and its employees by providing greater flexibility to respond to changing business conditions. HR planning becomes more rational and proactive, and results in overall increased organizational capability.

HR Development

The Framework for the Future profiles also served as the organizing data for the department's HR development activities. Strategic development is based on business strategy and strategic HR planning (needs minus existing resources). R&CA had developed a comprehensive base of skills, knowledge, and developmental experiences for each of its functions. This base would provide selection criteria for the department's major jobs, a curriculum for job skills training (when skills are matched with courses or development resources), and development and career pathing information to guide individual managers and subordinates. Using one source of data for these systems ensures that they are internally consistent and all developing the same competencies. In the final form, the function profiles developed by R&CA were comprehensive selection and development aids that could be used by any employee or manager. The profiles listed selection criteria (skills, knowledge, and experience) for different types of new hires (intra-departmental, within the company, and off the street), development criteria (technical, managerial, and interpersonal skills; technical and company knowledge; and on-job developmental experiences), and career movement guidelines for lateral movement or advancement within the department. In addition, the criteria specified on the function profiles could be used for performance management by individual managers, if desired.

As long as the information in the profiles is kept up-to-date, ongoing planning and development will be integrated and strategic. A process needs to be put in place to revisit the competencies listed in the profiles on a yearly or semiannual basis. In addition, the department occasionally needs to ask questions that go beyond the assumptions inherent in the function profiles. What are the operating assumptions about the future, and are they still valid? Are there areas of opportunity for the department that have not been recognized? Will new external trends suggest decreases in areas of functioning currently managed by the department? The department's HR competitive position is only as good as its information about these items and its flexibility to act when new information is encountered.

CHALLENGES

Although logically compelling, the process of making HR planning and development strategic is not an easy step for many corporations to make. There are several challenges for organizations to overcome if they are going to be successful at introducing real change.

First is recognizing that there is a problem. The forces pushing organizations to become more strategic are initially quite subtle. It is not until there is a resource crisis that many organizations are willing to look closely at their planning processes. The earlier a group begins to examine its needs and resources, the less discomfort it will experience as its internal or external environments change. Some of the signs a company may see that could suggest that its human resources are not strategically deployed include complaints from customers or managers about employee skills, a lack of career movement or development within certain groups, and poor morale and job satisfaction among employees. In addition, managers should be alert for changes in their industry or related businesses and internal demographic shifts (in skills or retirement eligibility, for example) that may influence the skill mix they will have available to meet future business needs.

Once a visionary manager sees the need for a shift in HR planning and development, it remains another task to convince the right people that the process should be reviewed. There are many reasons why top managers will *not* want to look at their people planning processes. The investigation is relatively unstructured and may threaten management's sense of security about its work and business strategy. At R&CA the HR manager spent a great deal of time educating the senior management team about the need for change by presenting information about the changing internal demographics at every opportunity. She called in external experts to address the management team about changing industry trends and the need for proactive HR planning. Even so, the response was not enthusiastic. The Personnel Steering Committee wanted to proceed cautiously and shelter the department head from surprises. A top management ally is probably essential, and buy-in must come from all levels of the organization.

Another challenge inherent in the process is focusing on flexibility and not the "right" answers. It is not possible to determine exactly what the future will look like for any organization. Consequently, groups need to remain open to many possible futures and develop their flexibility to respond instead of developing new responses that are equally as rigid as their old ones.

Finally, the process of reviewing what the business needs from its human resources and what competencies are available to meet those needs must be ongoing. A structure must be put in place to visit the planning and development process on a continual basis.

CONCLUSION

Strategic HR planning and development increasingly will be seen as a key component of a company's competitive advantage into the twenty-first century. Linking human resources with a company's business plans is a logical move, but one that may be perceived to be unstructured and risky for the status quo. In fact, the risk lies in *not* examining one's current resources and future needs, and thereby being unprepared for changes in the environment or internal demographics. Strategic HR planning and development is not a complex or expensive process, and actually serves to *reduce* the risk associated with a company's resource deployment policies and practices.

HR managers can play a vital role in educating top management about the need for such a shift, and should emphasize the benefits for all involved. Managers will have a much greater incentive to do development activities with their people if they believe that those activities are directly connected to the company's competitive position and success. People development becomes a business imperative instead of something that managers wish they had more time to do.

Part V

Organizational Reactions to a Changing Environment

This final section of the book describes some of the programs that organizations have initiated and will be initiating in response to environmental trends and employee needs and expectations.

Martin Greller and David Nee, who have had considerable managerial and planning experience, focus on organizational implications of a major demographic trend: the aging workforce. They argue that people aged fifty to seventy or older are a largely untapped, experienced resource that may help to resolve labor shortages. Companies may re-hire employees who have retired, and they may do more to develop current older workers who have not yet retired. Both pre- and post-retirement employees are often looking for increased job involvement and opportunities to demonstrate their skills, and are willing to accept responsibility. Unfortunately, corporate practices frequently force mid-career workers out of the organization, replacing them with lower-priced and more recently trained younger people. However, with smaller selection pools of younger workers, the career-extended worker (the person who might otherwise have retired but who was persuaded to remain) may be vital to meeting the organization's HR needs. Greller and Nee cover ways to recruit the older worker (e.g., through job fairs) and manage the current older workforce with better HR planning and pension and savings programs (which should be viewed as strategic business tools, not as welfare benefits or entitlements). In addition, the authors suggest ways to shift business strategy to take advantage of demographic shifts—for instance, by becoming a higher margin service-oriented firm because there are not sufficient numbers of employees for high-volume business. Another strategic shift is to rely on people outside the organization by contracting for services as needed. The aging workforce will mean that more older people will establish themselves as independent contractors or consultants and can be hired by firms to meet specific short-term requirements.

The next chapter in this section focuses on new work roles resulting from changing work-family relationships. An increase in dual-career couples and women staying in the workforce while they raise children has led to new types of work structures and work schedule designs. These have been facilitated by advanced telecommunications and computer technologies, termed "telematics." The author, Nicholas Beutell, has investigated alternative work-family conflicts and alternative work schedules. Here, Beutell describes telecommuting work arrangements that allow people to work in remote locations, often at home, using telematics. He addresses the traditional separate relationship between work and family and examines the work-family conflicts (e.g., time pressures, the strain from being overloaded, and conflicts in behavioral expectations—for instance, the need to be mild-mannered at home and aggressive in the office). The chapter indicates how personality and career stage influence the appropriateness of telecommuting. For instance, a person who has strong social needs would probably not do well working at home alone most of the time. A person who is just starting to work for the organization would probably not do well telecommuting because he or she would probably need to be around the office in order to "learn the ropes." The presence of children may make working at home more stressful, but on the other hand, it may also reduce time conflicts and the need for child care. Conflicts that result from telecommuting can be reduced through support systems, such as ensuring that there is enough space in which to work and personal support from family members. Managers of telecommuting subordinates need to be flexible in scheduling and controlling work. Moreover, the work itself must allow a certain amount of autonomy. Telecommuting can be a part-time arrangement, in that subordinates may have the understanding that they can work at home when the job demands allow. From the perspective of HR management, telecommuting presents some challenges, for instance, in performance appraisal and tracking attendance. However, telecommuting makes sense in many cases, given the demographics of the anticipated workforce in the year 2000, the increase in computer-based work, and the increase in decentralized organizational structures in many firms. Finally, to make telecommuting work, telecommuters may need special training skills, such as time management and work-family conflict resolution. Also, managers of telecommuting subordinates may need training in how to allocate their work load, maintain communications, and monitor their work performance.

The final chapter is an in-depth analysis of what is probably the most serious demographic trend facing organizations in the United States—the increasingly diverse workforce. The chapter shows that diversity can be a strategic advantage to the firm if it is managed well. Written by John P. Fernandez, a sociologist with considerable business experience, and by his associate, Jacqueline Dubois, the chapter highlights the results of a major corporate survey of 30,000 respondents and comments from more than 2,000 additional employees. Throughout the chapter, results of survey questions and significant quotes from open-ended questions provide substance and richness to this review. The authors address the degree to which employees accept diversity in the workplace, discussing reactions to language conflicts, cultural differences (e.g., what people from different cultures consider praise), and their support for pluralism (e.g., the extent to which they want their employers to ensure equal employment opportunity). Fernandez and Dubois recognize that two of the major problems organizations face with respect to HR utilization are racism and sexism. They examine forms of sexist stereotypes and gender discrimination as well as racist stereotypes and race discrimination. They also cover employees' reactions to people with alternative sexual preference. The final part of the chapter indicates that solutions to the productivity crisis in the United States in the coming decades include employing a multi-cultural workforce (not only to reduce the labor shortage, but also to add diversity as a competitive advantage) and dealing with resistance to pluralism. They describe a workshop to help employees recognize their reactions to differences in people and how to overcome resistance to these differences and promote more effective work relationships. Fernandez and Dubois note that truly good managers have always been able to utilize their subordinates by recognizing individual strengths and weaknesses and by maintaining flexibility when faced with new problems and challenges. The chapter concludes with specific steps that companies should take to maintain equal employment opportunity and incorporate diversity into the employee body.

CHAPTER 14 _____

HUMAN RESOURCE PLANNING FOR THE INEVITABLE—THE AGING WORKFORCE

_____ MARTIN M. GRELLER AND DAVID M. NEE

Much of human resource (HR) planning is absorbed in forecasting subtle changes in the business's strategy or the environment. Addressing these changes places the company at a competitive advantage. The demographic environment is neither subtle nor ambiguous. Changes are inevitable and have immense consequences for employers.

Details on the nature, depth, and likely course of demographic change have been covered elsewhere (see Coates 1987; Greller and Nee 1988, 1989; Johnston and Packer 1987; Russell 1987; Wattenberg 1987). The basic effects are (a) a sharp reduction in the traditional entry-level workforce (eighteen to twenty-five years of age) lasting at least through 2005 and probably beyond and (b) an increase in the proportion of workers in their mid-career years.

Although earlier warnings of the potential impact of demographic change were largely ignored (i.e., Malkiel 1983), its first consequences are already on our doorstep. The shortage of entry-level workers has become a pervasive problem. Half of the corporations that responded to an American Society for Personnel Administration (ASPA) survey (American Society for Personnel Administration 1989) reported that they were unable to fill open positions; the proportion of small businesses having trouble doing so was still larger ("Feeling the Pinch," 1989); and in a survey of HR forecasters, 90 percent were concerned about their company's ability to attract employees (Graddick, Bassman and Giordano 1989). But the shortage is only part of the problem that must be addressed. Equally important is the abundant middle-level labor pool (not just middle managers, but skilled craftspeople and professionals) being plateaued, displaced, and demotivated. For the most part, the surplus is simply being enjoyed by business, which does not view it as a problem. Nor is the baby boomers' role in solving the shortage fully appreciated.

But taking the problem from the point at which business currently feels discomfort, how can the shortage be addressed?

ON WHOM WILL BUSINESS CALL?

What makes the shortage so intense is that employers are looking for the people they would most like to hire—not the ones who are available. A reanalysis of data reported in the ASPA (1989) survey showed that the population from which employers most wanted to hire were students (see Figure 14.1). This is also the group that has been most reduced in size (i.e., the baby bust).

The next most preferred group was housewives. This has been the reserve of first resort in the past in the United States. The mythical Rosie the Riveter was there to fill in the empty places at the workbench when her man went off to war, and then (supposedly) retreated demurely to the kitchen when he came home. But Rosie no more retreated from the workplace than did her man at Omaha Beach. With only a slight hiccup after World War II, the proportion of women in the workforce has steadily increased. This group is no longer a reserve: women are an essential part of the workforce, and they are, in large measure, already in place.

Older workers placed third in the popularity contest. Of the three groups just mentioned, they have a unique advantage—they are available. In fact, they may represent the largest pool of underutilized human resources. Half of the fifty-five to sixty-four to-year-olds are not employed. Following Willie Sutton's approach (e.g., robbing banks because that is where money is to be found), HR managers must direct their attention to employing older workers because that is where the available human resources are to be found.

The fact that business will be recruiting older workers is not the problem; it is the solution. However, attitudes and current practice regarding older workers might suggest the opposite. Often it is these attitudes toward older workers, not their abilities or interests, that limit their participation in the workforce (Greller 1986). Examinations of life span development and worker performance have found that older workers are generally well able to do their jobs (McEvoy and Cascio 1989). Often older workers have relevant job experience and understand what is expected by employers.

Advocates for those groups that fell lower on the preference list (e.g., the hardcore unemployed and physically challenged) sometimes argue that the older workers are used to avoid employing these disadvantaged people. The relative lack of enthusiasm for employing the disadvantaged is based on two factors. First, a smaller portion of employers tried to make use of these populations, so even if they were very satisfied, their small number would limit the popularity score. Second, even those with experience hiring from these

Figure 14.1
Index of Success with Nontraditional Labor Pools

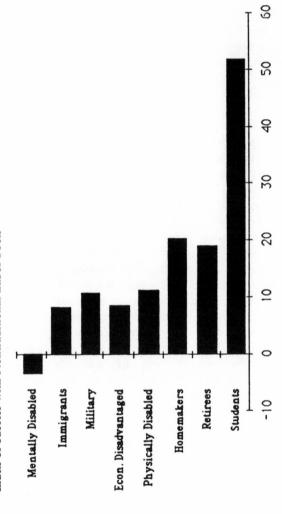

Note: The data on frequency of use and satisfaction were combined to form a −200 to +200 scale. Thus, a population that had been very well received but by only a small number of businesses would score a modest positive, whereas a moderately positive reaction by a large number of businesses might rate a higher score. The result is a preference index, not an indication of how well a given segment of the labor pool might work out if it were more thoroughly utilized.

groups often have not invested the time and effort required to be successful. The battle on behalf of the disadvantaged is not against the older worker, but is more properly waged against the apathy and inexperience of employers.

WHO IS AN OLDER WORKER?

When audiences are asked to indicate how many of them are older workers, usually only a small percentage raise their hands. One fellow in his eighties (still actively employed) refused to do so. One American Association of Retired Persons activist did, and was told by friends to put her hand down because she wasn't "old." A forty-year-old said he was an older worker because he felt that way. Stereotypes affect the older workers as much as they do the people who consider hiring them.

Although definitions differ, for current purposes, consider the population from fifty to seventy years of age as the older worker pool. In terms of careers, they have decided on the directions they find personally rewarding, and their work identity has crystalized (Greller and Nee 1989; Hall and Nougaim 1968; Levinson 1978; Super and Hall 1978). As they pass through these ages, most will make a decision about the point at which their careers have ended: retirement.

Retirement is a career choice independent of employment. An employee may retire on the job, being employed but uncommitted to work or the job. Other people have left their employers, receive pensions, but take jobs that they view as post-retirement employment (e.g., the one-time sales executive who now captains a fishing boat in Florida). Others have been forced out of their jobs (i.e., early retired), yet they do not accept that their careers have ended. Thus, the fact that one is older and not employed does not mean that one is retired. There are three types of older workers: post-retirement workers, un-retired workers, and career-extended workers (Greller 1989a). The distinction helps to define the workers' motivation, the positions that may be of interest to them, and how they may be induced into employment.

The *post-retirement worker* is the one most often pictured when discussing older workers. These are people who have completed a career and now seek employment that requires lower commitment. Convenience and flexibility are attractions. They may accept positions for which they are far more than qualified. They are not looking for full-time, regular employment, so they are well suited to a contingent workforce that the employer uses as a cushion against periods of high volume. But they are sensitive to the costs of employment. They are less willing to accept a difficult commute or an inhospitable work environment.

These are the older workers companies currently seek. They are used in place of young people (in the exploration stage of their careers) who also seek low commitment roles. Companies that attend job fairs for older workers are looking for part-time tellers, clerks, and salespeople.

The *un-retired worker* is a very different employee. These people may be out of a job but do not see their careers as ended. They may have been caught in a downsizing. They may have retired from their original employers only to discover that this was the wrong choice. However, they are seeking to continue their careers. Using the skills developed throughout their careers and building on past experiences are important for this group. They are looking for involvement and opportunities to demonstrate their skills, and are willing to accept responsibility.

This group has been tapped in a limited way. The insurance companies, which maintain large reserves of post-retirement processing clerks, will occasionally make a deal with a highly experienced actuary or other specially skilled person. A consulting arrangement is worked out that allows part-time work along with retirement benefits (Nye 1988).

Companies will occasionally go to this group when entering a new market. They hire a few experienced managers, professionals, or craftspeople who have extensive experience in the new area. They provide leadership and training for the company's own personnel. The expectation that these knowledgeable (and expensive) people will retire shortly after the market has been entered is viewed positively by the employer.

Both the post-retirement worker and the un-retired worker are found in the external labor market. For the most part, they have been displaced from employment. In large measure, they have been made into "retired" workers by the action of their prior employers. And this may occur even when workers are in their early fifties.

Corporate practices force mid-career workers out of the organization (see Greller and Nee 1989, ch. 2). Faced with an abundant supply of entry-level workers in the 1960s and 1970s, a generation of managers accustomed themselves to churning middle-level talent, replacing them with lower-priced and more recently trained younger people. Larger selection pools allowed employers to apply more stringent criteria to the new (replacement) hire than had been applied to the original employee. But the labor market situation is now reversed. This means that companies need to retain those workers who they currently push out of the organization.

The *career-extended worker* is the person who might otherwise have retired but has been persuaded to remain. As the average age of the labor pool increases, employers will be recruiting people of approximately the same age as those they just caused to retire. But the people who already work for a company understand its unique features. The employees' strengths and shortcomings are already known to the employer. Maintaining the committed involvement of these people will reduce the need for external recruiting and give the employer a competitive advantage.

The motivations of the career-extended worker are less clear, but they are subject to influence by the employer (Howard and Bray 1988; London and Mone 1987). These employees cannot be conscripted in violation of a psychological contract that says they are entitled to retire. Instead, the employer must offer an attractive picture of the career satisfactions to be had and offer a compensation package (including benefits) that is tailored to their needs.

RECRUITING THE OLDER WORKER

The greatest difficulty in recruiting older workers is the inadvertent discouragement communicated by many employers. Whether it is advertising that emphasizes youth or interviewers whose attitudes are unwelcoming, employers too often turn away the very people they must increasingly rely on.

When it comes to using older workers to replace missing entry-level labor, companies are becoming experienced. The most difficult aspect of such recruiting is figuring out where older workers are located. Going to a senior citizens' center (which has been tried with some success) has the disadvantage that these people have already found something else to do. Using newspaper advertising can work, but one must be careful of the paper's demographics, as retail advertisers are looking for the twenty-five- to forty-five-year-old.

Many cities organize job fairs that bring a large number of potentially interested seniors into one place (e.g., New York's Senior Employment Service). The group is assembled based on their interest in employment. The company can prepare its interviewers. For the most part, company recruiters deem these events successful. But HR planners must understand that each such event is relatively low yield.

For example, at one such senior job fair a major accounting firm found seven good prospects. The cost, in terms of dollars and time, was favorable compared with newspaper advertising, screening, and interviews. The victories in such recruiting occur one by one. It is a fact that reminds one of the importance of retention.

The looming issue in recruiting older workers is selection. The focus is currently on replacing entry-level workers using post-retirement workers. However, as business increasingly looks to older workers as a source of middle-level hiring, whether to fill out the ranks or to expand the knowledge base of the business, employers will need to become more discerning (Atwater, Bres, and Niehaus 1988; Gaertner 1988).

The challenge is dealing with the variety of backgrounds that experienced workers possess. The simpler profiles used in screening young candidates may not work. There are more ways in which older workers may have developed and demonstrated their skills. This will demand more flexibility and judgment on the part of recruiters.

MANAGING THE WORKFORCE YOU HAVE

The premier HR management issue may be aligning personnel policies, practices, and procedures with the goal of attracting and retaining older workers. One of the reasons we cannot entirely trust conclusions based on current company experience is that older workers are often denied the resources that might encourage growth and enthusiasm (Nye 1988; Rosen and Jerdee 1977). But four HR areas clearly require attention: HR planning, organizational and salary structure, pension and savings programs, and managing exit.

HR planning can be weak in an abundant labor market without costing the company much. When the projections are wrong, hiring is increased or layoffs occur. Errors become consequential when staff resources cannot be easily acquired, and that is the scenario for the future. Companies may be prevented from entering new businesses or markets because of a lack of human resources. For example, one health care organization was forced to shift from growth through internal development to acquisition because they could not hire enough people to staff new facilities.

For the most part, current HR planning practices are not up to the job. Of companies with HR forecasting functions, 60 percent focus on the short term (Graddick, Bassman, and Giordano 1989). Most of the HR planning is conducted separately from strategic business planning. Yet most projections indicate that human resources will be increasingly critical as companies face more limited staff availability, increased corporate change in the face of international competition, and technology demanding new skills from the workforce (Adler 1986; Goldstein and Gilliam 1990; Johnston and Packer 1987).

Employers need to clarify what kind of people they will need, with which skills, and in what numbers. This provides the rationale for hiring, training, and retention programs. It requires integrating information on the internal workforce, the external labor market, and the company's business plans.

The *organizational hierarchy* will change to match the changing workforce. Organizations will be flatter. This reflects the larger number of people in mid-career. It also allows those people to be better utilized.

Change is occurring without intervention by HR professionals. The labor market has responded to the baby boom by reducing the premium paid for people in this age group. Similarly, market forces have driven up the relative wages paid to the baby bust group (Greller and Nee 1988).

Another factor flattening the wage hierarchy is tenure. As employees stay in middle-level jobs longer, they progress further through the salary range. Promotions no longer require a raise to bring the employee up to the new position's salary minimum.

But organizational flattening is something that will be accelerated and formalized to help retain and attract older workers. The old salary structures of many narrow steps (with limited range of skills and responsibilities), each offering a small increment in salary, focus employees on advancement and limit management's flexibility in deploying the people. In a unionized pressroom, it is possible to assign an employee several tasks and have to pay the person at three different rates for the work performed during a single shift. The automobile industry has already begun to negotiate a loosening of the rigid restrictions that once limited the work an employee was allowed to do.

By expanding the range of activities associated with each pay grade (and broadening the range of salaries allowable within the grade), the company increases its flexibility and the employees' opportunities. If competitive pressures cause a shift in the work required, the employee can be moved to a new assignment. Workers with increased experience and a broader range of skills can be called on to use these skills in a variety of ways. Finally, the company has the freedom to reward the employee—based on performance, seniority, or whatever its strategy values—using the broader salary range. The employees' opportunities for new assignments are increased. Their risk of being laid off or "bumped" is decreased.

The flatter organization makes it easier to recruit experienced workers from outside the organization. There is no struggle to fit them into narrow slots. A range of work can be assigned that capitalizes on their skills and experiences. There is even more flexibility in the compensation that can be offered.

The flatter organization also helps to communicate more realistic expectation. It encourages employees to look toward the intrinsic nature of their work and not hierarchical advancement as a source of satisfaction (Brousseau 1989; vonGlinow, Driver, Brousseau, and Prince 1983).

Pension and savings programs are sometimes viewed as welfare benefits or entitlements. They are actually tools of the business strategy, which should reinforce the desired relationship of the company with its employees. Ideally, these should be reviewed as part of the HR planning process; however, they are so powerful and so expensive that they warrant special attention.

Over the past twenty years, the fashion in pension programs has changed. Originally, the defined-benefit pension (in which the pension received varies as a function of salary and tenure) was the model. Supplemental savings programs were offered to help employees prepare for their retirement. With the savings plans, one knows what was contributed, but the actual benefit received is determined by how well the plan's investments perform (hence the name "defined-contribution plan").

The importance of defined-contribution plans has increased. First, they became "the third leg" of support for employees" retirement. The other two were the company's defined-benefit pension and social security. More recently increasing regulation, accounting demands, and periodic pillaging of pension programs by corporate raiders have led companies to make the defined-contribution plans their primary pension vehicles.

For many companies, defined-contribution plans are the right tool with which to address an aging workforce. They are an attraction for the older worker who is being recruited. There is no disadvantage to short tenure. For employees who leave in mid-career, the savings may offer a launch pad to a new career.

Many plans match individual contributions with a tax-free contribution by the employer. These matching funds can be used to manage retention or exit. The company's matching funds may vest over a three- to five-year period. If the employee quits before they vest, the matching funds revert to the company. Vesting can be accelerated in the event of retirement at some designated time, layoff, or termination at the company's initiative.

Defined-contribution plans have advantages for the company seeking flexibility, especially for those employers who expect shifts in their staffing requirements. However, for businesses that require stability and need employees deeply knowledgeable about their proprietary processes, defined-benefit plans may still be appropriate. These systems encourage lifelong employment commitments. If that is what an employer wants, these continue to be sensible vehicles.

Programs to *manage exit* are another tool for making the most of the people already employed (Greller and Nee 1989). No matter what the company does in terms of planning, structure, or benefits, it is the employees' choice to stay or go (and to grow or stagnate) that determines the sort of workforce one has.

Companies can help their employees make that choice by accurately communicating what the employee may expect. What options and opportunities are offered by remaining with the company? What must the employee do to improve these prospects? What are the alternatives in the external labor market?

Essentially, a program to manage exit is very much like career counseling, pre-retirement, or outplacement programs. It invites employees to look at themselves, their career options, and their plans. The difference between this and other programs is that the company varies the input based on the decision it would like to see the participants reach.

For high-potential employees, the emphasis is on internal opportunities. The company wants them to know the good things apt to happen if they remain. They should also know what they must do to be successful. The target jobs are realistically previewed. Although this may discourage some people and mess up neatly drawn succession plans, it also saves the cost of grooming a candidate with a low probability of success.

In the face of changing business emphasis, companies may want some portion of the workforce to go away. These are not problem performers, but employees whose skills are no longer needed in the abundance they

once were. Ward (1988) noted that the traditional organizationally controlled layoff is far costlier than a program that involves employee choice
and retraining. Showing employees what they can expect, including the likely
limits to their opportunities, will lead a portion of them to decide to leave.
Others will use this as an opportunity to renew their career commitment,
redefine their goals within the company, and approach their tasks with new
vigor.

BUSINESS STRATEGIES THAT CAPITALIZE ON THE OLDER WORKFORCE

Human resources are as much a strategic factor as capital or raw materials.
If the supply of one of these other resources were to change as markedly
as is the case of human resources, there would be an immediate shift in
business strategy. It is also possible to modify the business's strategy to take
advantage of the demographic shifts.

A *higher-service strategy* has several advantages (Greller 1989b). First, it
depends on workers who are available in greatest abundance, those in mid-
career. Second, it recognizes the limited opportunities to expand one's business through increased volume of activity.

The individual employee is asked to know the customers better and respond to their needs through knowledge of how the company works. High
service expectations can attract and retain customers. But if a company offers
customers Mr. Goodwrench, he'd better be there when the customer's car
needs to be repaired (Davidow and Uttal 1989). In the 1990s, the average
experience of the workforce will be greater. Consequently, it will be easier to
find the people who can deliver on those high service expectations.

Companies can shift to *higher-margin* businesses. If the number of trans-
actions performed is limited by staffing, profit can still be increased if each
transaction is of higher value. One route to doing this is offering value
added services, which are distinctive in the market and for which customers
will pay a premium.

One direct mail house found that it was increasingly difficult to hire the
unskilled labor required for its large mail-handling operations. The traditional method of growth had been to increase the volume of mail. This
required more staff. So they took a different route. Maintaining the same
volume, they sold value added services such as merging mailing lists with
the client's credit card records to create customized mailings. The additional
work was done by higher skilled (mid-career) employees.

This is also a point at which technology can be used to augment the
capability of workers. Rather than thinking of technology as a way of
displacing labor, it can be viewed as a way to extend the skilled employee's
capabilities (Herold 1989).

The unbundled organization (Greller and Nee 1989) also takes advantage of changes in the workforce, but in a different way. Originally, such organizations received their impetus from financial considerations. To minimize exposure to risk, all commitments were made as tenuous as possible. Plants and equipment were leased rather than purchased. Research and development were accomplished through joint ventures or consortia-sponsored work at universities.

The unbundled organization similarly reduces its commitment to employees. Staff services are purchased from the outside rather than provided within the company. Components are not manufactured, but purchased. The unbundled organization relies on wholesalers, manufacturers' representatives, and franchisees to distribute its products.

Its HR strategy is to rely on people outside the company. As the workforce ages, increasing numbers of people will seek to establish themselves independently of any employer. At professional levels, these may be consultants. Skilled craftspeople become service providers or contractors. Others will form small businesses offering the manufacturing and distribution capacity on which the unbundled organization relies.

There is nothing to suggest that vendors to the unbundled corporation will have an easy time. Not all professionals or craftspeople are well suited to the demands of running a small business. However, the existence of such vendors allows a corporation to unbundle. Whether or not the choice is good for the individual, the evidence is that this is the choice being made by many people at mid-life.

CONCLUSION

Changing demographics will turn companies into case studies of successful or unsuccessful adaptation. How each employer forecasts, plans, and takes action to accommodate the change is what will determine the difference.

Although the older workers are not the only resource (Greller and Nee 1989; Nye 1988), they represent one of the most available alternatives. There is no way any employer will avoid the aging of its workforce. The challenge for HR planning is to make creative use of the change, doing so in ways that enhance the businesses.

REFERENCES

Adler, P. 1986. New technologies, new skills. *California Management Review, 29,* 9–25.

American Society for Personnel Administration. 1989. *1988 ASPA labor shortage survey.* Alexandria, VA.: American Society for Personnel Administration.

Atwater, D. M., E. S. Bres III, and R. J. Niehaus. 1988. Analyzing organizational strategic change using proactive labor market forecasts. In R. J. Niehaus and K. Price (eds.). *Creating the competitive edge through human resource applications* (pp. 119–35). New York: Plenum.

Brousseau, K. R. 1989, April 30. *Career dynamics in the baby boom and baby bust era*. Presented in the symposium: Alternatives for Dealing with the Demographic Boom/Bust. Society for Industrial and Organizational Psychology Conference, Boston.

Coates, J. R. 1987. An environmental scan: Projecting future human resource trends. *Human Resource Planning, 10,* 219–35.

Davidow, W. H., and B. Uttal. 1989. Service companies: Focus or falter. *Harvard Business Review, 67,* 77–85.

Feeling the pinch. 1989, April 3. *Business Week,* p. 82.

Gaertner, J. N. 1988. Managerial careers and organization-wide transformation. In R. J. Niehaus and K. Price (eds.). *Creating the competitive edge through human resource applications* (pp. 85–96). New York: Plenum.

Goldstein, I. L., and P. Gilliam. 1990. Training systems issues in the year 2000. *American Psychologist, 45,* 134–43.

Graddick, M. M., E. Bassman, and J. Giordano. 1989, April 30. *Demographics and their impact on industry.* Presented in the symposium: Alternatives for Dealing with the Demographic Boom/Bust. Society for Industrial and Organizational Psychology Conference, Boston.

Greller, M. M. 1986. Policies and programs for employing the aging. In *Employment and the aging* (pp. 15–23). New York: Brookdale Foundation.

Greller. M. M. 1989a, May 23. *Building the work force 2000: Tapping ability and experience.* Presentation for the Senior Employment Service, Department of Aging, City of New York.

Greller, M. M. 1989b. Making the aging work force a strategic advantage in your organization. In *Perspectives in human resources: Managing the work force revolution* (pp. 5–13). Alexandria, VA.: American Society for Personnel Administration.

Greller, M. M., and D. M. Nee. 1988. Baby boom and baby bust: Corporate response to the demographic challenge of 1990–2010. In R. J. Niehaus and K. Price (eds.). *Creating the competitive edge through human resource applications* (pp. 17–34). New York: Plenum.

Greller, M. M., and D. M. Nee. 1989. *From baby boom to baby bust: How business can meet the demographic challenge.* Reading, MA.: Addison-Wesley.

Hall, D. T., and K. Nougaim. 1968. An examination of Maslow's need hierarchy in an organizational setting. *Organizational Behavior and Human Performance, 3,* 12–35.

Herold, D. M. 1989, April 30. *Technology as an important component of human resource planning.* Presented in the symposium: Alternative for Dealing with the Demographic Boom/Bust. Society for Industrial and Organizational Psychology Conference, Boston.

Howard, A., and D. W. Bray. 1988. *Managerial lives in transition: Advancing age and changing times.* New York: Guilford.

Johnston, W. B., and A. H. Packer. 1987. *Workforce 2000: Work and workers for the 21st century.* Indianapolis, IN: Hudson Institute.

Levinson, D. J. 1978. *Seasons of a man's life.* New York: Knopf.

London, M., and E. M. Mone. 1987. *Career management and survival in the workplace.* San Francisco: Jossey-Bass.

McEvoy, G. M., and W. F. Cascio. 1989. Cumulative evidence of the relationship between employee age and job performance. *Journal of Applied Psychology,* *74,* 1–5.

Malkiel, B. G. 1983. Long run economic and demographic outlook: Implications for government policy and human resource planning. *Human Resource Planning, 6,* 143–52.

Nye, D. 1988. *Alternative staffing strategies.* Washington, D.C.: Bureau of National Affairs.

Pazy, A. 1987. Sex difference in response to organizational career management. *Human Resource Management, 26,* 243–56.

Rosen, B., and T. H. Jerdee. 1977. Too old or not too old? *Harvard Business Review, 53,* 97–106.

Russell, C. 1987. *100 predictions for the baby boom.* New York: Plenum.

Super, D. E., and D. T. Hall 1978. Career development: Exploration and planning. *Annual Review of Psychology, 29,* 333–72.

vonGlinow, M. A., M. J. Driver, K. R. Brousseau, and J. B. Prince. 1983. The design of a career oriented human resource system. *Academy of Management Journal, 8,* 23–32.

Ward, D. L. 1988. Layoffs: What does flexibility really cost? In R. J. Niehaus and K. Price (eds.). *Creating the competitive edge through human resource applications* (pp. 169–78). New York: Plenum.

Wattenberg, B. J. 1987. *The birth dearth: What happens when people in free countries don't have enough babies?* New York: Pharos.

CHAPTER 15

TELEMATICS, TELECOMMUTING, AND WORK-FAMILY RELATIONSHIPS: NEW WORK ROLES FOR THE FUTURE

NICHOLAS J. BEUTELL

Work arrangements such as telecommuting present a number of challenges to human resource (HR) planners. Managing the interaction of work and family life is particularly critical in light of workforce 2000 demographics and the restructuring of organizations. Women will constitute a large segment of new entrants into the workforce; many will be members of dual-career families. Work will not be nearly so closely tied to a centralized work environment, and organizations will be much flatter and leaner. Flexibility in work arrangements may well be an important source of competitive advantage for companies.

Managers need to understand the potential advantages and disadvantages of telecommuting as they plan for future assignments and work structures and respond to people's needs. Also, people need to know what to expect when they try telecommuting. This chapter examines some of the issues of telecommuting using telematics from a work-family conflict perspective (e.g., Greenhaus and Beutell 1985).

Telematics refers to the combination of telecommunications technology and computers (cf., Coates 1987; Martin 1981). Examples of telematics include computerized information systems, integrated services digital networks, satellites, and facsimile machines. The telematics revolution is having a profound impact on the nature of work, the structure of organizations, and the meaning of work and productivity (Coates 1987). Telematics technology means that work is not limited by time and space (Coates 1987; Pava 1986). Work can be performed virtually anywhere and at any time. This presents a major challenge to U.S. managers who find it difficult when there is interference with the direct line of sight of employees (Coates 1987). Yet this technology offers potential productivity gains from employees who are seeking to balance work and other life interests. Parents, for example, may find that more flexibility in reporting to the organization allows them to continue to be productive and at the same time manage family responsibilities more effectively.

Telecommuting refers to work that is performed in a remote location (frequently the home, although it can be any location away from the central office) using telematics. Many U.S. workers employed in traditional work arrangements already perform some of their work at home using telematics technologies. Many other employees perform all or a great portion of their work from home or remote locations. Although central work sites are not apt to disappear in the near future, the technology offers tremendous flexibility in where and how work is done. For the remainder of this chapter I will use telecommuting to indicate work that is performed using telematics from home.

WORK-FAMILY CONFLICT

The notion that work and family are separate worlds has been relegated to the realm of mythology (Kanter 1977). Work and family are mutually interactive systems. Pressures from work and family can interfere with each other such that participation in work (family) is made more difficult by virtue of participation in family (work). Greenhaus and Beutell (1985) identified three types of work-family conflict: time-based, strain-based, and behavior-based. Time spent in one role cannot be spent on the other role. Strain within one role can spill over into the other domain. Behaviors required for "successful" work (family) performance are not the same behaviors needed for effective family (work) performance (e.g., shifting gears from work to family for business executives or professionals). Work-family conflict is intensified when work and family roles are central to the person's self-concept and when there are strong negative sanctions for noncompliance with role demands (Greenhaus and Beutell 1985).

The work-family conflict literature raises some interesting questions: how are conflicts affected when both work and family roles are enacted in the same (or approximately the same) home environment? When work and family roles are geographically separated the most commonly reported cause of conflict is time. Are time conflicts reduced or exacerbated by telecommuting? When does the workday begin and end? What effect does telecommuting have on the family structure and function? How are the quality of work and family life affected? What about strain and behavior conflicts? Does work stress experienced in the home work environment have a more direct effect on other family members than stress experienced at a more traditional work site? How difficult is it to switch gears from work to family and vice versa? Work-family conflict has received little attention in the context of telecommuting and work-at-home.

Although the use of flexible work arrangements such as telecommuting appears to be advantageous for certain employees, it is also important to present a realistic picture by identifying potential work-family conflicts. The next section discusses some possible variables that affect work-family conflict from the individual, family, and work domains. The variables are not completely independent and are not intended to be an exhaustive list.

FACTORS THAT AFFECT WORK-FAMILY CONFLICT AMONG TELECOMMUTERS

Individual Factors

Sex. Many telecommuters/homeworkers will be women with children who are part of dual-career marriages (Coates 1987). Women, who have traditionally shouldered greater responsibility for the home, face the problem of simultaneous responsibilities for work *and* family (Hall 1972) when they work outside the home. In other words, women have generally been expected to gear work demands to children and the family. Work-at-home would be expected to increase the salience of such simultaneous demands. At the same time women have more experience in managing roles simultaneously and may be able to handle such demands more effectively than men. Men, on the other hand, who have traditionally performed their roles in a successive (Hall 1972) manner (i.e., work, then family) may find it difficult to avoid simultaneous role pressures if working from home.

Although telecommuting might be expected to reduce work-family conflict caused by geographical separation of work and family, preoccupation with family while at work (Fernandez 1986), and time pressures (e.g., reduced commuting) (Shamir and Salomon 1985), very little is known about the types of behaviors or structures that will enhance performance in both work and family roles. Caring for children while attempting to work at home may lead to decreased effectiveness as a parent *and* as an employee. Do family role pressures affect the work performance of men and women in the same way? Much more work is needed to understand how work and family roles can be structured to enhance the quality of life when work and family roles are performed within the home.

Personality. The strength of a person's social needs appears to be particularly important for telecommuters. Work-family conflict will be heightened to the extent that a telecommuter has strong social needs that would be better satisfied within a traditional office environment. Part-time telecommuters may be able to satisfy social needs better than full-timers through weekly trips to the office, but the stimulation provided by the social environment of the office can be especially important to women who have voluntarily reduced their work schedule to accommodate family needs (Beutell 1989). For some people the office social activity patterns signal that one is "at work." It is reasonable to expect that the office offers a social facilitation effect that heightens work involvement and perhaps achievement motivation (Becker 1982; Reichle 1980).

Career development. Becker (1982) has suggested that telecommuting is more suited to people who are beyond the early career stage. Early career employees need to learn the ropes and fit in with the social and competitive system at work. The relation between career stage and family stage is also an important factor. It is possible to speculate that successful telecommuting would occur when employees have passed beyond early career *and* their family stage is moderate (i.e., children are school aged or older). The rationale for this idea is as follows: Such employees have developed a realistic assessment of life at work, and family demands are less rigorous than at early family stages (i.e., when children are more dependent and require a lot of parental attention).

Self-expectations. Self-generated or reflexive role expectations can increase pressures for high levels of work performance that generate work stress that can spill over and affect family role performance and involvement (Greenhaus and Beutell 1985). There are a couple of issues here. First, high self-expectations might be manifested in workaholism (e.g., people who think that they must work constantly to keep up with office-based coworkers) and reduced interest and participation in family activities. Second is the phenomenon called "technostress" (Brod 1984) or the "inability to cope with new computer technologies in a healthy manner" (p. 16). People with high self-expectations who work in isolation with computer equipment can develop various problems, including a technocentered approach to life. As Brod (1984) has argued:

Technocentered people tend to be highly motivated and eager to adapt to the new technology. Unwittingly, however, they begin to adopt a mindset that mirrors the computer itself. Signs of the technocentered state include a high degree of factual thinking, poor access to feelings, an insistence on efficiency and speed, a lack of empathy for others, and a low tolerance for the ambiguities of human behavior and communication. At its most serious, this form of technostress can cause aberrant and antisocial behavior and the inability to think intuitively and creatively. In some cases spouses report that their technostress partners began to view them as machines. (P. 17)

There are dangers here, and it appears that a "high touch" or human response may be helpful in dealing with technostress (Naisbitt 1982). Brod (1984), however, has argued that high-touch responses are unlikely because of the seductiveness of the technology. People with very high self-expectations and jobs that require high levels of concentration may be most at risk to the damaging effects of technostress.

Family Factors

Family size and composition. The presence of children would be expected to heighten conflict because of increased family demands on home-based workers. By the same token, telecommuting has been suggested as a possible work structure to reduce work-family conflicts because of the opportunities to deal with family issues in a direct and immediate manner. Both of these statements are essentially correct. Research is needed, however, to identify the conditions (e.g., family role structure, ages of children, and presence of role supports such as babysitters and nannies) that make telecommuting effective. To date, most of the telecommuters have been high-achievement, career-involved people who are single or who are married but have no children; they have generally engaged in telematics on a voluntary and self-selected basis (Becker 1982).

Space requirements. Modification of the home environment to accommodate telematics technology is a major issue. The placement of computers, fax machines, and other equipment in order to minimize the effects on family life is not well understood. Becker (1982) reported that telephone lines frequently dictate the placement of such devices. Because the location of telephones usually precedes installation of telematics, phones are typically located in public areas where is a lot of traffic. Even when new telephone lines are installed, the placement of the lines can have unintended consequences on the family system. Telematics equipment could also affect family interaction patterns. Such consequences often result from multiple uses for the same space. Further, inadequate space in the home could lead to strain or behavior conflicts, and additions or modifications to the house could be quite expensive. (The issue of who assumes such costs, employee or employer, is also relevant.)

Support system. Work-family conflict among telecommuters can be reduced through support systems that include environmental support (i.e., enough space to physically separate work and family) and personal support from family members, especially the spouse. In effect, the support person serves as a gatekeeper on family interference when the "employee" role is enacted. Environmental supports serve to preserve the boundaries that separate work and family roles. Becker (1982) has argued that

the availability and use of particular support systems (or their absence), in turn, have a series of consequences both for the other family members, and for the organization which employs the individual. For family members, a series of support systems that is effective and functional from the perspective of one person (the worker) may be dysfunctional and disruptive for the remainder of the family. The nature of the activities that children are allowed to engage in, for example, may be restricted to accommodate office work in the home: more quiet, clean, and space-conserving play (e.g., reading) than messy, noisy, and space-consuming play (e.g., learning a musical instrument or setting up a model railroad). (P. 186)

Work Factors

Work schedule. Flexibility in performing work and family roles is presumed to be one of the major motivations in undertaking a telecommuting work arrangement. To the extent that the organization dictates work schedules and imposes tight time limits for work completion, however, much of the employee discretion and flexibility in scheduling can disappear. Further, when companies monitor employee performance electronically, additional stress can occur. This type of situation could approximate the "electronic sweatshop" (Toffler 1980) and engenders many of the potentially dehumanizing aspects of computer technology suggested by Zuboff (1986). Indeed, Garson (1988) has expressed concern over the computer's ability to monitor employees' behavior in a way that can potentially lead to oppressive control of workers.

Task characteristics. Shamir and Salomon (1985) have examined work-at-home in light of the major task characteristics identified by Hackman and Oldham (1976): autonomy, feedback, task significance, skill variety, and task identity. Autonomy related to work hours and methods would be expected to increase, but autonomy related to home demands would be expected to decrease. Feedback, which depends in part on contacts with superiors, peers, and clients, would be expected to decrease in quantity and in quality. Task significance would decrease, since the person "has less chances to observe other people at work, and has reduced opportunities for informal communication with members of the same organization" (Shamir and Salomon 1985, p. 458). Finally, the authors indicated that the effects of telecommuting on skill variety and task identity (referred to as task meaningfulness by Shamir and Salomon) were rather difficult to predict.

ALL-OR-NONE APPROACH TO TELECOMMUTING

The electronic cottage notion popularized by Toffler (1980) envisioned large numbers of people working at home within a supportive, integrated work-family environment. This vision has been questioned by Forester (1988) on several grounds: the rate of growth of telecommuting has not been as great as expected; most of the literature on telecommuting has been written by people with no experience with work-at-home who underestimate the psychological problems of working at home; some employees simply do not have enough space available to work at home; many employees choose not to work at home; and developments in home informatics are unlikely to lead to substantial increases in work-at-home. These observations do have some validity, but primarily in the context of viewing work-at-home as an all-or-none phenomenon.

Permanent, full-time telecommuting may not be the preferred work arrangement for vast segments of the "information economy" workforce or for organizations. However, telematics allows for flexibility in pursuing various work arrangements, including telecommuting, across the span of employees' careers. Forester (1988) has suggested an increase in part-time work-at-home as flexible work arrangements become more widespread. In this vein, Ramsower (1985) reported that part-time telecommuting did not produce as many negative outcomes as full-time telecommuting.

Consider Susan, a twenty-eight-year-old information researcher employed by a large telecommunications company. She has a five-year-old child and would welcome the opportunity to telecommute on a part-time basis for two salient reasons: flexibility in her child care arrangements and the chance to write up her research projects without the constant interruptions of the central office. As her child grows older, Susan may make adjustments in the time spent in the office versus telecommuting time.

New learning, as well as unlearning, will be necessary to take advantage of this new flexibility. Gordon (1985) has suggested that barriers to telecommuting are managerial rather than technical. Many of the organizational barriers are psychological and represent remnants of a Theory X mentality (i.e., workers are lazy and require close supervision). Telecommuting arrangements are threatening to middle managers who are already being squeezed out by telematics. Individuals, on the other hand, must consider new behaviors and structures for the integration of work and family.

Flexibility is also important for stimulating creativity and innovation. Working under several arrangements can provide a chance to develop a broader perspective that will help in personal and family as well as organizational development. Restricting all employees to one centralized work environment does not seem to be an optimal strategy for HR development. Telematics can provide such flexibility in a cost-effective manner.

HR IMPLICATIONS

Telematics presents an opportunity for organizational flexibility, but the technology must be managed in a proactive manner (e.g., Pava 1986). Several HR implications of these trends are discussed below.

Recruiting

Increasingly, employees are seeking employers who can provide opportunities to deal effectively with family needs (e.g., child and elder care) across the life span. Employers who can provide such alternative work arrangements using telematics will be perceived as employers of choice. Telematics can be one strategy for fostering a more family-sensitive workplace. Indeed, the electronic cottage (or the electronic sweatshop) is not a necessary corollary of telecommuting. It is likely that HR departments will experience an increase in the number of inquiries about the range of work structures available to prospective employees.

Selecting Telecommuters

It is generally agreed that telecommuting is not an appropriate work arrangement for all employees. Selecting prospective telecommuters should be done on the basis of a need for this work arrangement as well as certain personal characteristics. Needs might be work-related or an family-related, or both. Candidates for telecommuting should be self-motivated, self-disciplined, and results-oriented, and be able to work independently (Hamilton 1987). Successful selection is also enhanced when employees have had experience in the company (as opposed to new employees). Such a strategy gives the employee time to develop commitment to the organization (Hamilton 1987). Hamilton (1987) also suggested that family members of prospective telecommuters could be interviewed to make sure that they understand the realities of telecommuting.

Performance Monitoring

Determining whether telecommuters are actually working may be a source of concern for some employers. This presents a paradox. Computer monitoring smacks of Theory X—employees cannot be trusted to do their work. Such monitoring may also be perceived by employees as an invasion of privacy. On the other hand, the organization does have a legitimate right to know that work is getting done. Perhaps setting up a performance contract would facilitate agreement on a set of expectations, including timetables for completion of various tasks or reports. The effects of performance monitoring on family life is not currently known.

Training Telecommuters and Managers

Telecommuters need to be trained in time management skills as well as the ability to work in a relatively unstructured environment (Gordon 1985). Gordon (1985) has noted that "Telecommuters must be able to deal with distractions presented by families, friends, and neighbors. They must also be coached in their role in maintaining contact with the office, a duty shared by the manager and their coworkers who remain at the office" (p. 8).

Those who manage telecommuting employees must be trained to manage from a distance (Gordon 1985). This requires learning new role behaviors for managers and the employees who report to them. Face-to-face interactions will increase in importance, but many significant communications will increasingly occur by way of telematics. Developing performance and career expectations will require additional effort for managers and their employees.

HR Planning

New work roles such as telecommuting can play an important part in ensuring that an organization has the right people in the right place at the right time. Offering alternative work arrangements can help to retain valued employees, particularly those who are trying to balance their work and family lives. Implementation of telematics and telecommuting, while perhaps providing a more family-sensitive workplace, will also lead to a rethinking of HR utilization. For example, organizations will need to think in terms of equivalent head count as well as actual head count. Organizations will also have opportunities for force reductions, more decentralized operations, and increased flexibility and responsiveness.

These changes have major implications for HR planning. HR planners will need to anticipate the retraining of employees, providing outplacement assistance, redesigning jobs, and understanding the impact of various work structures on family life. More flexible work structures will mean more organic organizational forms, which will make planning more difficult. Environmental scanning and HR information systems will help to manage external and internal factors. The planning staff must be more directly involved in the strategic planning process. HR planners will need to be flexible and adaptable to meet these challenges.

REFERENCES

Becker, F. D. 1982. *Workspace: Creating environments in organizations*. New York: Praeger Publishers.

Beutell, N. J. 1989. Employee reactions to part-time work schedules. Unpublished research data.

Brod, C. 1984. *Technostress: The human costs of the computer revolution*. Reading, MA: Addison-Wesley.

Coates, J. F. 1987. An environmental scan: Projecting future human resource needs. *Human Resource Planning, 10,* 219–35.

Fernandez, J. P. 1986.*Child care and corporate productivity: Resolving work/family conflicts*. Lexington, MA: Lexington Books.

Forester, T. 1988. The myth of the electronic cottage. *Futures, 20,* 227–40.

Garson, B. 1988. *The electronic sweatshop: How computers are transforming the office of the future into the factory of the past*. New York: Simon & Schuster.

Gordon, G. E. 1985, Aug./Sept. Telecommuting: A management challenge. *Data Processing Management,* 1–12.

Greenhaus, J. H., and N. J. Beutell. 1985. Sources of conflict between work and family roles. *Academy of Management Review, 10,* 76–88.

Hackman, J. R., and G. R. Oldham 1976. Motivation through the design of work:

Test of a theory. *Organizational Behavior and Human Performance, 16,* 250–79.

Hall, D. T. 1972. A model of coping with role conflict: The role behavior of college-educated women. *Administrative Science Quarterly, 17,* 471–89.

Hamilton, C-A. 1987. Telecommuting. *Personnel Journal, 66,* 91–101.

Kanter, R. M. 1977. *Work and family in the United States: A critical review and agenda for research and policy.* New York: Russell Sage Foundation.

Martin, J. 1981. *Telematic society: A challenge for tomorrow.* Engelwood Cliffs, NJ: Prentice-Hall.

Naisbitt, J. 1982. *Megatrends: Ten new directions transforming our lives.* New York: Warner Books.

Pava, C. 1986. Managing new information technology: Design or default? In R. E. Walton and P. R. Lawrence (eds.), *HRM Trends and Challenges.* Boston: Harvard Business School Press.

Ramsower, R. M. 1985. *Telecommuting: The organizational and behavioral effects of working at home.* Ann Arbor, MI: UMI Research Press.

Reichle, J. 1980. *The effect of technology on the possible decentralization of the office environment: Home vs. office.* Unpublished manuscript, Department of Design and Environmental Analysis, Cornell University. Cited in Becker (1982).

Shamir, B., and I. Salomon. 1985. Work-at-home and the quality of working life. *Academy of Management Review, 10,* 455–64.

Toffler, A. 1980. *The third wave.* New York: William Morrow & Co.

Zuboff, S. 1986. Technologies that informate: Implications for human resource management in the computerized industrial workplace. In R. E. Walton and P. R. Lawrence (eds.), *HRM Trends and Challenges.* Boston: Harvard Business School Press.

CHAPTER 16

MANAGING A DIVERSE
WORKFORCE IN THE 1990s
___ JOHN P. FERNANDEZ AND JACQUELINE A. DUBOIS

In the late 1980s we have witnessed a proliferation of books and articles that describe the changing demographics in the United States. The authors are virtually unanimous in their predictions of a shrinking labor pool. They point out that the workforce of the 1990s will be increasingly composed of people of color, women, and foreign workers, as they account for almost all of the workforce growth. However, these authors fail to answer many key questions. For example, how does today's workforce *feel* about these demographic changes? Are workers aware of the changes? Perhaps more important, are they willing to *accept* a truly diverse workforce at all levels and in all jobs in their companies? In addition, these publications do not discuss the problems that corporate America will confront as its workforce is increasingly composed of different people with unique problems. Examples of these problems include the persistence of racism, sexism, ageism, and ethnocentrism; religious intolerance; the clash of many cultures and emerging lifestyles; and the language problems that will surface for those who use English, not only as a second language, but also as a first language.

In this chapter we present figures to concisely illustrate the demographic trends. It is important to understand the magnitude and scope of the changes. However, most of the discussion focuses on data from a major survey that John P. Fernandez conducted in 1987–88, with 30,000 respondents, as well as comments from more than 2,000 employees who participated in Fernandez's workshops on managing diversity. Using this information as a backdrop, we can paint a picture of the problems caused by the changing face of corporate America and also propose solutions to those problems. Note, these problems are not caused by the *changes* themselves, but by the inability of corporations to integrate a truly heterogeneous workforce at all levels. We must emphasize that companies that are willing to accommodate diversity will reap rewards in traditional dollars-and-cents terms as they listen to their most valuable resource: people. We predict that those corporations that refuse to attend to pressing employee concerns will be split by conflict as they find potential workers more difficult to find and much more apt to work in organizations where they are fully appreciated.

THE CHANGING DEMOGRAPHICS: AN OVERVIEW

In the next ten years or so, given moderate economic growth, there will be a total of twenty-one million new jobs in the United States. The following is a list of major demographic trends that will impact the workforce and our society as a whole in the next decade and beyond:

- U.S. manufacturing will be a much smaller share of the economy in the year 2000 than it is today. Service industries will create most of the new jobs and most of the new wealth over the next decade.

- Service industries require a greater level of skill and education, for the most part, than do manufacturing jobs. Filling these jobs requires more than simply the correct number of "bodies" it requires a qualified pool of workers from which to choose.

- Defining literacy as the ability to write, think systematically and logically, and speak with clarity and precision, 30 percent of all adult Americans are illiterate.

- More jobs will require not only basic skills but also problem-solving analytical and communication skills, yet a growing percentage of the projected labor force entrants are expected to lack these skills.

- No matter which analysis you look at, 65 percent of the new jobs will be filled by women, and most of these women will have children at some time during their careers.

- By the year 2000, approximately 47 percent of the civilian workforce will be women and 62 percent of all women will be at work. The numbers for men will be 53 percent of the workforce, and 75 percent of all men.

- The number of single-person households has increased from seven million in 1960 to more than twenty-one million in 1986. While only 13 percent of the adult population lived alone in 1960, the figure for the year 2000 is projected to be 26 percent.

- By 1990 two-income families are expected to compose as much as 90 percent of the working married population. The rise in multi-earner families has been one of the most important socioeconomic developments of the last twenty years.

- The generation of people who are responsible for both child and elder care (sandwich generation) will continue to grow as a result of the increased number of dual-earner families and the increased number of aged Americans.

- People with alternative lifestyles, such as homosexuality, will continue to become more visible.

- Between 1990 and 2000, the white population will decrease by more than 10 percent.
- Of the twenty-one million new jobs, 92 percent will be filled by women, people of color, and immigrants.
- The Asian American population grew by 142 percent between 1970 and 1980. By the turn of the century, the number of Asian Americans will double again to more than eight million. By the middle of the next century, they will be as large a minority as Hispanics are now.
- One fact to keep in mind when reviewing statistics about people of color is that many representatives from these groups are not counted. Those who are functionally illiterate cannot complete census forms, and many immigrants enter the country illegally and are not part of official counts.
- The Hispanic share of labor force growth (between 1985 and 2000) is projected as 22 percent. The black share of labor force growth for the same period is projected as 20 percent.
- Immigrants represented 28 percent of U.S. population growth during 1980–85; this represents an almost 50 percent increase from 1975–79. Experts predict that immigrant representation will increase to 35 percent through the 1990s.
- The number of foreigners receiving advanced degrees in engineering, computer science, an other sciences will continue to increase at a rapid rate.
- By 2050 one in two Americans will be black, Hispanic, or Asian.
- U.S. economic growth and world growth are tightly linked. However, the total U.S. foreign investment is only $3.3 billion, which is 0.3 percent of foreign investment in the United States.
- As U.S. companies become global corporations, they will have to make foreign employees integral collaborators in their organizations, not only in foreign territory but also in the United States.
- Older employees (aged more than forty-five years) will represent a share of labor force growth of 65 percent from 1985 to 2000.
- The size of the age group between eighteen and twenty-four will decrease about 25 percent.
- The average age of Americans will increase from thirty-four years to thirty-nine.
- The prime working-age group (twenty-five to forty-four years of age) is projected to represent 73 percent of the labor force in the twenty-first century, compared with 67 percent in 1986.
- More than 90 percent of those who will be working in the year 2000 are already in the workforce.
- Particularly hard hit by poor education are the nation's people of color, blacks, Hispanics, and Native Americans. Remember, these groups will account for most of the new entrants into the workforce in the coming decade.

These changes paint a picture of a United States that could either present great opportunities or be riddled with problems. For example, if we start investing in education from every source (private donations of various types and funding from all levels of government), we can truly have a literate country and a labor pool of qualified candidates. If we ignore the statistics about workforce composition and education, we will have a severe shortage of qualified workers and a country that continues to have large pockets of extremely disadvantaged people of color.

Although all of these changes are inevitable and have been discussed at length, little, if anything, has been written about employee perceptions and acceptance of these changes. We now turn our attention to the employee views about this increasingly pluralistic environment. In the remainder of the chapter, the terms "pluralism" and "diversity" will be used synonymously.

EMPLOYEE ACCEPTANCE OF DIVERSITY

Unfortunately, the idea of a diverse nation and workforce is not palatable to many Americans. With the reemergence of neo-Nazi groups, the swelling popularity of racist and anti-Semitic groups as typified by the ominous skinhead groups, we are witnessing a violent backlash to increased immigration and greater numbers of blacks, Hispanics, and Asians already in the United States. These supremist groups would like to create a country that is male dominated and "lily white." They may be extreme examples of hierarchist thinking, but there are many who adhere to at least some of their principles. They cling to the notion that the United States is/should be a "Western European civilization." They don't realize the degree to which "Western civilization" is made up of different cultures. For example, Asian influences have long been felt in Europe (i.e., the Chinese noodle became the staple Italian pasta). In Russia, the Tsarist regimes were criticized for being "too European." In the United States, many experts now agree that the founding fathers were influenced by Iroquois government when they developed our governing principles. Jazz, the original American music, is the creation of African Americans and stems from their cultural heritage.

As a starting point, then, we are a culture infused with pieces of every other culture around the world. It would be difficult to deny the flourishing evidence of this multiculturalism in the United States. It is not uncommon to be able to buy fast-food versions of teriyaki and pizza in the same restaurant. A Vietnamese family may own a shop that sells Guatemalan crafts and clothing. Many of the architects in the U.S. West and Southwest are Native Americans and Hispanic. In short, a walk down any major U.S. city street will provide an earload and eyefull of different languages, crafts, music, and *people*. The United States is truly an immigrant country, but many of its citizens want it to become a homogenized shadow of a fictitious "Western" ideal.

In the following sections we discuss specific diversity issues that managers

Figure 16.1
Who is Bothered by Hearing Different Languages?

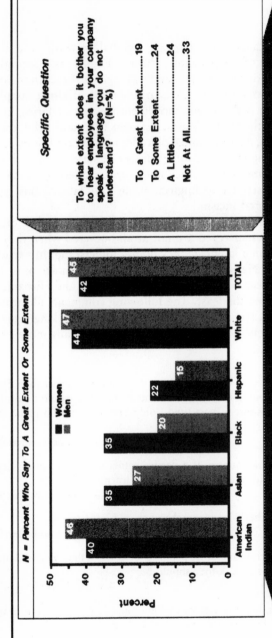

Specific Question

To what extent does it bother you to hear employees in your company speak a language you do not understand?   (N=%)

To a Great Extent..........19
To Some Extent.............24
A Little.........................24
Not At All.......................33

N = Percent Who Say To A Great Extent Or Some Extent

(chart: American Indian — Women 40, Men 46; Asian — Women 35, Men 27; Black — Women 35, Men 20; Hispanic — Women 22, Men 15; White — Women 44, Men 47; TOTAL — Women 42, Men 43)

Analyses

- More than 2 out of 5 employees say hearing a person speak a language they do not understand bothers them to some extent.

- The chart shows that Hispanic (15%) and Black (20%) men are least likely to be bothered. White (47%) and American Indian (46%) men are most likely to be bothered.

in the United States (and the rest of the world) must confront in the coming decades.

Language Conflicts

As corporate America becomes part of a global network, and as our workforce is composed of more people who use English as a second language, the issue of accepting and understanding languages other than English becomes crucial to corporate success. One of the most striking examples of anti-pluralistic thinking is the strong movement toward declaring English the official language of the United States. Between 1985 and 1989, thirteen states, including Florida, Arizona, and Colorado, passed resolutions making English their official language. The total number of states with such a resolution is seventeen. Some twenty other states are considering similar measures to limit public discourse to English. Some have labeled this type of law government-sponsored racism.

Specifically from Fernandez's research, Figure 16.1 shows that only 33 percent of the employees surveyed are not at all bothered when they hear other employees speak in a language they do not understand. In particular, white (47 percent) and Native American (46 percent) men are most likely to be bothered "to a great extent" or "to some extent," and Hispanic men (15 percent) are bothered the least. The following comments illustrate the numerous opinions and feelings employees have about the language issue. Some of the reactions reflect a progressive attitude, but many more express reactionary intolerance.

I think it is an advantage to be bilingual. If you use a language other than English, some individuals feel offended in the department. A minority would be dismissed or demoted for lesser reasons, in past times, only because he is Hispanic, black, Asian, or Indian.

—Hispanic, occupational man

This is an English-speaking country. If a person wants to advance in an English-speaking country he should learn the language and learn it well.

—white, lower-level man

If I don't understand another's language, then I should learn it.

—white, middle-level man

I have to work on not discounting other people's ideas when their English language skills are not as "good" as I think they should be.

—white, lower-level woman

I have difficulty listening beyond accents and grammar imperfections to hear (understand) the content of the message of the person I am dealing with.

—white, middle-level man

Language and the way I speak is one of the problems in communicating with others. I have been dealing with my present work group the last two and one-half years and have no problem (so far!) in dealing with them.

—Asian, lower-level man

Some Americans tend to spend more effort to understand European's English, but not Asian's. Some people think that women are inferior in science and mathematics. Some people think that Asians cannot speak good English.

—Asian, middle-level man.

There are times that I feel uncomfortable with someone who has an accent, because I think they don't understand me, so I start talking to them as if they were illiterate.

—white, middle-level woman

I am impatient with non-English speaking or poorly speaking people; tend to generalize about behavior; brought up in a household where the male is the breadwinner.

—white, middle-level man

I tend to expect minorities to be difficult to communicate with today, which leads me to believe that it takes more effort to get information from minorities.

—white, middle-level man

I also do not like the fact that Americans (people born and raised in America) do not make an extra effort in understanding a foreign-speaking person. Sometimes, they even make fun of foreigners.

—white, lower-level woman

In the work place, I do not like to be excluded from conversations because I cannot speak the language.

—white, occupational woman

Communication with Americans is not very easy since I didn't grow up here. Many times during conversations I am reminded that I don't totally belong here.

—Asian, lower-level woman

Language is an important form of communication and source of unity. Therefore, when in a common situation, it is important for two persons to be able to converse. In the United States, the vast majority of the population speaks English fluently or at least has some working knowledge of the language. In the interest of basic practicality, immigrants and other residents use English when imparting most public information. However, there are large segments of some states, and especially cities, in which the use of foreign languages is the normal way to conduct business and personal affairs. No one would argue that we should use another language as the *primary* mode of communication in this country. We would argue, however, that important signs should be printed in several languages to make their messages clear to everyone. We would also argue that private discussions (even if they take place in public) should not be subject to racist legislation. We believe that, in certain situations and communities, speaking in a foreign language is much more productive for business purposes than speaking in English. For example, many Hispanics who are new arrivals would be much more of a marketing target if advertisements and salespeople used Spanish. Similarly, business between prospective Japanese clients and U.S. business leaders might be much more productive if discussed in Japanese.

Notice that the question in the survey was worded such that it asked respondents whether they were bothered by simply *hearing* a foreign language. Also, the new statutes seek to limit *all* public discourse to English. Neither of these has anything to do with the mere practicality of English use; it has more to do with U.S. fear of "foreigners" taking over the country. Many forget that it was not long ago that their ancestors arrived, speaking their native tongues. Visitors to the United States are expected to enter the country equipped with a full knowledge of English. Interestingly, many Americans expect to visit other countries and hear and speak nothing but English. Most don't bother learning how to speak Spanish when they visit Mexico, for example. This extreme ethnocentrism is dangerous, given the emerging global marketplace. With rapid modes of transportation and business deals to be cut, Americans will increasingly find themselves in other countries and will find foreigners in their own country. They must not only get used to hearing languages other than English but also actually *learn* them in order to maintain a competitive edge.

Different Culture

When one discusses the introduction of a truly diverse workforce, there are some subtle issues that must be raised. "Accepting diversity" means much more than being able to look at another employee whose skin is a different color. As we have already mentioned, it can also mean listening to an accent, or speech in a different language. It can also mean accepting people who dress differently. Perhaps more difficult ways to accept diversity include learning what members from non-American cultures consider "praise" and "reward." For example, if you point out an Asian man in the office and publicly disclose what his accomplishments have been, he may be embarrassed by the spectacle. An alternative that he may prefer is a private letter of recognition. We must be able to recognize competence in new packages. A culture may have a more laid back style, but that doesn't necessarily mean that members of that culture are lazy, and their approach may be even more appropriate in a crisis.

When women entered the workforce, a big question was, What should they wear? Many women donned severe suits that made them look more masculine. They wore little makeup, and their hair was cut short or "neatly" pulled back. Much of this transformation was aimed at minimizing the differences between the appearance of women and men. After having been in the workforce for twenty years and attaining a limited level of acceptance, women can now begin to dress femininely in the workplace. Even still, there is much more attention paid to the "appropriateness" of a woman's attire than to that of a man.

As we noted in the demographic overview, immigrants represented 28 percent of U.S. population growth during the 1980–85 period, representing an almost 50 percent increase from 1975 to 1979. Most demographers project that immigrant representation will increase to 35 percent through the 1990s. In addition, for the first time in U.S. history, immigrants (about 50,000 per year) will be allowed into the United States if they possess technical, scientific, or other skills needed in this country. Consider these facts in light of the globalization of U.S. business, and the inevitable increase in foreign nationals who will come into this country and become an integral part of day-to-day business here. It is clear that unless employees are managed properly, the different cultures will clash and U.S. corporate competitiveness will suffer.

Although participants in Fernandez's surveys were never asked specifically about foreign culture, their responses paint a picture of conflict and intolerance in such areas as hygiene, dress, food, religious holidays, praise, eye contact, modesty, and aggressiveness. The comments suggest a host of potential problems that managers must learn to recognize and solve. Below are examples of these conflicts.

I feel socially uncomfortable with people outside of the structure of work—with minorities I feel even more uncomfortable, interacting very little outside of the work environment.

—white, lower-level man

I think the whole issue of white male/white female/people of color issue is a cultural problem. If we ever get to a point where we treat people as individuals and not part of a group then we've taken a giant step toward pluralism.

—white, occupational woman

Cultural differences in the way problems are viewed and in patterns of communication create conflict.

—white, middle-level man

I think it [managing diversity workshop] should be a mandatory course, but you have people that are angered by this because they feel they have been violated. Why can't they understand that violating others' rights hurts also. It's OK because we are a different color.

—Hispanic, occupational man

Inability to "warm up" to culturally different people—not being myself—walking on eggs to avoid offending others in the belief that they are super-sensitive, or I am insensitive.

—white, lower-level man

My biggest issue is dealing with people from other countries and cultures where communication (spoken language, writing skills, and the way in which a person thinks) is difficult.

—white, middle-level man

Lack of understanding and involvement in other cultures! I need to participate in the activities that will help me to understand other cultures.

—white, occupational woman

Cultural prejudice—not so much with European cultures, more with Asian, less with Hispanic.

—white, middle-level man

Basic message: openness to diversity of difference instead of rejecting people who are different because we are unsure of ourselves. We tend to see our own faults in others, but overlook them in ourselves.

—white, middle-level man

Work ethic standards are different for ethnic minorities. No one acknowledges my presence when I walk in someone's office and they are in a conversation. Key word is "ACKNOWLEDGE."

—Asian, occupational man

Have been brought up in a macho environment. Hence, tend to relate to the more aggressive males in a group, sometimes ignore the more timid people.

—Hispanic, occupational man

Certain ethnic groups (Asians) tend to stick together more so than others, thus shutting out other people.

—Hispanic, occupational man

I tend to presume how someone of a particular background will react to me before allowing them to react on their own.

—white, middle-level woman

I don't like to be around anyone with personal hygiene problems. Unfortunately, this seems to apply to Orientals, Asians (although not all). And of course, if this was a white with the same problem, I wouldn't like it either.

—white, lower-level woman

I don't seem to have trouble working with "Americans" of any race or creed. I do have trouble working with people from other countries (non-English-speaking countries).

—white, occupational woman

Fear of groups of minorities—feeling intimidated when surrounded by non-white people.

—white, lower-level man

I have an inherent bias to prefer someone who looks/acts like me without consciously realizing it.

—white, upper-level man

Asians are usually quiet in the meetings. This happened to me that I did not speak enough in the meeting and other people think I am stupid and cannot participate.

—Asian, middle-level man

Employee Support for Pluralism

In the 1987–88 survey, Fernandez measured employee support for pluralism (race, gender, foreign background, and lifestyle diversity) by asking a series of questions related to employee perceptions of certain groups of people. As Figure 16.2 shows, the vast majority (84 percent) of employees believe that it is important for their company's workforce to reflect the cultural makeup of customers and stockholders. Interestingly, only 38 percent of the employees believe that their supervisor should be compensated for her or his pluralistic efforts. Employees are least supportive of their company's financially assisting employee organizations that act as support groups for specific racial minority and gender groups. They indicate, through responses to open-ended questions, that they consider such groups to be segregationist and insist that if they exist, they should exist without direct company assistance. When these questions are grouped into an index, we find that blacks are much more likely (95 percent) to respond supportively to at least four of the of the questions than are whites (51 percent).

When the same information is broken down by gender, we find that women and men respond similarly, but whenever there is a difference, women are more likely to indicate support for pluralism. For example, women are more likely to believe that hiring, promotion, goals, and time-tables should be part of pluralistic efforts (71 percent for women, 61 percent for men) and that the company should financially support special race/gender interest organizations (36 percent for women, 27 percent for men). Women (55 percent) are also less likely to believe that these organizations increase segregation (men 66 percent). Employee comments add flavor to the data.

Create the understanding that diversity among employees involves much more than just race or sexual differences.

—white, middle-level man

We are working against age-old prejudices and culturally entrenched bias. Change will occur slowly and only as a result of constant vigilance, effort and sacrifice.

—Asian, lower-level man

Figure 16.2
Employee Support for Pluralism

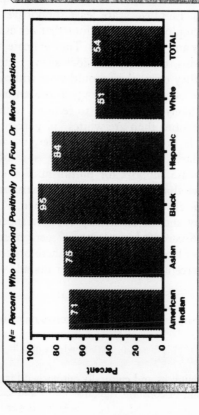

N= Percent Who Respond Positively On Four Or More Questions

Percent chart:
- American Indian: 71
- Asian: 75
- Black: 95
- Hispanic: 84
- White: 51
- TOTAL: 54

Questions Which Make Up the Index

- To what extent do you believe it is important for this company's employee makeup to reflect diversity similar to its customers and stockholders? (N=% who say at least to some extent)..........84

- To what extent do you agree or disagree with each of the following statements: (N=% who agree or strongly agree)
  Hiring, promotion goals and time tables should be part of pluralistic efforts..........67

  Attendance at company sponsored pluralism workshops, forums, etc. should be mandatory..........47

  My supervisor should be compensated on his/her pluralistic efforts..........38

- To what extent do you agree or disagree with the following statements about special interest organizations that discuss specific issues such as race/gender concerns:

  This company should allow such organizations to exist in the company. (agree or strongly agree)..........78

  These organizations merely increase segregation. (disagree or strongly disagree)..........58

  The company should financially support such organizations. (agree or strongly agree)..........33

- What is your position on interracial marriages? (supportive or very supportive)..........55

- To what extent does it bother you to hear employees at this company speak in a language you do not understand? (N=% who say not at all)..........31

Analyses

- As the above chart shows, there are extreme differences in responses among the different races. For example, 95% of the Blacks compared to only 51% of Whites respond in a supportive manner on at least 5 of 9 questions.

- When analyzing the data by gender, one finds no significant differences.

- Among the various major company units, the range of employees who respond positively on at least 5 questions is 46% to 69%.

I agree with pluralism, but it's a catch 22. So often I see minorities who expect something for nothing. They act like the world owes them and take advantage.
                                                                —Asian, occupational woman

Until the old people are gone who have grown up with these attitudes, we won't see much of a difference on discrimination. I feel I am very open-minded. I see and hear more discrimination against gay people than any other minority.
                                                                —white, occupational woman

Where are the black, handicapped, gay cowboys in the TV ads?
                                                                —white, lower-level man

The primary premise of pluralism sounds worthy, but may not be true nor completely practical in terms of potential for growth and profitability of a business in a free enterprise system.
                                                                —white, middle-level man

I understand the values and need for a pluralistic workforce. We must do special things to achieve this. We must not forget, however, the individual's responsibility to perform in a manner that creates value to the corporation.
                                                                —white, vice president man

I grew up in a family where women were subservient. These attitudes and expectations are deeply rooted within me. As hard as I fight them, I'll never be free of those attitudes. I fear I have become too militant in my feminist strivings, and I too often look down on women who choose to stay home and raise a family, for instance.
                                                                —white, middle-level woman

Having self-doubts about my own desire/efforts to achieve "color blindness," or "gender blindness." I doubt that I am as aware of my prejudices as I would like to believe.
                                                                —white, lower-level man

I have learned that diversity is very important to the corporate environment and its success. Diversity is something to accept and spread.
                                                                —white, middle-level man

Not letting my feelings on reverse discrimination get in the way when I'm interviewing candidates.
                                                                —white, lower-level woman

I accept relationships among races for other people, but I couldn't marry a black man, for example, because of the way society feels about it. But it doesn't affect me when I see it.
                                                                —white, lower-level woman

One explanation of the difference between the responses of whites and people of color with respect to pluralism in the workplace is the theory that people in positions of power prefer the status quo and people who have less power prefer change. This theory makes intuitive sense because those in power have much to lose with a shift in the equilibrium, and those who have less power have much to gain. Figure 16.3 dramatically demonstrates some of these concepts. The greatest differences in response to this question are by race. The only race to believe that its opportunities will worsen within a pluralistic environment is the white race. White women are only somewhat inclined to believe this, (15 percent) but the men are significantly more likely to believe that their opportunities will *decrease* in number (50 percent).

Fernandez's previous research provides some interesting insight into the patterns of responses, which will be discussed in this chapter. There are factors that influence which racial groups will be the objects of stereotyping and discrimination. Economic issues are probably the most important of these factors. Competition for desirable land, money and good jobs determines, in large part, the intensity and depth of threat felt by the dominant (in this case, white) society. Other important factors are the size and skin color of the group. Therefore, even though each group has experienced racism and discrimination, there are differences with respect to the type and degree of these problems. Each group has different positive and negative stereotypes placed on it, not only by the white majority but by other people of color.

As we study racial groups more thoroughly, we discover historical and cultural reasons for patterns of responses. White men, who are responsible for designing and implementing the meritocracy of corporate United States, are often hesitant to recognize the flaws in the system. Native Americans, who were subjected to forced deculturalization, often relate more to white culture than to "Indian culture". Another factor is that many Native Americans have little Indian blood. Even though they may prefer to call themselves "Native Americans," they look and act like whites because the majority have less than one-quarter Indian blood and have been raised in a white culture. Asians, who have been deemed "the model minority," and who are fewer in number than both blacks and Hispanics, are less supportive of pluralism than those two groups. Blacks, who have been subjected to the most prejudice in this country, are the most likely to find racism in the workplace, and the most committed to pluralism in their company. The responses of Hispanics fall in between Asians and blacks (as a rule); this trend is not surprising, since they experience the second-most amount of prejudice.

RACISM AND SEXISM

Of all the problems corporate America must face in the approaching decades, two of the biggest with respect to HR utilization will be the issues surrounding race and gender bias. These factors impact everyone, and will be the cause of many obstacles to corporate productivity. For more than twenty years, Fernandez has conducted studies on corporate life, and he

Figure 16.3
The Effect of Pluralism on Personal Career Opportunities

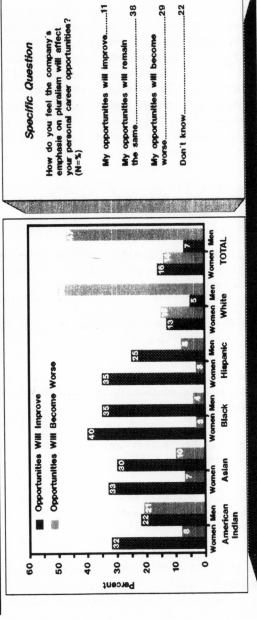

Specific Question

How do you feel the company's emphasis on pluralism will affect your personal career opportunities? (N=%)

My opportunities will improve......11

My opportunities will remain the same..............38

My opportunities will become worse..............29

Don't know..............22

Analyses

- Almost triple the percentage of employees (29%) believe their opportunities have become worse rather than improved (11%); however, these overall figures mask some major differences.

- The above chart shows that only 5% of the White men and 13% of the White women believe their opportunities have improved. This compares to between 22% to 40% of the other race/gender groups.

- With regard to opportunities becoming worse, 50% of the White men believe this versus only 3% to 21% of the other race/gender groups.

has found that a consistent majority of the employees subscribe to at least some sexist and racist stereotypes. These are the stereotypes that translate into race and gender discrimination.

Some people would argue that racism and sexism no longer exist in corporate America because there are regulations to ensure fair treatment regardless of race or gender. But as the following comments illustrate, people still harbor many negative feelings about co-workers who are in different race and gender groups. Keep in mind that many people don't disclose the full extent of their biases. There is a phenomenon known to social scientists as the "social desireability effect." People don't want to appear to hold "socially incorrect" views, so they temper their responses to appear reasonable. With the media and laws dictating nondiscrimination, those who still hold racist and sexist views may be more hesistant to express them. Yet, many employees are candid about negative feelings they have or perceive in the workplace.

People should be hired on qualification, not race! This pluralism crusade is garbage! And I'm A MINORITY!!

—Asian, occupational woman

I don't believe race should ever be an issue, either to exclude or to include an individual in any job or function. We have reached a time when intelligent people regard one another as equals and further efforts became superfluous.

—white, occupational man

I've discovered that I tend to be in awe of white male supervision, but not of female, black, or Asians, no matter how high up they are.

—white, occupational woman

The assumptions I automatically make about who they are, what they do/are, how they are likely to respond to me. Also, automatic sticking with people with whom I'm most comfortable.

—white, lower-level woman

The ones [white men] that are qualified have no problems, especially if they are secure in themselves, and most are.

—black, lower-level woman

White males are the ones who need most to be exposed to education on pluralism. They don't understand the reasons for it and don't want to. It would help them understand themselves and their feelings toward pluralism.

—Hispanic, lower-level woman

Brought up in a household where the male is the breadwinner. For example:

1. I have a hard time listening to Asians with heavy accents.
2. I am sometimes slow in recognizing technical abilities in women.
3. I feel Asians are not assertive enough.
4. I have difficulties with "Uncle Tom" minorities, for example, who say things

like "there is no discrimination," or those who try to neutralize the instructor to please the white males around with power.

—white, middle-level man

Although most of the white males I work with are sensitive to the emergence of women and minorities in the workforce, there are still the "informal networks" of men which are difficult or uncomfortable for women and minorities to enter.

—white, lower-level women

Many white males will blame another's race or sex as the reason they were not promoted.

—white, lower-level man

There is still a cultural basis for chauvinist behavior that cannot be mandated to go away; 500,000 years of custom don't disappear in one generation.

—white, lower-level man

I have witnessed white males talking about reverse discrimination and I can't help but wonder if they thought discrimination didn't exist in the first place, then how can reverse discrimination exist?

—black, middle-level man

Company emphasis on longevity has created a large pool of incompetent white males in USW—well-meaning good people, but incompetent.

—white, upper-level man

The company treats white men like second class citizens. They are saying "go to the back of the bus."

—Native American, occupational man

White men seem to be given more responsibilities and are expected to perform better. This may trigger stress on individuals who are not that capable. This may cause a lot of alcoholism which is prevalent in white male managers.

—Asian, occupational woman

They [white men] are human beings with the potential to learn and change.

—black, occupational woman

White men will help each other more than anyone else.

—black, occupational woman

We are a white male, good ole boy company that needs to fire a few.

—white, occupational woman

History speaks for itself. Look at the numbers. They are not good. White men promote white men.

—white, occupational woman

Young white males aren't even considered for employment.

—white, occupational woman

Stereotyping groups of people is dangerous because when you have a preconceived notion about who a person is, or how they are going to act, you fail to notice important things about them that don't conform to your theory. Often you even begin to mold how they act. For example, for a long time it was thought that women could only hold jobs that were low pressure and clerical. Women were treated in a patronizing way and handed little responsibility and training. In many cases, women were under the impression that they "had it good." Many men, and some women, believed that if women were placed in the vice president's chair, they would have had a difficult time adjusting to the position of power. The assumption that women could not handle pressure was tested by men who placed women who had demonstrated extreme competence in positions of moderate responsibility and authority. Not surprisingly, given their abilities, the women excelled, weakening the predominating assumption about them. Their success surprised both men and women who had let their sexist stereotypes govern their perceptions of women's competence.

Although we traditionally associate racism and sexism with white treatment of people of color or male treatment of women, this is an oversimplification. Stereotyping is a pervasive cultural malady. We all tend to make assumptions about people (that may initially help us categorize and understand our world) that eventually become dangerous "truths" about people (i.e., "homosexuals are immoral and unhealthy," "blacks are unclean," "Asians are trying to take over American"). Women stereotype other women, people of color stereotype themselves and other groups. Whites are the subjects of stereotypes; the illusion that white men are *always* in control, highly educated, competent, and so on may bring on an unusual amount of stress and pressure to perform. Whites who are sympathetic to the concerns of people of color may still be the targets of frustrated racial violence merely because they are white. It is interesting to note how different cultures stereotype differently. In China, older people are highly regarded because of their advanced years and accumulated knowledge. In the United States, older people are often viewed as frail, set in their ways, and useless to society.

Sexist Stereotypes and Gender Discrimination

We will now look at data that further illustrate the pervasiveness of sexist stereotypes in corporate America. Overall, the two most frequently held stereotypes about women are that many women obtained their current positions only because they are women (36 percent) and that the increasing employment of women has led to the breakdown of the U.S. family (33 percent).

When we analyze these issues by race and gender, we find significant differences. Overall, women are less likely to subscribe to three to six stereotypes against women. Among women, however, there are some differences. Figure 16.4 shows that Native American women (13 percent), black

Figure 16.4
Sexist Stereotypes and Attitudes

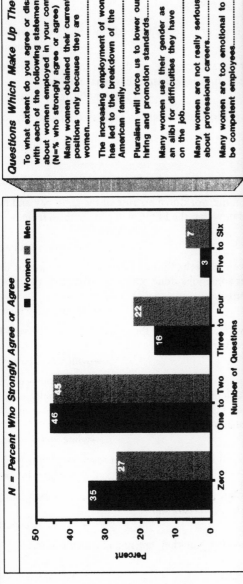

N = Percent Who Strongly Agree or Agree

Legend: ■ Women ▨ Men

Bar chart — Number of Questions (x-axis), Percent (y-axis):
- Zero: Women 35, Men 27
- One to Two: Women 46, Men 43
- Three to Four: Women 16, Men 22
- Five to Six: Women 3, Men 7

Questions Which Make Up The Index

To what extent do you agree or disagree with each of the following statements about women employed in your company: (N=% who strongly agree or agree)

Many women obtained their current positions only because they are women...............36

The increasing employment of women has led to the breakdown of the American family...............33

Pluralism will force us to lower our hiring and promotion standards..........30

Many women use their gender as an alibi for difficulties they have on the job...............23

Many women are not really serious about professional careers.........19

Many women are too emotional to be competent employees...............9

Analyses

- While no individual question has a majority of employees who agree with it, the above chart shows that many women and even more men do have sexist stereotypes and attitudes.

- Blacks (50%) are less likely to agree with sexist stereotypes than other race groups. The range among other races is from 30% for Whites to 37% for Hispanics and Asians.

- Among major company units, the percentage range of women who do not agree with any stereotypes is 27% to 54%. For men the range is 14% to 35%.

women (14 percent) and Hispanic women (14 percent) are less likely to stereotype than white women (20 percent). Among men, the differences are great. Black men (20 percent) and Asian men (23 percent) are the least likely to stereotype, compared to white men (44 percent) and Native American men (41 percent). Among the many sexist comments we have encountered in our research are the following:

Discrimination based on emotional decisions made by female supervisors.

—white, occupational man

Women are being forced to wear dresses before they are considered properly dressed. What's wrong with a jacket and slacks? Isn't that what men wear?

—Native American, occupational woman

Some of the men I have worked around want us to be sweet and pretty to be looked at.

—Asian, occupational woman

Women get power happy!

—Hispanic, occupational man

A lot of women are only in the workforce because of the good pay and not because they like their jobs. They know that the EEOC will protect them from being relieved of the jobs.

—Hispanic, occupational man

Women often do not have the mechanical or physical background or the "rain in the face" discipline to get some jobs done. Once in a new job, they try to "catch up" on prequisites they missed.

—Hispanic, occupational man

Frequent discussions on women's "time of the month," pregnancy, and issues that would never be considered with males.

—white, occupational woman

Working with outside plant techs and their foreman over a number of years, it has been a very prevalent problem because it has been a traditionally male area. If a manager gets mad and loses his temper, that's OK. If a woman loses it, she's a bitch or on her cycle. It's a problem that only time will solve.

—white, occupational woman

Women are more moody and less consistent in approach to similar problems.

—white, lower-level man

You, and your entire group, can't change the fact that a woman belongs in the home, no matter what -ism you dream up.

—white, occupational man

Prejudice against women—feel that they are not effective leaders, too weak and indecisive.

—white, occupational man

I like having a wife at home, mother at home. I see women in this role. I was brought up in the South, and must constantly battle stereotypes of blacks as lazy, inferior, etc. I have a difficult time accepting persons (as equals) with strong accents or poor English.

—white, lower-level man

Latent anger/disgust feelings with women who have children and then return to work within six months when they do not need to financially. I think it is somewhat selfish on their part (of course this implies that the male also works; it would be OK if he stayed home with the children. I have no problem with this in single parent families—that's necessity).

—white, middle-level man

I tend to categorize people, especially women, into those I am interested in romantically, and those I have no interest in. The liberalism I preach is not inherent, but intellectualized, or imposed by my intellect. Often I will catch myself and must consciously take steps to adjust my thinking and actions.

—white, lower-level man

I write off men who are arrogant, like they are probably sexist. I view blacks without education (i.e., not working and poor) as if they're representative of all blacks. I worry that women who aren't understanding their work aren't performing well, like they reflect other attitudes about me.

—white, lower-level man

Although it is difficult to find 50 percent or more employees who agree to any one stereotype about women, employees are often able to pinpoint specific areas in which they witness gender discrimination. More than a majority of employees, overall, have witnessed the following examples of discrimination in their company: women have a harder time finding sponsors in the company (72 percent); women are excluded from informal networks (63 percent); women must be better performers to get ahead (58 percent); and women are faced with sexual harassment on the job (56 percent).

Many corporate promotions result from the forming of a bond with one or more mentors and after-hours discussion and acquaintanceship. Often "the boys" go out after work to have a few drinks and discuss business (or pleasure). If a woman were to accompany them, it might be interpreted as a "come on" or may inspire jealousy and gossip at work or at home. The fact that women need to perform better than men to get ahead puts extra stress and pressure on them to overachieve, and the results (less pay, fewer promotions) are not necessarily worth the effort.

Not surprisingly, women perceive discrimination in all ten categories much more often than men. In particular, women (76 percent) believe that women have to be better performers than men to get ahead. Only 25 percent of the men agree with this statement. However, only 8 percent of men and 1 percent of women do *not* believe that there is any discrimination. The essential difference between women and men is not whether or not there is discrimination in the workplace, but the extent to which it exists.

Almost six times the percentage of women (35 percent compared with 6 percent of men) believe that there is a great deal of discrimination. Analysis by race and gender in Figure 16.5 reveals the extreme differences among various race/gender groups. The following comments graphically illustrate the reality of gender discrimination:

My boss once told me it'd be hard for me to move up any higher in the company because I'm a "small structured woman" (those of my ethnic background usually are). This kind of attitude, though unconscious, exists in all places. It makes people like me hold an unconscious "self-defeatist" attitude that I'll never go higher than lower-level management. I'm not a real activist on these kinds of issues, but it disturbs me enough to try harder, work harder, to prove him wrong. So far, I've had no luck or opportunities to make a step up. Sometimes I wonder if it's worth the effort.

—Native American, lower-level woman

Majority of women workers are still assigned clerical jobs. Apparently, little has been done to give them opportunities and advancements. This applies to both white and colored people.

—Asian, occupational woman

Talents and capabilities of women have always been great. Lack of recognition and self-worthiness keeps many women from development.

—Hispanic, occupational woman

It seems like women discriminate against women quite often.

—white, occupational woman

Much of the gender discrimination is cultural, and therefore, extremely subtle. There is a tendency to channel women into data base manipulation jobs and a willingness of women to be channeled in that direction. Not much done to develop truly technical women, who know why things work, in addition to what should happen. We need to see more technical women managers.

—white, occupational woman

Gender discrimination in the company is demonstrated in the number of middle- and higher-level women in management, compared with men.

—Asian, lower level woman

Older women have very few opportunities for advancement because they cannot attract sponsors or mentors.

—black, lower-level woman

All people are more productive in a supportive environment. The subtle everyday messages women receive telling them they are not competent is not supportive and causes an enormous loss of production.

—white, lower-level woman

Figure 16.5
Gender Discrimination

N = Percent Who at Least Agree or Say at Least Frequently to the Questions

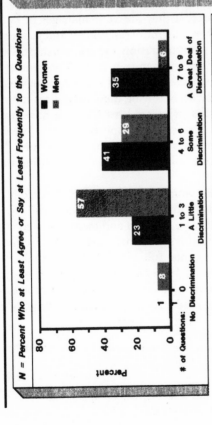

# of Questions:

| 0 No Discrimination | 1 to 3 A Little Discrimination | 4 to 6 Some Discrimination | 7 to 9 A Great Deal of Discrimination |

■ Women
▨ Men

Analyses

- Responses to the individual questions show that more than 1 out of 2 employees believe women face problems in 4 of the 9 areas.

- The above chart shows the extreme differences in opinions between men and women.

- By race, one finds that 50% of the Blacks compared to 15% of the Asians believe there is a great deal of discrimination. The range among the other race groups is 22% of the American Indians to 29% of the Hispanics.

- Among other major company units, the response for employees who see a great deal of gender discrimination range from 30% to 43% for women and 4% to 9% for men.

Questions Which Make Up the Index

To what extent do you agree or disagree with each of the following statements about women employed in your company? (N=% who strongly agree or agree)

In general, women have a much harder time finding a sponsor, or mentor than men do....................72

Many women are often excluded from informal networks by men...........63

In general, women have to be better performers than men to get ahead........58

Many women are faced with some type of sexual harassment on the job...56

Many women have a difficult time initiating informal work-related activities such as lunch and social-izing after work, because men mis-interpret their behavior as a "come on".......................................48

In general, customers do not accept a woman's authority as much as they accept a man's in similar situations.......42

In general, women are often placed in jobs with no future..................41

In general, women are penalized more for mistakes than men...............33

How frequently do you hear language in your organization which you con-sider sexist? (N=% who say at least frequently).............................29

Lots of "testing" of women, to see if they're as tough as men. Sometimes, it goes to the point where a woman is set up because she's perceived as weaker. Generally, things are much worse than they were a few years ago.

—white, lower-level woman

Pregnant women seem to be more discriminated against. There is an antiquated attitude about mothers as employees.

—white, middle-level woman

Racist Stereotypes and Race Discrimination

The most frequently cited racist stereotype is the notion that an employee of color could not be demoted without undeserved charges of discrimination (54 percent) (Figure 16.6). Coming in at a close second is the stereotype "people of color got their position only because they are people of color" (53 percent). These are particularly damaging stereotypes because they carry with them the heavy implication that people of color are getting jobs they don't deserve (are not qualified for) merely to meet arbitrary quotas or rules mandating fair treatment of people of color. If this is how you perceive people of color in the workforce, if they are your manager or co-worker, you will have less respect for them and more resentment and jealousy. These feelings interfere with smooth work operation and relationships. One of the notions that must be dispelled by companies is that 68 percent of the employees believe that even though they have prejudices against people who are different than they are, they do not bring these prejudices into work. It is interesting to note that blacks, who are least likely to have prejudices, are least likely to believe that they can accomplish this feat. For example, 55 percent of the blacks, compared with 71 percent of the whites, "strongly agree" or "agree" that they can hold prejudices and not bring them into work.

The only racist statement that women are significantly less likely to agree with is "pluralism will force us to lower our hiring standards" (women 25 percent, men 40 percent). Otherwise, women and men appear to concur on many of the statements. Predictably, Hispanics and blacks are least likely to agree with most racist statements, followed by Asians. Only 9 percent of blacks, compared with between 38 percent and 58 percent of other race groups, will agree that employees of color cannot be demoted without charges of discrimination being made. As the following comments indicate, many employees subscribe to strong racist stereotypes.

Manager afraid to discipline a poor, lazy, black worker because he may be accused of racism.

—white, lower-level woman

The U.S.A. is a racist country; it has a racist past. Company employees reflect the same prejudices exhibited by society in general.

—black, middle-level man

Figure 16.6
Racist Stereotypes and Attitudes

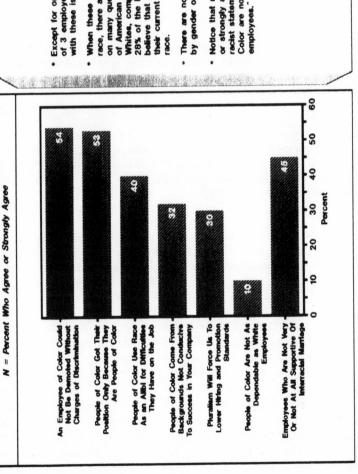

N = Percent Who Agree or Strongly Agree

An Employee of Color Could Not Be Demoted Without Charges of Discrimination — 54

People of Color Got Their Position Only Because They Are People of Color — 53

People of Color Use Race As an Alibi for Difficulties They Have on the Job — 40

People of Color Come From Backgrounds Not Conducive To Success in Your Company — 32

Pluralism Will Force Us To Lower Hiring and Promotion Standards — 30

People of Color Are Not As Dependable as White Employees — 10

Employees Who Are Not Very Or Not At All Supportive Of Interracial Marriage — 46

Percent

Analyses

- Except for one stereotype, at least 1 out of 3 employees agree or strongly agree with these issues.

- When these questions are analyzed by race, there are significant differences on many questions. For example, 67% of American Indians and 56% of the Whites, compared to 24% of the Hispanics, 28% of the Blacks, and 35% of the Asians believe that many People of Color got their current job merely because of their race.

- There are no significant differences by gender on most questions.

- Notice that most employees will not agree or strongly agree with an obviously racist statement such as "People of Color are not as dependable as White employees."

While overt racism seems to have declined; there is a considerable amount of subtle racism which continues to exist in the company.

—black, middle-level man

In some cases, people of color blame their problems on discrimination as an excuse, rather than facing the fact that they may have other problems or just messed up.

—white, middle-level woman

Racist attitudes are latent; they don't emerge until times are bad and scapegoats are needed.

—Asian, lower-level man

A basic belief that black culture, on average, is not compatible with technocratic/ academic institutions.

—white, upper-level man

When I see a black person, I feel they are less likely to be intelligent and serious about work (technical work). I feel some white males tend to take it for granted that I am less knowledgeable and I am inferior because I am not white. So I tend to look at them and deal with them with some reservations.

—Hispanic, occupational man

Asians are sneaky and often caught cheating. I get very impatient with cultures that cannot express themselves in the English language. The Chinese do not write documents with proper grammar. I feel it is their responsibility to improve this and I should not have to be subjected to reading these. People who have bad personal hygiene are from a foreign culture.

—white, occupational woman

Even though I am not racist/sexist, I am aware of prejudices and stereotypes. At times, a racist/sexist remark is made by myself, with no intent to harm, but in a joking way. Afterwards, I realize what I said could have really bothered some.

—white, occupational man

Figure 16.7 demonstrates the striking difference between whites and people of color with respect to perceived race discrimination. For every group except whites, at least twice as many employees perceived three to six problems as perceived no problems. The same percentage of white women believed there were no discrimination problems as believed there were three to six problems. More white men (40 percent) believed there were no discrimination problems than believed there were three to six problems (31 percent). Among the other race groups, black men (84 percent) and women (90 percent) were, by far, the most likely to report discrimination. The other groups ranged from 44 percent (American Indian men) to 52 percent (Asian women). Typical comments by our survey participants concerning race discrimination are as follows:

Figure 16.7
Race Discrimination

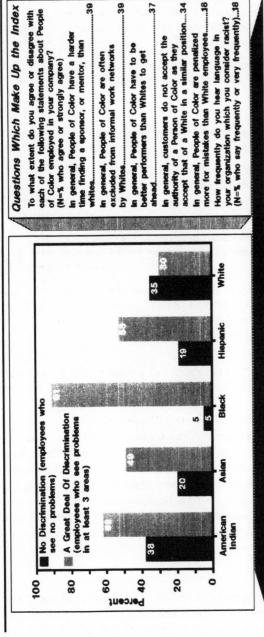

Questions Which Make Up the Index

To what extent do you agree or disagree with each of the following statements about People of Color employed in your company? (N=% who agree or strongly agree)

In general, People of Color have a harder time finding a sponsor, or mentor, than white...39

In general, People of Color are often excluded from informal work networks by Whites...39

In general, People of Color have to be better performers than Whites to get ahead...37

In general, customers do not accept the authority of a Person of Color as they accept that of a White in a similar position....34

In general, People of Color are penalized more for mistakes than White employees.........18

How frequently do you hear language in your organization which you consider racist? (N=% who say frequently or very frequently)...18

Analyses

- As the chart shows, Blacks are much more likely than other People of Color to perceive discrimination in at least three of the areas. Whites are by far least likely to believe this.

- When looked at by gender, it is clear that women (35%) are much more likely than men (20%) to see a great deal of race discrimination.

- Among major company units, between 22% and 32% of White employees, compared to between 35% and 93% of People of Color, feel that People of Color are subject to a great deal of discrimination. Conversely, between 27% and 40% of the White employees, compared to between 2% and 30% of the People of Color feel that People of Color face no discrimination.

Percent

■ No Discrimination (employees who see no problems)

▨ A Great Deal Of Discrimination (employees who see problems in at least 3 areas)

American Indian 38

Asian 20

Black 5 5

Hispanic 19

White 35 30

I do not see any blacks or Asians being promoted or mentored, and I know for a fact they are interested in being promoted.

—white, occupational woman

People of color are often excluded from the "cliques," so to speak. Supervisors tend to downplay any contribution employees of color can make to an organization.

—black, lower-level woman

People of color have to be three times as competent as whites in order to be recognized as competent and capable, whereas whites are assumed to be competent, merely because they are white.

—black, lower-level woman

The subtleties of discrimination are alarming; some people never understand that.

—Hispanic, lower-level woman

After WWII, my stepfather was refused employment with Mountain Bell on the basis of the color of his skin; the employment office would not even allow him to fill out an application. We've made some progress, but not nearly enough!

—white, lower-level woman

As an Asian-American, I feel I don't have much of a chance with this company. I'd like to see some improvement on advancement for Asian-Americans.

—Asian, occupational woman

Have some problems with Asian males. I have been affected by having an insensitive, biased (against blacks, black females and Asian females) manager when I first started with the company. I now feel I have to work harder when a male Asian is on the team to prove that I belong to the company.

—Hispanic, lower-level woman

Tendency to "wait and see" on the abilities of a minority in a job situation.

—white, upper-level man

We may have traveled some distance toward creating an environment in the office that is color and gender blind, but the comments and data from this section indicate that there is some distance to travel before these issues are merely memories. One of the many positive aspects to the new global marketplace may be that stereotypes and assumptions from all parties will be put aside and issues brought to a head and resolved. The only way to be truly productive and successful is in a spirit of cooperation and respect, rather than finger pointing and suspicion.

SEXUAL PREFERENCE

Sexual preference has greatly increased in importance in the past decade. In the late 1970s many gays "came out of the closet" and asserted their right to be understood and accepted. Unfortunately, in the early 1980s, the outbreaks of acquired immunodeficiency syndrome (AIDS) frightened a conservative U.S. population. Early information about the disease linked it only to homosexual males and implied that it could be contracted through casual contact (AIDS can only be transferred through bodily fluid exchange). Widespread reaction to AIDS inflamed existing prejudices against homosexuals. Some even claimed that the disease was "a sign from God that homosexuality was wrong." More recent and complete information shows that although the disease can be transmitted sexually, it is not necessarily a sexual disease. And furthermore, it can be transmitted through heterosexual as well as homosexual contact.

Homosexuality is not a new phenomenon. Throughout history, many cultures have been based on same-sex relationships (with arranged "marriages" for the purpose of having children). One of the most famous examples of a culture with large, accepted segments of the population who were homosexual, was ancient Greece. Highly educated men looked for other highly educated and cultured men to form long-lasting romantic bonds. Wives, who had lesbian lovers, were chosen for men to be the mothers of their children. These choices were based on family connections, and the woman stayed at home to raise the children. Not only is homosexuality common among human populations, it is also found in other species of animals. The point is that this alternative sexual lifestyle has been very common throughout history.

As we discussed earlier, many Americans are hesitant to acknowledge the multiple cultures that co-exist in the United States. They are often even more hesitant to accept many of the different lifestyles that exist, particularly alternative sexual lifestyles. It is a fact that multiple cultures and lifestyles exist; in the 1988 survey, 10 percent to 12 percent of the employee body indicates that it is gay. Some believe that this figure is high; it is difficult to discern, since the population is still hesitant to reveal itself. Their hesitance is understandable, given the violent, homophobic reaction many people have when they encounter a gay person. Fernandez measured the extent to which employees in the survey sample were bothered by the presence of subordinates and supervisors with sexual orientations different from their own. He found that 37 percent of the population was bothered by people with different sexual preferences. Keep in mind that the percentage of the population that is gay (10 percent to 12 percent or more) would not be inclined to be bothered. Fernandez discovered that a much higher percentage of men (46 percent) than women (29 percent) indicate that alternative sexuality is a problem for them (see Figure 16.8).

Corporations cannot and should not dictate a person's sexual behavior. In addition, to be competitive in the changing times, companies cannot afford to exclude or underutilize 10 to 12 percent of the population. The shortage of workers, especially well-qualified workers, should be a significant business reason to begin to deal with the homophobia of employees. Here are some comments to illustrate employee reaction to homosexuality and homosexual support groups:

Figure 16.8
Acceptance of Employees with Different Sexual Orientation

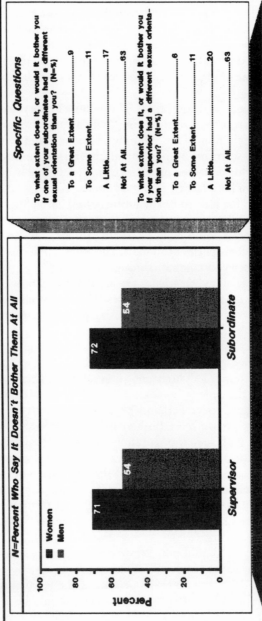

N=Percent Who Say It Doesn't Bother Them At All

■ Women
▨ Men

Supervisor: 71, 54
Subordinate: 72, 54

Percent (0–100)

Specific Questions

To what extent does it, or would it bother you
if one of your subordinates had a different
sexual orientation than you?   (N=%)

To a Great Extent......................9
To Some Extent.......................11
A Little....................................17
Not At All................................63

To what extent does it, or would it bother you
if your supervisor had a different sexual orientation than you?   (N=%)

To a Great Extent......................6
To Some Extent.......................11
A Little....................................20
Not At All................................63

Analyses

• Equal percentages of employees have no problem with other employees who have different sexual preferences (63%).
  Overall, almost 2 out of 5 employees are bothered at least a little.

• Women are much more likely than men not to be bothered by different sexual orientations of supervisors and subordinates.

• Just looking at those who are bothered at least to some extent, it is clear that White men (29%) and American Indian men
  (32%) are the most likely to respond this way about supervisors.   Between 0%–15% of the other race/gender groups concur.

• Similar trends occur with responses about subordinates.

Who cares anymore? The queers are going to take over anyway!
                                                —Hispanic, occupational man

EAGLES [a gay/lesbian organization] is a disgrace to our national bird.
                                                —Native American, occupational man

EAGLES is disgusting.
                                                —white, occupational man

A minimum of 10 percent to 15 percent of the company's employees and customers
are gay. It is past time they should be included in equal opportunities. Presently the
company is stifling this very creative, skilled resource and market.
                                                —white, occupational man

I have no problem with the company's pluralism efforts as far as race or gender
goes, but I DO have a problem with it as far as "gays" go; my personal belief is
that "gays" are mentally ill and should be treated as such.
                                                —white, lower-level man

EMPLOYEE PERCEPTIONS OF COMPANY SUPPORT FOR PLURALISM

Companies may face considerable opposition to pluralistic changes; they
must contend with a current workforce that is, at the least, skeptical of
company commitment to pluralism and, at the most, blatantly opposed to
diversity. In order to make a successful transition to a new corporate culture,
there must be a total commitment from the organization, not only in terms
of the image the company projects, but also, and most important, in terms
of the leadership demonstrated by top executives. Below are some comments
that illustrate employee perceptions of company support for pluralism. You
will notice that many are tentatively optimistic, but most are skeptical of
the long-term commitment being made by their company.

A very interesting course/meeting. I hope the company is not conducting this meeting
for just the purpose of "it is good to have AA meetings" or "good to have AA
awareness." From the bottom of the heart everybody should go back and re-evaluate
their values for life and for the people who live in this country. It might also be a
good idea to share with others—not from mainstream, obviously.
                                                —Asian, lower-level man

I hope pluralism stays with our company objectives for a long time—not just another
matter that will phase out in a couple of years.
                                                —Asian, occupational woman

I'm not convinced that the company supports a pluralistic environment, but does a
great job giving it lip service. A pluralistic workforce does indeed exist at first and
second levels where I might add, it potentially "does the least damage" in that first
and second levels have the least decision/policy making power. At the other end of
the spectrum, the company has also achieved a pluralistic workforce in its executive

levels. These individuals, because of the nature of their responsibilities, and stature in the company, receive extensive media and public attention. Those outside the company are left with the impression therefore, that all management levels must be pluralistic if the executive levels are. Our own company statistics prove this erroneous.

—white, lower-level woman

Top management must be sincere in their efforts. There are too many exceptions made for employees to really believe the company is serious about this.

—white, lower-level woman

Continue to make pluralism a highly visible and supported program.

—white, middle-level woman

The company should have a minority forum. We need to express our thoughts to upper management. I feel they care somewhat.

—black, occupational woman

The fact that it is even mentioned in this age of pseudo-political conservatism is commendable for my company.

—Hispanic, occupational man

The company's pluralistic efforts are accepted at the top levels and bottom levels but not at the middle where a person's career is determined.

—Asian, lower-level man

I still feel the company's pluralistic efforts are "lip service." I have seen two white males promoted into jobs that I was equally qualified for. I brought it to my fourth level's attention, but all I got was an apology. I was never even considered for the jobs.

—black, lower-level woman

All efforts thus far appear to exist only on paper and in the motion (mime). Until the jobs of those who practice prejudice and bias in their work practices are placed in jeopardy, there will be no pluralism.

—black, lower-level woman

The employees were asked a series of questions to ascertain whether or not they believe that their company supports pluralistic ideals (Figure 16.9). Overall, except for the black employees, more than three out of five employees believe that their company is supportive in four out of the seven areas. It is interesting to note that although a healthy percentage of employees believe that their company supports pluralism, only 6 percent believe that there will be no resistance to pluralistic efforts. Perhaps this is an acknowledgment of the fact that many employees will have problems accepting diversity, but their "company" as an entity supports it. Employees need to realize that a company is nothing more than a collection of employees, and if these employees don't support a program, the company doesn't support it either.

There are contradictions in the employee responses. Although more than

Figure 16.9
Employee Perceptions of Company Support for Pluralism

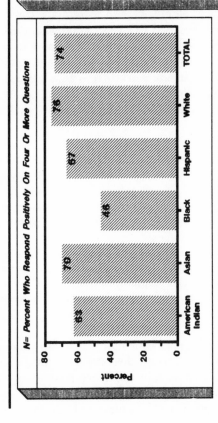

N= Percent Who Respond Positively On Four Or More Questions

American Indian	Asian	Black	Hispanic	White	TOTAL
63	70	46	67	76	74

Analyses

- As one can see from the individual questions, at least 67% of the employees respond favorably on all questions except for their perceptions of resistance to pluralism.

- As the above chart shows, the greatest difference in responses by race is between Blacks (46%) and Whites (76%). The other race groups fall in between: Hispanics (67%), American Indians (63%) and Asians (70%).

- There is no response difference between men and women.

Questions Which Make Up the Index

To what extent do you agree or disagree with each of the following statements? (N=% who agree or strongly agree)

The company publications I see reflect a pluralistic commitment.......89

The company's public advertisement reflect its commitment to pluralism......75

Top management exhibits behavior which is suitable to lead a pluralistic workforce......70

To what extent do you believe your supervisor's age impacts negatively on his/her ability to work effectively in a pluralistically driven company? (N=% who say to a small extent or no extent)......83

To what extent do you believe the following? (N=% who say to some extent or to a great extent)

Your supervisor's supervisor supports pluralism......78

Your supervisor supports pluralism through her/his behavior.......67

At what level do you believe this company's pluralistic efforts will meet the greatest resistance? (Select only one answer)

No resistance will occur......6

two out of three employees believe that their leadership at various levels is supportive of pluralism, only 6 percent believe that their company's pluralistic efforts will not meet any resistance. Many employees (36 percent) believe that there will be equal resistance at all levels. Among those employees who believe one level will be more likely to resist, the highest percentage of employees indicate that the greatest resistance will occur at the occupational level (16 percent). This percentage is followed closely by lower-level managers (14 percent), middle and upper-level managers (12 percent), and officers (4 percent). These data suggest that any improvement in pluralism cannot be targeted at any one group, but at all groups equally.

WHAT SHOULD BE DONE?

The overall solution to the potential productivity crisis in the United States in the coming decades has two major and inevitable components. First, we must employ a multicultural workforce, not only to fill job slots left vacant by the baby bust in the white population but also to add diversity and infuse corporate America with the "new blood" needed to retain a competitive edge. Enlightened chief executive officers (CEOs) agree that what the United States needs is an increase in productivity and quality; they no longer place most of the blame for U.S. deficits on unfair trade barriers and taxes. ITT CEO Rand Araskog believes that a diverse workforce is an advantage. "It's a help in terms of new ideas and flexibility. The cultural diversity of America is a major advantage in the long run." The issues that run parallel to this first component are pressing.

- We must make a concerted, well-planned effort to educate this new potential pool of workers, many of whom come from groups with backgrounds in poverty and disadvantage.

- Companies need to invest in the communities from which they hope to draw workers. They must also train employees who may be functionally or marginally illiterate when they are hired.

- With more and more women in the workforce, the whole issue of quality child care must be addressed and problems attacked. We must find ways to accommodate the need for both parents to work to make monthly payments as well as the desire of both parents to forge a rewarding career with everyone's need to assure that our next generation is cared for at all stages of its development.

There is a whole aspect to the diversity issue that many who are opposed to it may have overlooked: an emphasis on diversity includes the general concept of diversity of *ideas* as well as cultures. When companies start to accommodate different ideas and lifestyles, they must employ a degree of creativity and flexibility that has positive effects for everybody. Furthermore, not all white men have the same idea of how corporate America should be run. As with any other group, there are differences of opinion, and many risky or creative ideas get overlooked in favor of the status quo. The only people who stand to lose in the new environment are those who cling to outmoded ideas without testing their assumptions against those being proposed by a varied workforce. Issues such as these transcend race, gender, and age. The incorporation of different ideas will benefit everyone.

The second component of corporate America's solution to competitive problems is that we must deal with resistance to pluralism. This issue is discussed in the remainder of the chapter. To convince a reluctant workforce, raised in a society of prejudice and discrimination, that it is in the best interest of *everybody* to diversify the office will require creative short- and long-term management techniques. To begin, below are some comments from employees that reflect varied opinions about company pluralistic efforts and suggested solutions to the problems:

I appreciated the point that it's a two-way road: white males need to put time and energy into understanding minorities and women; minorities and women need to speak up more on what is bothering them.

—white, middle-level man

I feel that managers have an important role to play in understanding their subordinates. Several things can be done to understand cultural diversity and appreciate individuals.

—black, middle-level man

Pluralism should be the product of a discrimination-free work environment. However, there are people who need it but won't go to the workshop. It would be ideal for our company to reach those who do need it!

—Hispanic, occupational man

Workshops and seminars are fine, but a personal commitment from all employees is necessary to make pluralism work.

—Asian, lower-level woman

It's just a way to get employee organization groups off the company's back. Until something is done about the people who are *discriminating*, pluralism is a waste of time. When discrimination is brought to management's attention, they say it doesn't exist. *Nothing changes.*

—black, lower-level woman

Some employees with power to promote and supervise think the effort is a joke because they have not been demanded to promote the idea. For example, one third-level director said, "The only way I will be made to attend one of those workshops is if my job depended on it."

—black, lower-level man

I think it's a right thought; I'm not so sure we are implementing it appropriately. People are seeing only minorities getting promoted, some less qualified than other candidates. Let's train them, develop them, get them qualified, not promote them regardless. If we don't, it will hurt the minorities and the corporation.

—white, lower-level woman

I feel supervisors should be compensated based upon their ability to effectively and efficiently manage a work group; they should not be compensated if they maintain a bigoted attitude, though. Compensation should not be based solely on pluralistic efforts.

—white, lower-level woman

A totally pluralistic company would not base its employee makeup on the makeup of its customers or stockholders, but on the true meaning of pluralism. For example, if the customer base is 1 percent of a particular group in top management, does the company, if faced with exceeding that 1 percent, not promote or hire such an individual? I think and hope not. I also feel that correlating employee makeup to such barometers only initially identifies how our company compares to those factors which, of course, can be skewed positively or negatively depending on the statistics used.

—Asian, middle-level woman

Remove all subjectiveness from staffing, promotion and salary decision making and you will find that previously invisible people of color will rise to the top.

—black, middle-level man

The laudable efforts of the company have yielded mixed results, poor morale and have ignored the obvious: hiring only the best and promoting only the best will draw the best people of all races and colors.

—white, middle-level man

Orders like "your next hire will be a woman or minority" undermine the program. Saying, "I expect you to commit to hiring outstanding women and minorities" boosts the program!

—white, officer man

We live in an area with a small minority population. We must recruit more effectively people of color to gain the required input from different people in order to be effective.

—white, upper-level man

Train middle managers and hire supervisors in techniques which turn chaos of diversity into creativity.

—white, middle-level woman

Perform by actions rather than words. We've made greater progress than is always known. Implement it through the education of the management team.

—white, officer man

Educate employees. Offer more involvement.

—Native American, occupational woman

I believe you need to have equality between men and women first. Get new blood into management. The old timers are too set in their ways.

—Asian, occupational woman

Have company sponsored get-togethers on weekends, holidays.

—Asian, occupational man

Let employees know what it [pluralism] means. That it's not a threat. Show some diversity at the top office levels as well as throughout the organization.

—black, occupational woman

Provide a forum where people can see the benefits of pluralism. Show them the forward thinking and strengths of a united company as opposed to one mired in fighting.

—white, upper-level man

Make successful minorities visible. We have so many competent minorities around that they are not that strange.

—white, occupational woman

Encourage people to know one another on personal, social and spiritual levels, not just professionally.

—white, occupational woman

Make it mandatory for everyone to attend pluralism workshops. When instances occur there should be consequences involved.

—white, occupational woman

I have my own unspoken ideas on this but I've heard pluralism talked about so much that I feel people are turning a deaf ear to it because they're tired of hearing about it. Let's stop talking and just do it!

—Native American, lower-level woman

Enforce it by tying it to money. Get into the purse and it's amazing how fast people change.

—black, lower-level woman

Encourage people to talk about their prejudices and to find out where the stumbling blocks are. Enlighten middle management. Let's have black, Asian, etc. counselors available.

—black, lower-level woman

Make sure pluralistic seminar attendance is mandatory and make sure company policies are followed.

—black, lower-level woman

Compete aggressively in the marketplace for extremely high quality employees of color! Go all out and recruit from high quality educational institutions with a high percentage of students of color. Recruit the very best these schools produce.

—black, lower-level man

Continue in current direction, however should focus on changing or getting rid of employees who are an obstacle to pluralism.

—Hispanic, lower-level woman

Look to the future—you will not change the way people have been brought up, but they may change the way they raise their kids.

—white, lower-level man

Get rid of those that already have openly refused to support this effort.

—black, middle-level woman

Workshops: One Way to Increase Awareness

The employee suggestions for corporate initiatives to foster a pluralistic attitude include many references to mandatory workshops. These seminars are designed to increase awareness of issues, particularly stereotyping and the subjective process of hiring and promotion. One of the most instructive and revealing parts of Fernandez's workshops is the use of a design that asks participants to evaluate employees for promotion. All of the candidates are highly "qualified," talented individuals who under a strictly meritocratic corporate system would be promoted. Nevertheless, each candidate has committed some "faux pas" and has been subjected to rumors. Most of the participant groups fail to promote any of the candidates because they focus on the social blunders and rumors rather than the candidate's accomplishments. The exercise demonstrates that employees are as much a part of the problems and solutions as the "company" as a whole. Here are a few reactions from workshop participants concerning what they learned from this exercise:

I learned a lot today. My mind has been opened up. The case studies made me realize that I paid attention to personal traits instead of a person's ability. I did not want people to treat me this way; however, I acted this way myself.

—black, lower-level woman

The most revealing event was the case problem. It reminded me of how easily one can be swayed. That is focusing on a limited set of information, and selecting what you want. This lesson, while not new, was a solid reminder that all information should be weighed.

—Hispanic, occupational woman

The employee evaluation was very useful, mainly because it made me realize that my own personal feelings get in the way of making sound judgments. Actually, the discussion afterward is what brought about this realization.

—white, lower-level woman

I think it was very interesting how we view people subjectively without realizing it. If we were totally objective and free from bias, then our responses in the first exercise should not have been that different, whether we judge ourselves or others.

—white, middle-level man

Excellent program. I had never thought about AA issues this way. You gave a new perspective on the whole program—namely, we are part of the problem. On the whole, a very useful day. I think for many, we started the day wondering how we would fare. I am taking home many new thoughts.

—Asian, lower-level man

I enjoyed having some of my own self-images challenged. I've often resented people whom I perceived as extremely different. I think I may have gained an insight into dealing with that resentment.

—white, occupational man

Overall message: judging performance of others the way I'd like to be judged. Tendency to get hung up on issues which don't pertain to real criteria.

—black, lower-level man

What Can Managers Do?

In order to manage a diverse workforce, corporate America needs to train and reward excellent managers. Truly good managers have always been able to utilize their subordinates by recognizing individual strengths and weaknesses and by maintaining flexibility when faced with new problems and challenges. The demographic changes are presenting challenges that our top managers, with training, will have more than enough expertise to successfully maneuver through. The following is a list of important factors that managers must keep in mind as they confront the coming years.

1. Managers must be conscious about the nature of bureaucracy and its limitations. Specifically, there are only so many slots at the "top of the heap" and only so many traditional resources (mainly money) to go around. Many people who meet all the criteria for promotion will be disappointed and frustrated if there is no way to reward their achievements other than promotion.

2. Strategies must be developed and implemented to increase fairness and equity in promotions and hiring. We have discussed, with the case study example, how subjective the process of hiring and promotion can be, with attention paid to characteristics that have nothing to do with "getting the job done right."

3. Managers should strive to develop a realistic corporate culture, one that strikes a balance between the inherent frailties and limitations of the bureaucratic structure and yet seeks to find creative ways to overcome some of the obstacles.

4. Communication between managers and subordinates is the key to corporate success. Managers must be trained in the utilization and career development of those who work for them, and subordinates must be trained on their individual responsibility for the direction of their careers.

5. Implement incentives for managers who successfully utilize workers. These incentives can come in the traditional money and bonus forms, but also in the form of special assignments, recognition, and other, nontraditional rewards.

6. Recognizing that there are limited promotional opportunities for large numbers of people who desire and expect promotions, corporations must develop reward systems that focus on team efforts.

7. Beware the traditional "merit award" system that only awards one person at a time for exceptional performance. This system has potentially destructive psychological consequences for those who do not get recognized. It also doesn't recognize that often the high performance of one person rests on the high performance of all those who work for and with her or him.

8. Team awards can be based on the results of the company as a whole or on the success of individual units within the company.

9. Develop pay incentives for those employees who are top talents, but must, for corporate reasons, stay in jobs for long periods of time because of their expertise, thus being taken out of the mainstream of promotional candidates.

Heterogeneous Workforce Issues

The preceding suggestions are useful in managing any workforce, but now we will mention measures for managing a heterogeneous mixture of employees. Companies should consider

- comprehensive training for employees at all levels, including top management, and

- integration of affirmative action and equal opportunity and diversity awareness and activities throughout the company's existing functions, in all departments and at all levels.

Here are specific steps companies should take with respect to equal opportunity (EO) priorities and incorporating diversity in general:

1. Establish goals and timetables for all departments and levels of the corporation, with respect to hiring and promotion of people of color, women, and where white males are underrepresented establish similar goals and timetables.

2. Conduct multicultural events and strongly encourage employees to attend.

3. Make certain that all training programs and systems related to managerial and supervisory skills development have modules with some aspect of racism, sexism, ageism, and pluralism.

4. Develop managing differences awareness workshops using trained volunteer facilitators drawn from high-potential, middle-level and above managers, whose participation should be mandatory.

5. Require higher-level managers to become mentors and sponsors to high-potential women and people of color. Measure and reward their success in this task.

6. Develop concrete performance measurement criteria to evaluate all managers' efforts in the managing differences area. Establish rewards for those who demonstrate a positive record in these areas and penalties for those who do not.

7. Demonstrate the company's commitment to managing differences by promoting people who directly work in these areas and do an outstanding job.

8. Make certain that issues concerning managing differences have time slots on all middle- and upper-management meetings.

9. As companies globalize, they should send high-potential people, at all levels, to other countries to be immersed in foreign culture to become familiar with and learn from it.

10. Hire more people who have studied the liberal arts, especially foreign cultures, for managerial positions.

11. Devise ways to utilize and maintain the dynamism of an aging workforce.

How to Increase Company Credibility—Lip Service Versus Action

Modern employees are savvy to slick company tactics that give the appearance of taking action, but in reality do nothing. Today's workers are much more likely than their predecessors to walk into a CEO's office and demand, "Whatever happened to pluralism?" There are ways to have visible company involvement.

- Have top executives circulate within the company, discussing problem areas.
- Make sure that the executive staff attend workshops and seminars along with rank-and-file employees.
- Publish companywide material to document any changes; provide a forum for debate, etc.
- Conduct large-scale surveys as a measure of employee attitudes with plenty of opportunity for written comments. Publish the results.

We would like to emphasize that corporations must recognize that these issues must be managed just like other corporate problems; they will not disappear without action. People are socialized into becoming racist, sexist, and ageist through methods both subtle and overt. Companies implement multiple strategies to influence, educate, and, it is hoped, change employees. This is going to be a long-term process because the current socialization is pervasive and has been shaping employees over a lifetime. Probably the best way to ensure that this is a priority for managers is to tie monetary rewards to those who come up with creative and effective ways to manage diversity. We end this chapter with two comments from the people who must be the instigators of change and acceptance:

Quit talking so much about it and make upper- and officer-level management jobs and bonuses dependent in some way on the steps they prove they've implemented for pluralism.

—black, middle-level man

Actions speak louder than words; pay should be used for reward and punishment.

—white, upper-level woman

INDEX

ABOUT THE CONTRIBUTORS

EMILY S. BASSMAN is currently a district manager with Pacific Bell, in the area of human resource planning and organizational capability. Before joining Pacific Bell in 1989, she spent ten years at AT&T, the last seven of which were in the human resources department. Bassman earned a Ph.D. in psychology from Stanford University and a B.A. from Indiana University.

NICHOLAS J. BEUTELL is professor and chair of the management department in the W. Paul Stillman School of Business, Seton Hall University. He received his Ph.D. in human resource management from Stevens Institute of Technology in 1979. His publications have appeared in the *Academy of Management Review, Journal of Applied Psychology*, and *Personnel Administrator*. He is the co-author of a personnel text, *Effective Personnel Management*. Beutell is the 1989/90 president of the Eastern Academy of Management. His research interests include work-family conflict, human resource information systems, and globalization of the human resource function.

JOSEPH F. COATES is president of J. F. Coates, Inc., a policy research organization specializing in the study of the future. Educated at Brooklyn Polytechnic Institute, Pennsylvania State University, and the University of Pennsylvania, Coates received an honorary doctorate in 1985 from the Claremont Graduate School. He is the co-author of *What Futurists Believe* (1989) as well as the author or co-author of more than 200 articles and papers. Coates started his career as an industrial chemist, and he holds nineteen patents. He was also formerly head of exploratory research at the Congressional Office of Technology Assessment. Coates is an adjunct professor at the George Washington University, where he teaches graduate courses on technology and on the future.

JACQUELINE A. DUBOIS graduated magna cum laude, Phi Beta Kappa from the University of Washington in 1987. She received her B.S. in psychology with an emphasis in social psychology and law. She is currently senior research consultant with Advanced Research Management Consultants.

TROY DUSTER is currently professor of sociology and director of the Institute for the Study of Social Change at the University of California, Berkeley. He is the recipient of a number of research fellowships, including awards from the Swedish government (1962) and the Guggenheim (1971) and Ford Foundations (1979). He has been a member of the Assembly of Behavioral and Social Sciences of the National Academy of Sciences. Duster's books and monographs include *The Legislation of Morality* (1970), *Aims and Control of the Universities* (1974), and *Cultural Perspectives on Biological Knowledge* (with Karen Garrett, 1984). He is also the author of a number of articles on theory and methods.

DANIEL C. FELDMAN (Ph.D., Yale University) is professor of management and Business Partnership Foundation fellow at the University of South Carolina College of Business Administration. He has previously served on the faculties of Yale University, the University of Minnesota Industrial Relations Center, Northwestern's J. L. Kellogg Graduate School of Management, and the University of Florida Graduate School of Management. Feldman has published widely in the area of career development, and is the author of four books, including *Managing Careers in Organizations* (1988). A member of the Academy of Management and the American Psychological Association, he has served on the editorial boards of the *Academy of Management Journal* and the *Journal of Management* and on the executive committees of the Organizational Behavior and Careers Divisions of the Academy of Management.

JOHN P. FERNANDEZ graduated magna cum laude from Harvard University in 1969 and received his Ph.D. in sociology from the University of California at Berkeley, in 1973. He has extensive experience, both as a researcher and teacher and as a manager with AT&T for fifteen years. While with AT&T, John served as a division-level manager in the areas of operations, labor relations, personnel, and human resources forecasting and planning. He is currently the president of Advanced Research Management Consultants, a Philadelphia-based consulting firm that specializes in human resource issues such as survey research, needs assessment, managing a diverse workforce, and dependent care.

MIRIAN M. GRADDICK is currently division manager of Leadership Systems for AT&T with responsibility for corporatewide programs aimed at the identification and development of high-potential managers. Graddick received her B.A. in psychology from Hampton University and her M.A. and Ph.D. from Pennsylvania State University in industrial and organizational psychology. She has had a variety of assignments in human resources since joining AT&T in 1981. These include the design and validation of entry-level selection tests, management of an assessment center designed to evaluate middle management potential, human resource planning, and succession planning. Graddick has conducted research and written numerous papers on such topics as the analysis of managerial jobs, correlates of advancement of women into middle and upper management, the selection and development of U.S. expatriates, integrating business planning and human resource planning, and corporate philosophies of management development.

MARTIN M. GRELLER is president of Personnel Strategies, Inc., a human resource consulting firm in Warren, New Jersey. He has previously been director of human resource planning and development for The New York Times Company and an assistant professor of management at New York University's Graduate School of Business. He received his Ph.D. from Yale University for work in the administrative sciences department and an undergraduate degree from Tufts University.

LORI HEWIG is a statistician for the New York State Department of Civil Service. Her work in workforce planning analysis focuses on the development of employee turnover models and forecasts of labor supply and demand. Before joining the Department of Civil Service in September 1988, Hewig worked for four years performing quantitative investment research for the New York State Teachers' Retirement System in Albany, New York. She has a B.A. from the State University of New York at Albany and an M.S. in operations research and statistics from Rensselaer Polytechnic Institute.

JENNIFER JARRATT is vice president of J. F. Coates, Inc., an organization committed to studies of the future. She is the co-author of *What Futurists Believe* (1989) along with other works on human resource and environmental trends. Jarratt holds a B.A. from Goddard College and a master's degree in future studies from the University of Houston, Clear Lake. Formerly communications director for a nonprofit agency, Jarratt has been the speaker at conferences on technology transfer and the future of the workforce. She has been the analyst on at least sixteen futures studies since 1983, including "The Electronic and Photonic World of 2005: An Exploration of Business Opportunities in Information Technology."

PAMELA C. JONES is district manager of Human Resource Strategies for AT&T. She has had a variety of corporate experiences within AT&T's marketing and human resource departments. Most recently she has been responsible for contributing to the development of human resource policies and programs to match the increasingly competitive and global direction of the company.

DIANA KRAMER received her B.A. in education from Glassboro State College in 1972. In 1975, she received her M.A. in psychology from the New School for Social Research, and in 1979, she received her Ph.D. in psychology from Fordham University. Kramer has been involved in managing, developing, and implementing systems and policies in succession planning, executive development, human resource strategic planning, and management development. She began her corporate career with AT&T in 1980. Since 1987 she has worked for BASF Corporation, where she has been responsible for human resource planning and development.

FRANK M. J. LAFASTO is vice president for human resource planning and development for Baxter Healthcare Corporation, a position that involves him in succession planning, performance measurement, executive development, and selection standards. An author and guest lecturer on management issues, LaFasto has extensive experience in building effective management teams. He holds a Ph.D. in organizational communications from the University of Denver.

CARRIE R. LEANA (Ph.D., University of Houston) is assistant professor of organizational behavior at the Katz Graduate School of Business at the University of Pittsburgh. She has published extensively in the areas of participative management and job loss in such journals as *Journal of Applied Psychology, Academy of Management Journal,* and *Academy of Management Review.* Leana is co-author of *Individual and Institutional Responses to Job Loss.* A member of the Academy of Management, Leana has also served on the faculty of the University of Florida Graduate School of Business.

MANUEL LONDON is professor and director of the Labor/Management Studies Program at the State University of New York at Stony Brook. Before joining Stony Brook in April 1989, London worked for twelve years for AT&T, where he held a series of assignments in the human resource and training departments. One assignment was working with John Fernandez and Emily Bassman to establish AT&T's corporate human resource forecasting and planning group after the Bell System divestiture. Before joining AT&T, London was on the faculty of the University of Illinois at Champaign's business school for three years. He received his Ph.D. in industrial and organizational psychology from the Ohio State University and his bachelor's degree in psychology and philosophy from Case Western Reserve University. London is the co-author of *Managing Careers* (1982) and the author of *Developing Managers* (1985) and of other books and numerous articles on employee training, career development, and organizational change. His book *Change Agents: New Roles and Innovation Strategies for Human Resource Professionals* received the 1989 book award from the American Society for Personnel Administration. London is on the editorial boards of *Administrative Science Quarterly, Journal of Applied Psychology, Personnel Psychology, Human Resource Management Review,* and *Journal of Management Development.* He is currently treasurer of the Society for Industrial and Organizational Psychology and on the Board of Governors of the Academy of Management.

DAVID NASATIR is a professor of behavioral science at California State University, Dominquez Hills. He was educated at Massachusetts Institute of Technology, Stanford, and the University of California, where he received his Ph.D. He has authored several works on data archives for the social sciences and has been active in the study of topics as diverse as social change in Latin America and the epidemiology of alcohol use among college and university students.

DAVID M. NEE is executive director of the Ittleson Foundation, which sponsors work in the fields of mental health, the environment, the elderly, and criminal justice. Previously, he served as executive director of the Burden Foundation and director of program development of the Massachusetts Department of Correction. He received his M.A. from Yale University, an M.B.A. from Boston University, and his bachelor's degree from Harvard University.

ANTHONY J. RUCCI is senior vice president of human resources for Baxter Healthcare Corporation, a seven-billion-dollar market leader in the manufacture and distribution of health care products and services, headquartered in Deerfield, Illinois. Rucci has been on the editorial board of the *Journal of Applied Psychology* and is currently associate editor of the *Human Resource Planning Journal.* He holds a Ph.D. in industrial psychology from Bowling Green State University.

WILLIAM A. SCHIEMANN is president of Wm. A. Schiemann & Associates, a firm dedicated to the enhancement of organizational effectiveness. His expertise includes corporate culture audits, human resource effectiveness surveys, quality of service assessments, customer attitude surveys, and merger, acquisition, and downsizing strategy. Before founding Wm. A. Schiemann & Associates, Schiemann was senior vice president of Sirota &

Alper Associates and vice president of Opinion Research Corporation. He was also a manager of employment and selection for AT&T and a faculty member at Georgia Institute of Technology and the University of Iowa. He received his Ph.D. in organizational psychology from the University of Illinois, and he holds an M.B.A. from the Illinois Institute of Technology.

JAMES A. SHERIDAN is an independent consultant and entrepreneur. He is chairman of the board of Imaginative Materials Group, Inc., a new ventures real estate and business consulting firm. Sheridan has previously been affiliated with AT&T, where he worked on human resource forecasting and planning. He has also worked for Towers, Perrin, Forster & Crosby, Paradigm Consultants, the Western Consulting Group, and Right Associates. He received his M.A. from the University of Wichita and has done doctoral work at the University of Louisville in human factors engineering.

JAMES B. SHILLABER consults with private and public sector organizations on the strategic deployment and development of human resources. He is affiliated with the firm of Wm. A. Schiemann & Associates. Shillaber is also an associate with Rutgers University's Center for Applied Psychology and maintains a clinical practice in Colts Neck, New Jersey. He received his B.A. in psychology from Hampshire College and his Psy.D. in clinical psychology from Rutgers University.

CHRISTIE TEIGLAND is currently the director of workforce planning analysis, a new initiative started in 1988, in the New York State Department of Civil Service. Before that, Teigland was a principal econometrician with New York State for five years. She received a Ph.D. in economics from the State University of New York at Albany in 1986, and was an assistant professor of economics at St. Olaf College in Northfield, Minnesota, for two years. She has published articles in the *Journal of Money, Credit and Banking* and the *International Journal of Forecasting*.

DAVID ULRICH is on the faculty at the University of Michigan Business School. He has consulted in the areas of strategic planning and human resource planning and has worked with more than ninety of the current Fortune 200 companies. Ulrich holds a B.A. from Brigham Young University and a Ph.D. from the University of California, Los Angeles.

JAMES W. WALKER is a partner in The Walker Group, a consulting firm based in Phoenix. He specializes in assessing human resource and management effectiveness issues and developing strategies to address them. Walker is widely known for his speaking, writing, and other activities in the personnel field. He is the author of many articles and six books, including the award-winning *Human Resource Planning*. He was founder of the Human

Resource Planning Society and served as its charter president. Walker earned an M.A. in labor and management and a Ph.D. in business administration from the University of Iowa, and has served on the faculties at Indiana University and San Diego State University. Walker was vice president and director of Human Resource Consulting Services for Towers, Perrin, Forster & Crosby before leaving in 1986 to found The Walker Group. He created the Human Resource Business School, an eight-day program to help human resource professionals strengthen their business perspective and consulting skills vital to today's changing staff roles